Your All-in-One Resource

On the CD that accompanies this book, you'll find a fully searchable version of this *Step by Step* book as well as additional resources to extend your learning. The reference library includes an electronic version of this book, and the following eBooks and reference materials:

- *Microsoft Computer Dictionary, Fifth Edition*
- Sample chapters and poster from *Look Both Ways: Help Protect Your Family on the Internet* by Linda Criddle
- *Windows Vista Product Guide*

The CD interface has a new look. You can use the tabs for an assortment of tasks:

- Check for book updates (if you have Internet access)
- Install the book's practice file
- Go online for product support or CD support
- Send us feedback

The following screen shot gives you a glimpse of the new interface.

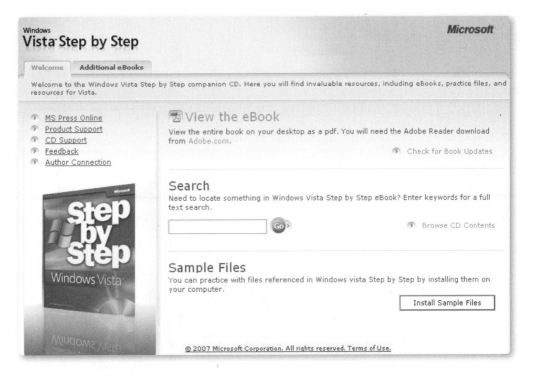

Microsoft® Office Excel® 2007 Step by Step

Curtis D. Frye

PUBLISHED BY
Microsoft Press
A Division of Microsoft Corporation
One Microsoft Way
Redmond, Washington 98052-6399

Library of Congress Control Number: 2006936146

Printed and bound in the United States of America.

14 15 16 17 18 19 20 21 22 23 QGT 6 5 4 3 2 1

Distributed in Canada by H.B. Fenn and Company Ltd.

A CIP catalogue record for this book is available from the British Library.

Microsoft Press books are available through booksellers and distributors worldwide. For further information about international editions, contact your local Microsoft Corporation office or contact Microsoft Press International directly at fax (425) 936-7329. Visit our Web site at www.microsoft.com/mspress. Send comments to mspinput@microsoft.com.

Acquisitions Editor: Juliana Aldous Atkinson
Developmental Editor: Sandra Haynes
Project Editor: Valerie Woolley
Editorial and Production Services: Studioserv

Body Part No. X12-49214

Contents

About the Author. ix

Acknowledgments x

Features and Conventions. xi

Using the Companion CD xiii

Getting Help xix

The Microsoft Business Certification Program xxi

Quick Reference xxvii

1   What's New in Excel 2007?   1

Becoming Familiar with the New User Interface 2

Managing Larger Data Collections. 3

Understanding the New Office File Formats. 4

Formatting Cells and Worksheets. 5

Managing Data Tables More Effectively 6

Creating Formulas More Easily 7

Summarizing Data. 8

Creating Powerful Conditional Formats. 9

Creating More Attractive Charts. 10

Controlling Printouts More Carefully. 10

Key Points 11

2   Setting Up a Workbook   13

Creating Workbooks. 14

Modifying Workbooks 18

Modifying Worksheets 21

Customizing the Excel 2007 Program Window 26

    Zooming In on a Worksheet 26

    Arranging Multiple Workbook Windows. 27

    Adding Buttons to the Quick Access Toolbar 28

    Maximizing the Usable Space 29

Key Points 33

3 Working with Data and Data Tables   **35**

Entering and Revising Data 36

Moving Data Within a Workbook. 41

Finding and Replacing Data. 44

Correcting and Expanding Upon Worksheet Data .48

Defining a Table. 53

Key Points 57

4 Performing Calculations on Data   **59**

Naming Groups of Data. 60

Creating Formulas to Calculate Values. 64

Summarizing Data That Meets Specific Conditions. 71

Finding and Correcting Errors in Calculations 75

Key Points 83

5 Changing Workbook Appearance   **85**

Formatting Cells. 86

Defining Styles. 92

Applying Workbook Themes and Table Styles. 96

Making Numbers Easier to Read. 102

Changing the Appearance of Data Based on Its Value 106

Adding Images to Worksheets 113

Key Points 117

6 Focusing on Specific Data by Using Filters   **119**

Limiting Data That Appears on Your Screen. 120

Manipulating List Data 125

Defining Valid Sets of Values for Ranges of Cells. .130

Key Points 135

7 Reordering and Summarizing Data   **137**

Sorting Data Lists. 138

Organizing Data into Levels. 145

Looking Up Information in a Data List. 151

Key Points 155

8 Combining Data from Multiple Sources   **157**

Using Data Lists as Templates for Other Lists. 158

Linking to Data in Other Worksheets and Workbooks. 164

Consolidating Multiple Sets of Data into a Single Workbook 170
Grouping Multiple Sets of Data 173
Key Points 175

9 Analyzing Alternative Data Sets   177
Defining an Alternative Data Set 178
Defining Multiple Alternative Data Sets 181
Varying Your Data to Get a Desired Result by Using Goal Seek 185
Finding Optimal Solutions by Using Solver. 189
Analyzing Data by Using Descriptive Statistics. 194
Key Points 197

10 Creating Dynamic Lists by Using PivotTables   199
Analyzing Data Dynamically by Using PivotTables 200
Filtering, Showing, and Hiding PivotTable Data. 209
Editing PivotTables 216
Formatting PivotTables. 221
Creating PivotTables from External Data. 228
Key Points 233

11 Creating Charts and Graphics   235
Creating Charts 236
Customizing the Appearance of Charts. 242
Finding Trends in Your Data. 248
Creating Dynamic Charts by Using PivotCharts. 251
Creating Diagrams by Using SmartArt. 256
Key Points 263

12 Printing   265
Adding Headers and Footers to Printed Pages 266
Preparing Worksheets for Printing. 271
Previewing Worksheets Before Printing. 273
Changing Page Breaks in a Worksheet 273
Changing the Page Printing Order for Worksheets. 275
Printing Data Lists 279
Printing Parts of Data Lists. 281
Printing Charts. 286
Key Points 287

13   Automating Repetitive Tasks by Using Macros   289

Introducing Macros. 290

Macro Security in Excel 2007. 290

Examining Macros 293

Creating and Modifying Macros. 297

Running Macros When a Button Is Clicked. 301

Running Macros When a Workbook Is Opened. 306

Key Points 309

14   Working with Other Microsoft Office System Programs   311

Including Office Documents in Worksheets 312

Storing Workbooks as Parts of Other Office Documents. 315

Creating Hyperlinks. 318

Pasting Charts into Other Documents. 323

Key Points 325

15   Collaborating with Colleagues   327

Sharing Data Lists 328

Managing Comments. 331

Tracking and Managing Colleagues' Changes 335

Protecting Workbooks and Worksheets 339

Authenticating Workbooks 344

Saving Workbooks for the Web 346

Sidebar: Saving a Workbook for Secure Electronic Distribution 350

Sidebar: Finalizing a Workbook. 351

Key Points 352

Glossary. 353

Index. 357

What do you think of this book? We want to hear from you!

Microsoft is interested in hearing your feedback so we can continually improve our books and learning resources for you. To participate in a brief online survey, please visit:

www.microsoft.com/learning/booksurvey/

About the Author

Curtis Frye

Curt Frye is a freelance writer and Microsoft Most Valuable Professional for Microsoft Office Excel. He lives in Portland, Oregon, and is the author of eight books from Microsoft Press, including *Microsoft Office Excel 2007 Step by Step*, *Microsoft Office Access 2007 Plain & Simple*, *Microsoft Office Excel 2007 Plain & Simple*, and *Microsoft Office Small Business Accounting 2006 Step By Step*. He has also written numerous articles for the Microsoft Work Essentials web site.

Before beginning his writing career in June 1995, Curt spent four years with The MITRE Corporation as a defense trade analyst and one year as Director of Sales and Marketing for Digital Gateway Systems, an Internet service provider. Curt graduated from Syracuse University in 1990 with an honors degree in political science. When he's not writing, Curt is a professional improvisational comedian with ComedySportz Portland.

Acknowledgments

Creating a book is a time-consuming (sometimes all-consuming) process, but working within an established relationship makes everything go much more smoothly. In that light, I'd like to thank Sandra Haynes, the Microsoft Press Series Editor, for inviting me back for another tilt at the windmill. I've been lucky to work with Microsoft Press for the past six years, and always enjoy working with Valerie Woolley, Project Editor at Microsoft Press. She kept us all on track and moving forward while maintaining her sense of humor.

I'd also like to thank Steve Sagman of Waypoint Press. I worked with Steve on a previous project, and was ecstatic when Sandra mentioned that I'd get to work with him and his crew again. Steve did a great job with the technical edit, Nancy Sixsmith kept me on the straight and narrow with a thorough copy edit, Audrey Marr brought everything together as the book's compositor, and Shawn Peck completed the project with a careful proofread. I hope I get the chance to work with all of them again.

Features and Conventions

You can save time when you use this book by understanding how the *Step by Step* series shows special instructions, keys to press, buttons to click, and so on.

Convention	Meaning
1 2	Numbered steps guide you through hands-on exercises in each topic.
⊙	This icon at the beginning of a chapter indicates information about the practice files provided on the companion CD for use in the chapter.
USE	This paragraph preceding a step-by-step exercise indicates the practice files that you will use when working through the exercise.
BE SURE TO	This paragraph preceding a step-by-step exercise indicates any requirements you should attend to before beginning the exercise.
OPEN	This paragraph preceding a step-by-step exercise indicates files that you should open before beginning the exercise.
CLOSE	This paragraph following a step-by-step exercise provides instructions for closing open files or programs before moving on to another topic.
Tip	These paragraphs provide helpful hints or shortcuts that make working through a task easier.
Important	These paragraphs point out information that you need to know to complete a procedure.
Troubleshooting	These paragraphs explain how to fix common problems that might prevent you from continuing through an exercise.
See Also	These paragraphs direct you to more information in this book about a topic.
Enter	In step-by-step exercises, keys you must press appear as they do on the keyboard.
Alt + Tab	A plus sign (+) between two key names means that you must press those keys at the same time. For example, "Press Alt + Tab" means that you hold down the Alt key while you press the Tab key.

Convention	Meaning
Program elements	In steps, program elements such as buttons, commands, and dialog boxes are shown in black bold type.
Glossary terms	Terms that are explained in the glossary at the end of the book are shown in blue italic type.
User input	Text that you are supposed to type appears in blue bold type in the procedures.
Files, folders, URLs, and emphasis	Files, folder paths, URLs, and emphasized words appear in italic type.

Using the Companion CD

The companion CD included with this book contains practice files you can use as you work through the book's exercises. By using practice files, you won't waste time creating samples and typing spreadsheet data. Instead, you can jump right in and concentrate on learning how to use Microsoft Office Excel 2007.

> Digital Content for Digital Book Readers: If you bought a digital-only edition of this book, you can enjoy select content from the print edition's companion CD.
>
> Visit *go.microsoft.com/fwlink/?LinkId=91308* to get your downloadable content. This content is always up-to-date and available to all readers.

CD Contents

The following table lists the practice files supplied on the companion CD.

Chapter	Folder\File
Chapter 1: What's New in Excel 2007	None
Chapter 2: Setting Up a Workbook	*Creating\Exception Summary.xlsx* *Creating\Route Volume.xlsx*
Chapter 3: Working with Data and Data Tables	*Data and Data Tables\2007Q1ShipmentsByCategory.xlsx* *Data and Data Tables\Average Deliveries.xlsx* *Data and Data Tables\Driver Sort Times.xlsx* *Data and Data Tables\Series.xlsx* *Data and Data Tables\Service Levels.xlsx*
Chapter 4: Performing Calculations on Data	*Formulas\ConveyerBid.xlsx* *Formulas\ITExpenses.xlsx* *Formulas\PackagingCosts.xlsx* *Formulas\VehicleMiles.xlsx*

Chapter	Folder\File
Chapter 5: Changing Document Appearance	Appearance\acbluprt.jpg
	Appearance\callcenter.jpg
	Appearance\CallCenter.xlsx
	Appearance\Dashboard.xlsx
	Appearance\ExecutiveSearch.xlsx
	Appearance\HourlyExceptions.xlsx
	Appearance\HourlyTracking.xlsx
	Appearance\VehicleMileSummary.xlsx
Chapter 6: Focusing on Specific Data Using Filters	Focusing\Credit.xlsx
	Focusing\ForFollowUp.xlsx
	Focusing\PackageExceptions.xlsx
Chapter 7: Reordering and Summarizing Data	Sorting\GroupByQuarter.xlsx
	Sorting\ShipmentLog.xlsx
	Sorting\ShippingSummary.xlsx
Chapter 8: Combining Data from Multiple Sources	MultipleFiles\Consolidate.xlsx
	MultipleFiles\Daily Call Summary.xlsx
	MultipleFiles\February Calls.xlsx
	MultipleFiles\Fleeting Operating Costs.xlsx
	MultipleFiles\January Calls.xlsx
	MultipleFiles\Operating Expense Dashboard.xlsx
Chapter 9: Analyzing Alternative Data Sets	Alternatives\2DayScenario.xlsx
	Alternatives\Ad Buy.xlsx
	Alternatives\Driver Sort Times.xlsx
	Alternatives\Multiple Scenarios.xlsx
	Alternatives\Target Values.xlsx
Chapter 10: Creating Dynamic Lists with PivotTables	PivotTables\Creating.txt
	PivotTables\Creating.xlsx
	PivotTables\Editing.xlsx
	PivotTables\Focusing.xlsx
	PivotTables\Formatting.xlsx
Chapter 11: Creating Charts and Graphics	Charting\Future Volumes.xlsx
	Charting\Org Chart.xlsx
	Charting\Revenue Analysis.xlsx
	Charting\Volume by Center.xlsx
	Charting\Yearly Package Volume.xlsx

Chapter	Folder\File
Chapter 12: Printing	*Printing\ConsolidatedMessenger.png*
	Printing\Corporate Revenue.xlsx
	Printing\Hourly Pickups.xlsx
	Printing\Pickups by Hour.xlsx
	Printing\Revenue by Customer.xlsx
	Printing\Summary by Customer.xlsx
Chapter 13: Automating Repetitive Tasks with Macros	*Macros\Performance Dashboard.xlsm*
	Macros\RunOnOpen.xlsm
	Macros\VolumeHighlights.xlsm
	Macros\Yearly Sales Summary.xlsx
Chapter 14: Working with Other Microsoft Office System Programs	*Other Programs\2007 Yearly Revenue Summary.pptx*
	Other Programs\Hyperlink.xlsx
	Other Programs\Level Descriptions.xlsx
	Other Programs\Revenue Chart.xlsx
	Other Programs\Revenue Summary.pptx
	Other Programs\RevenueByServiceLevel.xlsx
	Other Programs\Summary Presentation.xlsx
Chapter 15: Collaborating with Colleagues	*Sharing\Cost Projections.xlsx*
	Sharing\Projection Change Tracking.xlsx
	Sharing\Projections for Comment.xlsx
	Sharing\Projections Signed.xlsx
	Sharing\SecureInfo.xlsx
	Sharing\Shipment Summary.xlsx

Minimum System Requirements

To run Excel 2007, your computer needs to meet the following minimum hardware requirements:

- 500 megahertz (MHz)
- 256 megabytes (MB) RAM
- 1.5 gigabytes (GB) available space
- CD or DVD drive
- 1024 × 768 or higher resolution monitor

Installing the Practice Files

You need to install the practice files in the correct location on your hard disk before you can use them in the exercises. Follow these steps:

1. Remove the companion CD from the envelope at the back of the book, and insert it into the CD drive of your computer. If the **AutoPlay** window opens, click **Run startcd.exe**.

    The Microsoft Software License Terms appear. To use the practice files, you must accept the terms of the license agreement.

2. Click **I accept the agreement**, and then click **Next**.

    After you accept the license agreement, the CD interface appears.

> **Important** If the menu screen does not appear, click the Start button and then click Computer. Display the Folders list in the Navigation pane, click the icon for your CD drive, and then in the right pane, double-click the StartCD executable file.

3. Click **Install Practice Files**. If the **File Download** and/or **Internet Explorer Security** dialog boxes open, click **Yes** and/or **Run**.

4. On the **Welcome** page of the InstallShield Wizard, click **Next**. On the **License Agreement** page, click **I accept the terms in the license agreement**, and then click **Next**.

5. If you want to install the practice files to a location other than the default folder (*Documents\Microsoft Press\Excel2007SBS*), click the **Browse** button, select the new drive and path, and then click **OK**.

> **Important** If you are using Windows XP or earlier, the default folder will be *My Documents\Microsoft Press\Excel2007SBS*.

6. On the **Custom Setup** page, click **Next**, and then on the **Ready to Install the Program** screen, click **Install**.

7. After the practice files have been installed, click **Finish**.

8. Close the **Step by Step Companion CD** window.

9. Remove the companion CD from the CD drive, and return it to the envelope at the back of the book.

Using the Practice Files

When you install the practice files from the companion CD that accompanies this book, the files are stored on your hard disk in chapter-specific subfolders under *Documents\ Microsoft Press\Excel2007SBS*. Each exercise is preceded by a paragraph that lists the files needed for that exercise and explains any preparations needed before you start working through the exercise. Here are examples:

USE the *ForFollowUp* workbook. This practice file is located in the *Documents\Microsoft Press\Excel2007SBS\Focusing* folder.

BE SURE TO start Excel 2007 before beginning this exercise.

OPEN the *ForFollowUp* workbook.

You can browse to the practice files in Windows Explorer by following these steps:

1. On the **Windows taskbar**, click the **Start** button, and then click **Documents**.

    Or

    If you are using Windows XP or earlier, click **My Documents** instead.

2. In the *Documents* or *My Documents* folder, double-click *Microsoft Press*, double-click *Excel2007SBS*, and then double-click a specific chapter folder.

You can browse to the practice files from a dialog box by following these steps:

1. In the **Favorite Links** pane in the dialog box, click *Documents*.

    Or

    If you are using Windows XP or earlier, click *My Documents* on the **Places bar** instead.

2. In the *Documents* or *My Documents* folder, double-click *Microsoft Press*, double-click *Excel2007SBS*, and then double-click a specific chapter folder.

Uninstalling the Practice Files

You can free up hard disk space by uninstalling the practice files that were installed from the companion CD. The uninstall process also deletes any files that you created in the *Microsoft Press\Excel2007SBS* chapter-specific folders while working through the exercises. Follow these steps:

1. On the **Windows taskbar**, click the **Start** button, and then click **Control Panel**.

2. In **Control Panel**, under **Programs**, click the **Uninstall a program** task.

   Or

   In **Control Panel**, click **Add or Remove Programs**.

3. If you are using Windows Vista, in the **Programs and Features** window, click **Microsoft Office Excel 2007 Step by Step**, and then on the toolbar at the top of the window, click the **Uninstall** button.

   Or

   In the **Add or Remove Programs** window, click **Microsoft Office Excel 2007 Step by Step**, and then click **Remove**.

4. If a message box asks you to confirm the deletion, click **Yes**.

See Also If you need additional help installing or uninstalling the practice files, see "Getting Help" later in this book.

Important Microsoft Product Support Services does not provide support for this book or its companion CD.

Getting Help

Every effort has been made to ensure the accuracy of this book and the contents of its companion CD. If you do run into problems, please contact the sources listed below for assistance.

Getting Help with This Book and Its Companion CD

If your question or issue concerns the content of this book or its companion CD, please first search the online Microsoft Press Knowledge Base, which provides support information for known errors in or corrections to this book, at the following Web site:

www.microsoft.com/mspress/support/search.asp

If you do not find your answer at the online Knowledge Base, send your comments or questions to Microsoft Press Technical Support at:

mspinput@microsoft.com

Getting Help with Excel 2007

If your question is about Microsoft Office Excel 2007, and not about the content of this Microsoft Press book, please search the Office 2007 Solution Center or the Microsoft Knowledge Base at:

support.microsoft.com

In the United States, Microsoft software product support issues not covered by the Microsoft Knowledge Base are addressed by Microsoft Product Support Services. Location-specific software support options are available from:

support.microsoft.com/gp/selfoverview/

The Microsoft Business Certification Program

Desktop computing proficiency is becoming increasingly important in today's business world. As a result, when screening, hiring, and training employees, more employers are relying on the objectivity and consistency of technology certification to ensure the competence of their workforce. As an employee or job seeker, you can use technology certification to prove that you already have the skills you need to succeed, saving current and future employers the trouble and expense of training you.

The Microsoft Business Certification program is designed to assist employees in validating their Windows Vista skills and 2007 Microsoft Office program skills. The following certification paths are available:

- A Microsoft Certified Application Specialist (MCAS) is an individual who has demonstrated proficiency in Windows Vista or in a 2007 Office program by passing a certification exam in Windows Vista or in one or more of the 2007 Office programs, including Microsoft Office Word 2007, Microsoft Office Excel 2007, Microsoft Office PowerPoint 2007, Microsoft Office Outlook 2007, and Microsoft Office Access 2007.

- A Microsoft Certified Application Professional (MCAP) is an individual who has taken his or her knowledge of the 2007 Office system and of Microsoft SharePoint Products and Technologies to the next level and has demonstrated by passing a certification exam that he or she can use the collaborative power of the Office system to accomplish job functions such as *Budget Analysis and Forecasting*, or *Content Management and Collaboration*.

Selecting a Certification Path

When selecting a Microsoft Business Certification path that you would like to pursue, you should assess the following:

- The program and program version(s) with which you are familiar
- The length of time you have used the program
- Whether you have had formal or informal training in the use of that program

Candidates for MCAS-level certification are expected to successfully complete a wide range of standard business tasks, such as formatting a document or worksheet. Successful candidates generally have six or more months of experience with Windows Vista or the specific Office program, including either formal, instructor-led training or self study using MCAS-approved books, guides, or interactive computer-based materials.

Candidates for MCAP-level certification are expected to successfully complete more complex, business-oriented tasks that involve using the advanced functionality of the combined 2007 Office suite of products, as well as SharePoint. Successful candidates generally have at least six months and may have several years of experience with the programs, including formal, instructor-led training or self study using MCAP-approved materials.

Becoming a Microsoft Certified Application Specialist—Microsoft 2007 Office System

Every MCAS and MCAP certification exam is developed from a set of exam skill standards that are derived from studies of how the 2007 Office programs are used in the workplace. Because these skill standards dictate the scope of each exam, they provide critical information about how to prepare for certification.

To become a Microsoft Certified Application Specialist in one of the 2007 Office programs, you must demonstrate the proficiency in these areas:

Exam	Skill sets
77-601: Using Microsoft Office Word 2007	Creating and Customizing Documents
	Formatting Content
	Working with Visual Content
	Organizing Content
	Reviewing Documents
	Sharing and Securing Content
77-602: Using Microsoft Office Excel 2007	Creating and Manipulating Data
	Formatting Data and Content
	Creating and Modifying Formulas
	Presenting Data Visually
	Collaborating and Securing Data
77-603: Using Microsoft Office PowerPoint 2007	Creating and Manipulating Data
	Formatting Data and Content
	Creating and Modifying Formulas
	Presenting Data Visually
	Collaborating and Securing Data
77-604: Using Microsoft Office Outlook 2007	Managing Messaging
	Managing Scheduling
	Managing Tasks
	Managing Contacts and Personal Contact Information
	Organizing Information
77-605: Using Microsoft Office Access 2007	Structuring a Database
	Creating and Formatting Database Elements
	Entering and Modifying Data
	Creating and Modifying Queries
	Presenting and Sharing
	Managing and Maintaining Databases

Taking a Microsoft Business Certification Exam

The MCAS and MCAP certification exams for Windows Vista and the 2007 Office programs are performance-based and require you to complete business-related tasks using interactive simulation (a digital model) of the Windows Vista operating system or one or more programs in the Office suite.

Test Taking Tips

- Follow all instructions provided in each question completely and accurately.

- Enter requested information as it appears in the instructions, but without duplicating the formatting unless you are specifically instructed to do otherwise.

- Close all dialog boxes before proceeding to the next exam questions unless you are specifically instructed to do otherwise.

- Don't close task panes proceeding to the next exam questions unless you are specifically instructed to do otherwise.

- If you are asked to print a document, spreadsheet, chart, report, or slide, perform the task, but be aware that nothing will actually be printed.

- Don't worry about extra keystrokes or mouse clicks. Your work is scored based on its result, not on the method you use to achieve that result, and not on the time you take to complete the question.

- If your computer becomes unstable during the exam or if a power outage occurs, contact a testing center administrator immediately. The administrator will restart the computer and return the exam to the point where the interruption occurred with your score intact.

Certification Benefits

At the conclusion of the exam, you will receive a score report, which you can print with the assistance of the testing center administrator. If your score meets or exceeds the passing standard (the minimum required score), you will be contacted by e-mail by the Microsoft Certification Program team and mailed a printed certificate within approximately 14 days. The e-mail message you receive will include your Microsoft Certification ID and links to online resources, including the Microsoft Certified Professional site. On this site, you can order a welcome kit and ID card, view and send your certification transcript, build a personalized certification logo, and access other useful and interesting resources, including special offers from Microsoft and affiliated companies.

Using the Logo Builder, you can create a personalized certification logo that includes the MCAS logo and the specific programs in which you have achieved certification. If you achieve MCAS certification in multiple programs, you can include all of them in one logo, like this:

 Microsoft Office Access 2007 Certified
Microsoft Office Excel 2007 Certified
Microsoft Office Outlook 2007 Certified
Microsoft Office Powerpoint 2007 Certified
Microsoft Office Word 2007 Certified
Microsoft Windows Vista Certified

You can include your personalized logo on business cards and other personal promotional materials. This logo attests to the fact that you are proficient in the applications or cross-application skills necessary to achieve the certification.

For More Information

To learn more about the Microsoft Certified Application Specialist exams, the Microsoft Certified Application Professional exams, and related courseware, visit

www.microsoft.com/learning/mcp/msbc

Quick Reference

2 Setting Up a Workbook

To open a workbook

1. Click the **Microsoft Office Button**, and then click **Open**.
2. Navigate to the folder that contains the workbook you want to open.
3. Click the workbook, and then click **Open**.

To create a new workbook

1. Click the **Microsoft Office Button**, and then click **New**.
2. In the **New Workbook** window, click **Blank Workbook**.
3. Click **Create**.

To save a workbook

1. On the **Quick Access Toolbar**, click the **Save** button.
2. Type a name for the file.
3. Click **Save**.

To set file properties

1. Click the **Microsoft Office Button**, point to **Prepare**, and then click **Properties**.
2. In the **Document Information Panel**, click the type of properties you want to set in the **Property Views and Options** list.
3. Add information describing your file, and then close the **Document Information Panel**.

To define custom properties

1. Click the **Microsoft Office Button**, point to **Prepare**, and then click **Properties**.
2. In the **Property Views and Options** list, click **Advanced Properties**.
3. In the **Properties** dialog box, click the **Custom** tab.
4. In the **Name** box, type a property name, select the type of data contained in the property, and then type a value for the property.
5. Click **Add**, and then click **OK**.

To display a worksheet

→ Click the sheet tab of the worksheet you want to display.

To create a new worksheet

1. Right-click the sheet tab of the worksheet that follows the location where you want to insert a worksheet, and then click **Insert**.

2. In the **Insert** dialog box, double-click **Worksheet**.

To rename a worksheet

1. Double-click the sheet tab of the worksheet you want to rename.

2. Type the new name of the worksheet, and then press Enter.

To copy a worksheet to another workbook

1. Open the workbook that will receive the new worksheets.

2. Switch to the workbook that contains the worksheets you want to copy, hold down the Ctrl key, and click the sheet tabs of the worksheets you want to copy.

3. Right-click the selection, and then click **Move Or Copy**.

4. Select the **Create A Copy** check box.

5. In the **To Book** list, click the workbook to which you want the worksheet(s) copied.

6. Click **OK**.

To change the order of worksheets in a workbook

→ Drag the sheet tab of the worksheet you want to move.

To hide a worksheet

1. Hold down the Ctrl key and click the sheet tabs of the worksheets you want to hide.

2. Right-click any selected worksheet tab, and then click **Hide**.

To unhide a worksheet

1. Right-click any worksheet tab, and then click **Unhide**.

2. Click the worksheet you want to unhide, and then click **OK**.

To delete a worksheet

1. Hold down the Ctrl key and click the sheet tabs of the worksheets you want to delete.

2. Right-click the selection, and then click **Delete**.

To change a row's height or column's width

1. Select the rows and columns you want to resize.

2. Drag a row or column border until it is the desired size.

To insert a column or row

→ Right-click the column header to the right of, or the row header below, where you want the new column or row to appear, and then click **Insert**.

To delete columns or rows

1. Select the rows or columns you want to delete.

2. Right-click the selection, and then click **Delete**.

To hide columns or rows

1. Select the rows or columns you want to hide.

2. Right-click a row or column header in the selection, and then click **Hide**.

To unhide columns or rows

1. Click the row or column header of the row above or the column to the left of the rows or columns you want to unhide.

2. Hold down the Shift key and click the row or column header of the row or column below or to the right of the rows or columns you want to unhide.

3. Right-click the selection, and then click **Unhide**.

To insert a cell

1. Select the cells in the location where you want to insert new cells.

2. Display the **Home** tab.

3. In the **Cells** group, in the **Insert** list, click **Insert Cells**.

4. Select the option representing how you want to move the existing cells to make room for the inserted cells. Then click **OK**.

To delete cells

1. Select the cells you want to delete.

2. Display the **Home** tab.

3. In the **Cells** group, in the **Delete** list, click **Delete Cells**.

4. Select the option representing how you want the remaining cells to fill in the deleted space.

5. Click **OK**.

To move a group of cells to a new location

1. Select the cells you want to move.

2. Point to the outline of the selected cells.

3. Drag the cells to the desired location.

To zoom in or out on a worksheet

● Click the **Zoom In** control to make your window's contents 10 percent larger.

● Click the **Zoom Out** control to make your window's contents 10 percent smaller.

● Drag the **Zoom** slider control to the left to zoom out, or to the right to zoom in.

To zoom in or out to a specific zoom level

1. On the **View** tab, in the **Zoom** group, click **Zoom**.

2. Select the **Custom** option.

3. Type a new zoom level in the **Custom** field.

4. Click **OK**.

To change to another open workbook

1. On the **View** tab, in the **Window** group, click **Switch Windows**.

2. Click the name of the workbook you want to display.

To arrange all open workbooks in the program window

1. On the **View** tab, in the **Window** group, click **Arrange All**.

2. Select the desired arrangement.

3. Click **OK**.

To add a button to the Quick Access Toolbar

1. Click the **Customize Quick Access Toolbar** button, and then click **More Commands**.

2. In the **Choose Commands From** list, click the category from which you want to choose the command.

3. Click the command you want to add, and then click the **Add** button.

4. After you finish adding commands, click **OK**.

To move a button on the Quick Access Toolbar

1. Click the **Customize Quick Access Toolbar** button, and then click **More Commands**.

2. In the active command list, click the command you want to move.

3. Click the **Move Up** button or the **Move Down** button.

To remove a button from the Quick Access Toolbar

1. Right-click the button you want to remove.

2. Click **Remove from Quick Access Toolbar**.

To hide and display the Ribbon

● To hide the Ribbon, double-click the active tab label.

● To temporarily redisplay the Ribbon, click the tab label you want. Then click any button on the tab, or click away from the tab, to rehide it.

● To permanently redisplay the Ribbon, double-click any tab label.

To hide the formula bar

→ On the **View** tab, in the **Show/Hide** group, clear the **Formula Bar** check box.

To hide column and row headings

→ On the **View** tab, in the **Show/Hide** group, clear the **Headings** check box.

3   Working with Data and Data Tables

To enter a data series using AutoFill

1. Type the first label or value for your list.

2. Drag the fill handle to the cell containing the last label or value in the series.

To change how dragging the fill handle extends a series

1. Type the first label or value for your list.

2. Hold down the <kbd>Ctrl</kbd> key, and drag the fill handle to the cell containing the last label or value in the series.

To enter data by using AutoComplete

1. Type the beginning of an entry.

2. Press <kbd>Tab</kbd> to accept the AutoComplete value.

To enter data by picking from a list

1. Right-click a cell in a column with existing values, and then click **Pick from Drop-down List**.

2. Click the item in the list you want to enter.

To copy and paste cells

1. Select the cells you want to copy.

2. On the **Home** tab, in the **Clipboard** group, click **Copy**.

3. Click the cells into which you want to paste the values.

4. On the **Home** tab, in the **Clipboard** group, click **Paste**.

To transpose data when pasting

1. Copy the cells you want to transpose.

2. Click the cell in which you want to paste the contents of the top or left copied cell.

3. In the **Paste** list, click **Transpose.**

To copy and paste a row or column

1. Select the row or column you want to copy.

2. On the **Home** tab, in the **Clipboard** group, click **Copy**.

3. Click the header of the row or column into which you want to paste the values.

4. On the **Home** tab, in the **Clipboard** group, click **Paste**.

To find data within a worksheet

1. On the **Home** tab, in the **Editing** group, click **Find & Select**, and then, in the list, click **Find**.

2. Type the text you want to find, and then click **Find Next**.

To replace a value with another value within a worksheet

1. In the **Editing** group, click **Find & Select**, and then, in the list, click **Replace**.

2. Type the text you want to replace.

3. Type the text you want to take the place of the existing text, and then click **Find Next**.

4. For each search term located, click **Find Next**, follow any of these steps, and then repeat:

   ○ Click **Replace** to replace the text.

   ○ Click **Find Next** to skip this instance of the text and move to the next time it occurs.

   ○ Click **Replace All** to replace every instance of the text.

To edit a cell's contents by hand

1. Click the cell you want to edit.

2. In the formula bar, select the text you want to edit.

3. Type the new text, and then press [Enter].

To check spelling

1. On the **Review** tab, in the **Proofing** group, click **Spelling**. If you are asked whether you want to save your work, do so.

2. Follow any of these steps:

   ○ Click **Ignore Once** to ignore the current misspelling.

   ○ Click **Ignore All** to ignore all instances of the misspelled word.

   ○ Click **Add to Dictionary** to add the current word to the dictionary.

   ○ Click the correct spelling, and then click **Change** to replace the current misspelling with the correct word.

   ○ Click the correct spelling, and then click **Change All** to replace all instances of the current misspelling with the correct word.

   ○ Click **Cancel** to stop checking spelling.

3. Click **OK** to clear the dialog box that appears after the spelling check is complete.

To look up a word in the Thesaurus

1. Select the word you want to look up.

2. On the **Review** tab, in the **Proofing** group, click **Thesaurus**.

To translate a word to another language

1. Select the word you want to look up.

2. On the **Review** tab, in the **Proofing** group, click **Translate**.

To create a data table

1. Type your table headers in a single row.

2. Type your first data row directly below the header row.

3. Click any cell in the range from which you want to create a table.

4. On the **Home** tab, in the **Styles** group, click **Format as Table**.

5. Click the desired table style.

6. Verify that Excel identified the data range correctly.

7. If your table has headers, select the **My table has headers** check box.

8. Click **OK**.

To add rows to a data table

→ Click the cell at the bottom right corner of the data table and press `Tab` to create a new table row.

→ Type data into the cell below the bottom left corner of the data table and press `Tab`. Excel will make the new row part of the data table.

To resize a table

1. Click any cell in the table.

2. Drag the resize handle to expand or contract the table.

To add a Total row to a column

1. Click any cell in the table.

2. On the **Design** tab, in the **Table Style Options** group, click **Total Row**.

To change the Total row summary function

1. Click any cell in the table's **Total** row.

2. Click the down arrow that appears.

3. Click the desired summary function.

To rename a table

1. Click any cell in the table.

2. On the **Design** tab, in the **Properties** group, type a new value in the **Table Name** box.

4   Performing Calculations on Data

To create a named range

1. Select the cells you want to name.

2. On the formula bar, click the **Name Box**.

3. Type the name you want for the range.

4. Press `Enter`.

To create a named range from a selection

1. Select the cells you want to name as a range. Be sure either the first or last cell contains the name for the range.

2. On the **Formulas** tab, in the **Defined Names** group, click **Create from Selection**.

3. Select the check box that represents the cell that contains the range's desired name.

4. Click **OK**.

To display the Name Manager

→ On the **Formulas** tab, in the **Defined Names** group, click **Name Manager**.

To edit a named range

1. On the **Formulas** tab, in the **Defined Names** group, click **Name Manager**.

2. Click the named range you want to edit, and then click the **Edit** button.

3. Click the **Collapse Dialog** button.

4. Select the cells you want the range to include, and then click **Close**.

To delete a named range

→ In the **Edit Name** dialog box, click the range you want to delete, and then click the **Delete** button.

To create a formula

1. Click the cell into which you want to enter a formula.
2. Type =.
3. Type the expression representing the calculation you want to perform.
4. Press [Enter].

To create a formula using the Insert Function dialog box

1. On the **Formulas** tab, in the **Function Library** group, click **Insert Function**.
2. Select the function you want to use, and click **OK**.
3. Fill in the **Function Arguments** dialog box, and click **OK**.

To use a named range in a formula

1. Begin typing the formula.
2. Type the name of the named range as a function's argument.

To refer to a table column or row in a formula

1. Click the cell in which you want to create the formula.
2. Type =, followed by the function to include in the formula and a left parenthesis; for example, =SUM(would be a valid way to start.
3. Point to the header of the table column you want to use in the formula. When the mouse pointer changes to a black, downward-pointing arrow, click the column header.
4. Type a right parenthesis and press [Enter].

To create a formula using Formula AutoComplete

1. Begin typing the formula.
2. Click the desired function from the list that appears.

To create a formula that doesn't change when copied between cells

1. Begin typing the formula.
2. Precede all column and row references with a dollar sign (for example, $C$4).

To create a formula that does change when copied between cells

1. Begin typing the formula.

2. Type all column and row references without a dollar sign (for example, C4).

To create a conditional formula

1. Click the cell in which you want to enter an *IF* function.

2. On the **Formulas** tab, in the **Function Library** group, click **Logical**, and then click **IF**.

3. Type a conditional statement that evaluates to true or false.

4. Type the text you want to appear if the condition is true.

5. Type the text you want to appear if the condition is false.

6. Click **OK**.

To display cells that provide values for a formula

1. Click the cell you want to track.

2. On the **Formulas** tab, in the **Formula Auditing** group, click the **Trace Precedents** button.

To display formulas that use a cell's contents

1. Click the cell you want to track.

2. On the **Formulas** tab, in the **Formula Auditing** group, click the **Trace Dependents** button.

To remove tracer arrows

1. Click the cell you want to track.

2. On the **Formulas** tab, in the **Formula Auditing** group, click the **Remove Arrows** button.

To locate errors in a worksheet

1. On the **Formulas** tab, in the **Formula Auditing** group, click the **Error Checking** button.

2. Click the **Edit in Formula Bar** button.

3. Edit the formula.

4. Click the **Next** button to view the next error.

To step through a formula to locate an error

1. Click the cell with the formula you want to evaluate.
2. On the **Formulas** tab, in the **Formula Auditing** group, click **Evaluate Formula**.
3. Click **Evaluate** (one or more times) to move through the formula's elements.
4. Click **Close**.

To watch a value in a cell

1. On the **Formulas** tab, in the **Formula Auditing** group, click **Watch Window**.
2. Click **Add Watch**.
3. Select the cells you want to watch.
4. Click **Add**.
5. Click **Watch Window**.

To delete a watch

1. On the **Formulas** tab, in the **Formula Auditing** group, click **Watch Window**.
2. Click the watch you want to delete.
3. Click **Delete Watch**.
4. Click the **Close** button.

5   Changing Workbook Appearance

To change a cell's font, font style, font color, or background color

1. Select the cells you want to change.
2. On the **Home** tab, use the controls in the **Font** group to format the cells.

To add a border to a cell

1. Select the cells around which you want to draw a border.
2. On the **Home** tab, in the **Font** group, click the **Border** arrow, and then, in the list, click the type of border you want to apply.

To apply a style to a cell

1. Select the cells you want to change.
2. On the **Home** tab, in the **Styles** group, click **Cell Styles**.
3. Click a style.

To create a new style

1. On the **Home** tab, in the **Styles** group, click **Cell Styles**.

2. Click **New Cell Style**.

3. Type a new style name.

4. Click **Format**.

5. Specify the formatting you want this style to contain.

6. Click **OK** twice.

To delete a style

1. On the **Home** tab, in the **Styles** group, click **Cell Styles**.

2. Right-click the style you want to delete.

3. Click **Delete**.

To copy a cell's formatting onto another cell

1. Click the cell that contains the format you want to apply to another cell.

2. On the **Home** tab, in the **Clipboard** group, click the **Format Painter** button.

3. Select the cells to which you want to apply the formatting.

To apply a workbook theme

1. On the **Page Layout** tab, in the **Themes** group, click **Themes**.

2. Click the theme you want to apply.

To change theme fonts, colors, and graphic effects

→ Using the **Controls** on the **Page Layout** tab, in the **Themes** group, follow one of these steps:

   ○ Click the **Fonts** button and select a new font.

   ○ Click the **Colors** button and select a new color set.

   ○ Click the **Effects** button and select a new default effect.

To save a workbook's format as a new theme

1. Format your worksheet using the colors, fonts, and effects you want to include in your theme.

2. On the **Page Layout** tab, in the **Themes** group, click **Themes**.

3. Click **Save Current Theme**.

4. Type a name for your theme.

5. Click **Save**.

To create a new table style

1. On the **Home** tab, in the **Styles** group, click **Format as Table**, and then click **New Table Style**.

2. In the **Name** field, type a name for the table style.

3. In the **Table Element** list, click the element you want to format.

4. Click **Format**, and use the controls in the **Format** dialog box to format the table element.

5. Click **OK**.

6. Repeat as desired to format other elements, and then click **OK**.

To format a cell value as a phone number

1. On the **Home** tab, click the **Number** dialog box launcher.

2. Click **Special**.

3. Click **Phone Number**.

4. Click **OK**.

To format cell data as a currency value

→ On the **Home** tab, in the **Number** group, click the **Accounting Number Format** button.

To select a foreign currency symbol

→ On the **Home** tab, in the **Number** group, click the **Accounting Number Format** arrow, and then, in the list, click the currency symbol you want to apply.

To add words to a cell's value

1. On the **Home** tab, click the **Number** dialog box launcher.

2. Click **Custom**.

3. Click the format to serve as the base for your custom format.

4. Type the text to appear in the cell, enclosed in quotes (for example, "cases").

5. Click **OK**.

To apply a conditional format to a cell

1. Select the cells you want to change.
2. On the **Home** tab, in the **Styles** group, click **Conditional Formatting**.
3. Click **New Rule**.
4. Click **Format Only Cells That Contain**.
5. In the **Comparison Phrase** list, click the comparison phrase you want.
6. Type the constant values or formulas you want evaluated.
7. Click **Format**.
8. Specify the formatting you want and click **OK** twice.

To edit a conditional formatting rule

1. Select the cells that contain the rule you want to edit.
2. On the **Home** tab, in the **Styles** group, click **Conditional Formatting**.
3. Click **Manage Rules**.
4. Click the rule you want to change.
5. Click **Edit Rule**.
6. Use the controls to make your changes.
7. Click **OK** twice to save your changes.

To delete a conditional formatting rule

1. Select the cells that contain the rule you want to edit.
2. On the **Home** tab, in the **Styles** group, click **Conditional Formatting**.
3. Click **Manage Rules**.
4. Click the rule you want to delete.
5. Click **Delete Rule**.
6. Click **OK**.

To display data bars in one or more cells

1. Select the cells that contain your data.
2. On the **Home** tab, in the **Styles** group, click **Conditional Formatting**.
3. Point to **Data Bars**.
4. Click the data bar option you want to apply.

To display a color scale in one or more cells

1. Select the cells that contain your data.
2. On the **Home** tab, in the **Styles** group, click **Conditional Formatting**.
3. Point to **Color Scales**.
4. Click the color scale pattern you want to apply.

To display icon sets in one or more cells

1. Select the cells that contain your data.
2. On the **Home** tab, in the **Styles** group, click **Conditional Formatting**.
3. Point to **Icon Sets**.
4. Click the icon set you want to apply.

To add a picture to a worksheet

1. On the **Insert** tab, in the **Illustrations** group, click **Picture**.
2. Double-click the picture you want to insert.

To change a picture's characteristics

1. Click the picture.
2. Use the controls on the **Format** tab to edit the picture.

6 Focusing on Specific Data by Using Filters

To apply a filter to a worksheet

1. Click any cell in the range you want to filter.
2. On the **Data** tab, in the **Sort & Filter** group, click **Filter**.
3. Click the filter arrow for the column by which you want to filter your worksheet.
4. Select the check boxes next to the values by which you want to filter the list.
5. Click **OK**.

To clear a filter

1. Click any cell in the filtered range.
2. On the **Data** tab, in the **Sort & Filter** group, click **Clear**.

To display the top or bottom values in a column

1. Click the filter arrow at the top of the column by which you want to filter the list.
2. Click **Number Filters**.
3. Click **Top 10**.
4. Select whether to display the top or bottom values.
5. Select how many values to display.
6. Select whether the value in the middle box represents the number of items to display, or the percentage of items to display.

To create a custom filter

1. Click any cell in the list you want to filter.
2. If necessary, on the **Data** tab, in the **Sort & Filter** group, click **Filter** to display the filter arrows.
3. Click the filter arrow of the column for which you want to create a custom filter.
4. Point to **Text Filters**.
5. Click **Custom Filter**.
6. In the **Comparison Operator** list, click the comparison you want to use.
7. Type the value by which you want to compare the values in the selected column.
8. Click **OK**.

To generate a random value

→ Type the formula =RAND().

To generate a random value between two other values

→ Type the formula =RANDBETWEEN(low, high), replacing low and high with the lower and upper bound of values you want to generate.

To summarize data quickly using AutoCalculate

1. Select the cells you want to summarize.
2. View the summary on the status bar, at the bottom right of the Excel program window.

To summarize filtered data using a SUBTOTAL formula

→ Type the formula =SUBTOTAL(function, ref), replacing function with the desired summary function, and ref with the cell range you want so summarize.

To find list rows that contain unique values

1. Select the cells in which you want to find unique values.

2. On the **Data** tab, in the **Sort & Filter** group, click **Advanced**.

3. Select the **Unique Records Only** check box.

4. Click **OK**.

To create a validation rule

1. Select the cells you want to validate.

2. On the **Data** tab, in the **Data Tools** group, click the **Data Validation**, and then, in the list, click **Data Validation**.

3. In the **Allow** list, click the type of data you want to allow.

4. In the **Data** list, click the condition for which you want to validate.

5. Type the appropriate values in the boxes.

6. Click the **Input Message** tab.

7. Select the **Show input message when cell is selected** check box.

8. Type the message you want to appear when the cell is clicked.

9. Click the **Error Alert** tab.

10. Select the **Show error alert after invalid data is entered** check box.

11. In the **Style** list, click the icon you want to appear next to your message.

12. Type a title for the error message box.

13. Type the error message you want.

14. Click **OK**.

To identify which cells contain invalid data

→ In the **Data Validation** list, click **Circle Invalid Data**.

To turn off data validation in a cell

→ In the **Data Validation** list, click **Clear Invalidation Circles**.

7   Reordering and Summarizing Data

To sort a data list

1. Click any cell in the column by which you want to sort your data.

2. On the **Data** tab, in the **Sort & Filter** group, click the **Sort Ascending** button or the **Sort Descending** button.

To sort a data list by values in multiple columns

1. Select a cell in the data list or table you want to sort.

2. On the **Data** tab, in the **Sort & Filter** group, click **Sort**.

3. In the **Sort By** list, click the first column by which you want to sort.

4. In the **Sort On** list, click the criteria by which you want to sort.

5. In the **Order** list, click **A to Z** or **Z to A** to indicate the order into which the column's values should be sorted.

6. Click **Add Level**.

7. If necessary, repeat steps 3–6 to set the columns and order for additional sorting rules.

8. Click **OK**.

To add a sorting level

1. Select a cell in the data list or table you want to sort.

2. On the **Data** tab, in the **Sort & Filter** group, click **Sort**.

3. Click **Add Level**, and define the sort using the tools in the dialog box.

To delete a sorting level

1. Select a cell in the sorted data list.

2. On the **Data** tab, in the **Sort & Filter** group, click **Sort**.

3. Click the level you want to delete.

4. Click **Delete Level**.

To create a custom list for sorting

1. Click the **Microsoft Office Button**.
2. Click **Excel Options**.
3. Click **Popular**.
4. Click **Edit Custom Lists**.
5. Click **New List**.
6. Type the custom list you want. Separate each entry by pressing [Enter].
7. Click **Add**.
8. Click **OK** twice to close the **Custom Lists** dialog box and the **Excel Options** dialog box.

To sort worksheet data by a custom list of values

1. Click any cell in the list you want to sort.
2. On the **Data** tab, in the **Sort & Filter** group, click **Sort**.
3. In the **Sort By** list, click the column you want to sort by.
4. In the **Sort On** list, click the criteria you want to sort by.
5. In the **Order** list, click **Custom List**.
6. Click a custom list.
7. Click **OK** to close the **Custom Lists** dialog box.
8. Click **OK** to sort the data list.

To organize worksheet data into groups

1. Click any cell in the range you want to group.
2. On the **Data** tab, in the **Outline** group, click **Subtotal**.
3. In the **At Each Change In** list, click the value on which you want to base the subtotals.
4. In the **Use Function** list, click the subtotal function you want to use.
5. Select which columns should have subtotals calculated.
6. Click **OK**.

To show and hide levels of detail in a grouped data list

→ Follow either of these steps:
  ○ Click the **Show Detail** control on a hidden grouping level to display that level's contents.
  ○ Click the **Hide Detail** control to hide rows that are currently displayed.

To remove grouping levels from a data list

1. Click any cell in the subtotaled range.
2. On the **Data** tab, in the **Outline** group, click **Subtotal**, and then click **Remove All**.

To look up data in a data list

1. Create a sorted data list or data table that has column headers.
2. Create a VLOOKUP formula of the form *=VLOOKUP(lookup_value, table_array, col_index_num, range_lookup)*.
3. Type a value in the cell referred to by the *lookup_value* argument.

8   Combining Data from Multiple Sources

To create a workbook template

1. Click the **Microsoft Office Button**, and click **Save As**.
2. In the **Save As Type** list, click **Excel Template**.
3. Type the name you want for the template.
4. Click **Save**.

To create a new workbook that is based on a template

1. Click the **Microsoft Office Button**, and click **New**.
2. Click **Installed Templates**, and double-click the template you want to use to create your workbook.
3. Click the **Microsoft Office Button**, and click **Save As**.
4. Type a name for the file.
5. In the **Save As Type** list, click **Excel Workbook**.
6. Click **Save**.

To create a worksheet template

1. Remove all but one worksheet from a workbook, and format the worksheet as you want the template to appear.
2. Click the **Microsoft Office Button**, and click **Save As**.
3. In the **Save As Type** list, click **Excel Template**.
4. Type the name you want for the template.
5. Click **Save**.

To add a template-based worksheet to a workbook

1. Right-click a sheet tab, and then click **Insert**.
2. On the **Spreadsheet Solutions** tab, click the template you want to use.
3. Click **OK**.

To create a link between two cells

1. In the cell you want to be target of the link, type =, but do not press `Enter`.
2. On the **View** tab, in the **Window** group, click **Switch Windows**, and then click the workbook that contains the data for your target cell.
3. Click the cell that contains the data, and press `Enter`.

To open multiple workbooks simultaneously

1. Open the workbooks you want to open simultaneously.
2. On the **View** tab, in the **Window** group, click **Save Workspace**.
3. Type a name for the workspace.
4. Click **Save**.

9 Analyzing Alternative Data Sets

Define an alternative data set

1. On the **Data** tab, in the **Data Tools** group, click **What-If Analysis**, and then click **Scenario Manager**.
2. Click **Add**.
3. In the **Scenario Name** field, type a name for the scenario.
4. At the right edge of the **Changing cells** field, click the **Contract Dialog** button.
5. Select the cells to change, and then click the **Expand Dialog** button.

6. Click **OK**.

7. Type new values for the cells, and then click **OK**.

8. Click **Close**.

To change a worksheet's values using a scenario

1. On the **Data** tab, in the **Data Tools** group, click **What-If Analysis**, and then click **Scenario Manager**.

2. Click the scenario you want to display.

3. Click **Show**.

To summarize the values in multiple scenarios

1. On the **Data** tab, in the **Data Tools** group, click **What-If Analysis**, and then click **Scenario Manager**.

2. Click **Summary**.

3. Verify that the **Scenario summary** option is selected and that the correct cells appear in the **Result cells** field.

4. Click **OK**.

To determine the required inputs for a formula to generate a specific result

1. On the **Data** tab, in the **Data Tools** group, click **What-If Analysis**, and then click **Goal Seek**.

2. In the **Set cell** field, type the address of the cell that contains the formula you want to generate a target value.

3. In the **To value** field, type the target value.

4. In the **By changing cell** field, type the cell that contains the value you want to vary.

5. Click **OK**.

6. Click **Cancel** to close the **Goal Seek** dialog box without saving your changes.

To analyze data by using Descriptive Statistics

1. On the **Data** tab, in the **Analysis** group, click **Data Analysis**.

2. Click **Descriptive Statistics**, and then click **OK**.

3. Click in the **Input Range** field, and then select the cells you want to summarize.

4. Select the **Summary Statistics** check box.

5. Click **OK**.

10   Creating Dynamic Lists by Using PivotTables

To create a PivotTable from a data list

1. Click any cell in the data table.

2. On the **Insert** tab, in the **Tables** group, click **PivotTable**.

3. Verify that the proper table name or cell range appears in the **Table/Range** field and that the **New Worksheet** option is selected.

4. Click **OK**.

5. In the **PivotTable Field List** task pane, drag the available fields to the desired spots in the PivotTable.

To pivot a PivotTable

→ In the **PivotTable Field List** task pane, drag a field header to a new position.

To filter a PivotTable

1. On the PivotTable worksheet, click any cell in the PivotTable.

2. In the **PivotTable Field List** task pane's **Choose fields to add to report** section, click the target field header. Then click the down arrow next to the field header and clear the **(Select All)** check box.

3. Select the check boxes of the values you do want to show, and then click **OK**.

To show or hide the PivotTable Field List task pane

1. Click any cell in the PivotTable.

2. On the **Options** tab, in the **Show/Hide** group, click the **Field List** button.

To show or hide levels of detail within a PivotTable

→ In the body of the PivotTable, follow either of these steps:

   ○ Click the **Show Detail** control to display hidden rows.

   ○ Click the **Hide Detail** control to hide rows displayed in the PivotTable.

To rename a PivotTable

1. On the PivotTable worksheet, click any cell in the PivotTable.

2. On the **Options** contextual tab, in the **PivotTable** group, in the **PivotTable Name** field, type a new name for the PivotTable.

To control how and where subtotals and grand totals appear in your PivotTable

1. On the PivotTable worksheet, click any cell in the PivotTable.

2. On the **Design** contextual tab, in the **Layout** group, click **Subtotals**, and then click the option representing how you want subtotals to appear in your PivotTable.

3. On the **Design** contextual tab, in the **Layout** group, click **Grand Totals**, and then click the option representing how you want grand totals to appear in your PivotTable.

To change the PivotTable summary function

→ Right-click any data cell in the PivotTable, point to **Summarize Data By**, and then click the desired summary function.

To apply a number format to a PivotTable

1. On the PivotTable worksheet, right-click any data cell, and then click **Number Format**.

2. In the **Category** list, click **Number**.

3. Use the controls on the **Number** tab to create your format.

4. Click **OK**.

To apply a conditional format to a PivotTable

1. Select the cell ranges you want to format.

2. On the **Home** tab, in the **Styles** group, click **Conditional Formatting**, point to the type of conditional format you want to use, and then click the specific format you want to apply.

To apply a PivotTable Style to a PivotTable

1. Click any cell in the PivotTable.

2. On the **Design** tab, in the **PivotTable Styles** gallery, click the style you want to apply to the PivotTable.

To create a new PivotTable style

1. Click any cell in the PivotTable.

2. On the **Design** contextual tab, in the **PivotTable Styles** group, click the **More** button at the bottom-right corner of the style gallery.

3. Click **New PivotTable Style**.

4. In the **Name** field, type a name for the style.

5. In the **Table Element** list, click the element you want to change, and then click **Format**.

6. Use the controls in the **Format Cells** dialog box to format the element.

7. If desired, repeat step 6 for other elements.

8. Click **OK** twice.

To import data from an external source

1. On the **Data** tab, in the **Get External Data** group, click **From Text**.

2. Navigate to the folder that contains the source file, and double-click the file.

3. Verify that the **Delimited** option is selected, and then click **Next**.

4. In the **Delimiters** section, verify that the correct check box is selected, and also verify that the data displayed in the **Data preview** area reflects the structure you expect.

5. Click **Finish**.

11   Creating Charts and Graphics

To create a chart

1. Click any cell in the data table.

2. On the **Insert** tab, in the **Charts** group, click the desired chart type, and then click the desired chart subtype.

To change how Excel plots your data

1. On the **Design** tab, in the **Data** group, click **Select Data**.

2. In the **Legend Entries (Series)** area, click the data series you want to change.

3. Click **Remove**.

4. In the **Horizontal (Categories) Axis Labels** area, click **Edit**.

5. Select the cells you want to plot on this axis, and then click **OK**.

To remove a series from an axis

1. On the **Design** tab, in the **Data** group, click **Select Data**.

2. In the **Legend Entries (Series)** area, click the data series you want to remove from the chart.

3. Click **Remove**.

To add a series to an axis

1. On the **Design** tab, in the **Data** group, click **Select Data**.

2. In the **Legend Entries (Series)** area, click **Add**.

3. In the **Series name** box, type a name for the series.

4. Click in the **Series values** box, and select the cells to provide values for the series.

5. Click **OK**.

To move a chart to its own worksheet

1. Click the chart.

2. On the **Design** tab, in the **Location** group, click **Move Chart**.

3. Select the target sheet for the chart, and click **OK**.

To apply a Chart Style to a chart

1. Click the chart.

2. On the **Design** tab, in the **Chart Styles** gallery, click the style you want to apply.

To apply a different layout to a chart

1. Click the chart.

2. On the **Design** tab, in the **Chart Layouts** gallery, click the layout you want to apply.

To change the appearance of a chart's gridlines

1. Click the chart.

2. On the **Layout** tab, in the **Axes** group, click **Gridlines**, and then click the gridline settings you want.

To select a chart element for formatting

1. Click the chart.

2. On the **Layout** tab, in the **Current Selection** group, click the **Chart Elements** arrow and then, in the list, click the element you want to select.

To select a data point in a series

1. Click the chart.

2. Click any point in the data series.

3. Click the specific data point you want to select.

To format a chart element

1. Select the chart element you want to format.
2. On the **Layout** tab, in the **Current Selection** group, click **Format Selection**.
3. Use the controls in the **Format** dialog box to format the chart element.

To save a chart as a chart template

1. Click the chart.
2. On the **Design** tab, in the **Type** group, click **Save As Template**.
3. Type a name for the template.
4. Click **Save**.

To add a trendline to a chart

1. Select the chart.
2. On the **Layout** contextual tab, in the **Analysis** group, click **Trendline**, and then click **More Trendline Options**.
3. In the **Trend/Regression Type** area, click **Linear**.
4. In the **Forecast** area, in the **Forward** field, type the number of periods you want to project.
5. Click **Close**.

To create a PivotChart

1. On the data worksheet, click any cell in the data table.
2. On the **Insert** tab, in the **Tables** group, click the **PivotTable** arrow and then, in the list, click **PivotChart**.
3. Verify that the correct data source appears in the **Table/Range** field and that the **New Worksheet** option is selected.
4. Click **OK**.

To change the chart type of a chart or PivotChart

1. Click the chart.
2. On the **Design** contextual tab, in the **Type** group, click **Change Chart Type**.
3. Click the desired chart type and subtype.
4. Click **OK**.

To create a SmartArt diagram

1. On the **Insert** tab, in the **Illustrations** group, click **SmartArt**.

2. Click the desired graphic type.

3. Click the desired subtype, and then click **OK**.

To add text to a diagram shape

→ Click the shape, and type the text.

To add a shape to a diagram

1. Click the shape above or to the right of where you want the new shape to appears.

2. On the **Design** contextual tab, in the **Create Graphic** group, click the **Add Shape** arrow and then, in the list, click the option representing where you want the shape to appear.

To change the format of a diagram shape

1. Right-click the shape, and then click **Format Shape**.

2. Use the controls in the **Format Shape** dialog box to change the shape's appearance.

12 Printing

To display a worksheet in Page Layout View

→ On the **View** tab, in the **Workbook Views** group, click **Page Layout**.

To add a header or footer to a worksheet

1. On the **View** tab, in the **Workbook Views** group, click **Page Layout**.

2. Follow either of these steps:

   ○ At the top of the worksheet, click the target header section.

   ○ At the bottom of the worksheet, click the target footer section.

3. In the active header or footer section, type the text that you want to have appear, and press Enter .

To create an AutoHeader

1. On the **View** tab, in the **Workbook Views** group, click **Page Layout**.

2. At the top of the worksheet, click **Click to add header**.

3. Click in the target header section.

4. On the **Design** contextual tab, in the **Header & Footer Elements** group, click the auto text you want to add.

To add an image to a header or footer

1. On the **View** tab, in the **Workbook Views** group, click **Page Layout**.

2. Click the desired header or footer section.

3. On the **Design** contextual tab, in the **Header & Footer Elements** group, click **Picture**.

4. Double-click the picture you want to add to the header or footer.

To format an image in a header or footer

1. Click the image in the footer and then, on the **Design** contextual tab, click **Format Picture**.

2. Use the controls in the **Format Picture** dialog box to change the picture's appearance.

3. Click **OK**.

To change a worksheet's margins

→ On the **Page Layout** tab, in the **Page Setup** group, click **Margins**, and then click the desired margins, or click **Custom Margins** to enter the margins manually.

To change a worksheet's page orientation

→ On the **Page Layout** tab, in the **Page Setup** group, click **Orientation**, and then click the desired orientation.

To print a worksheet on a specific number of pages

1. On the **Page Layout** tab, in the **Scale to Fit** group, click the **Width** arrow and then, in the list, click the desired number of pages.

2. On the **Page Layout** tab, in the **Scale to Fit** group, click the **Height** arrow and then, in the list, click the desired number of pages.

To preview a worksheet before printing

→ While displaying the worksheet you want to preview, click the **Microsoft Office Button**, point to **Print**, and then click **Print Preview**.

To add a page break to a worksheet

1. Click the row or header below or to the right of where you want the page break to appear.
2. On the **Page Layout** tab, in the **Page Setup** group, click **Breaks**, and then click **Insert Page Break**.

To remove a page break from a worksheet

1. Click the row or header below or to the right of the page break.
2. On the **Page Layout** tab, in the **Page Setup** group, click **Breaks**, and then click **Remove Page Break**.

To change the order in which worksheets print

1. On the **Page Layout** tab, click the **Page Setup** dialog box launcher.
2. If necessary, click the **Sheet** tab.
3. In the **Page order** section, click the desired option.
4. Click **OK**.

To print a worksheet

→ Click the **Microsoft Office Button**, and then click **Print**.

To print part of a worksheet

1. On the **Page Layout** tab, in the **Page Setup** group, click **Print Titles**.
2. At the right edge of the **Columns to repeat at left** field, click **Collapse Dialog**.
3. Select the column header of the columns you want to repeat.
4. At the right edge of the **Columns to repeat at left** field, click the **Expand Dialog** button.

To center material on the printed page

1. On the **Page Layout** tab, click the **Page Setup** dialog box launcher.
2. On the **Margins** page of the dialog box, select the **Horizontally** and **Vertically** check boxes.
3. Click **OK**.

To print a chart

1. Select the chart.

2. Click the **Microsoft Office Button**, and then click **Print**.

3. Verify that the **Selected Chart** option is selected, and then click **OK** (or click **Cancel** if you don't want to print the chart).

13   Automating Repetitive Tasks by Using Macros

To save a workbook as a macro-enabled workbook

1. Click the **Microsoft Office Button**, and then click **Save As**.

2. In the **Save as type** list, click **Excel Macro-Enabled Workbook (*.xlsm)**.

3. Click **Save**.

To enable macros to run in a workbook

1. On the **Message Bar**, click **Options**.

2. Click **Enable this content**.

3. Click **OK**.

To view a macro

1. On the **View** tab, in the **Macros** group, click the **Macros** arrow and then, in the list, click **View Macros**.

2. Click the macro you want to view, and then click **Edit**.

To step through a macro

1. In the **Macros** list, click **View Macros**.

2. Click the macro you want to view, and then click **Step Into**.

3. Press F8 to execute the first macro step.

To run a macro

1. In the **Macros** list, click **View Macros**.

2. Click the desired macro, and then click **Run**.

To record a macro

1. In the **Macros** list, click **Record Macro**.

2. In the **Record Macro** dialog box, delete the existing name from the **Macro name** box, and then type a new name for the macro.

3. Click **OK**.

4. Perform the actions you want to record.

5. In the **Macros** list, click **Stop Recording**.

To edit a macro

1. In the **Macros** list, click **View Macros**.

2. Click the macro you want to view, and then click **Edit**.

3. Make any desired changes.

4. Click the Visual Basic Editor **Close** button.

To run a macro when a Quick Access Toolbar button is clicked

1. On the **Quick Access Toolbar**, click the **Customize Quick Access Toolbar** button, and then click **More Commands**.

2. If necessary, in the **Choose commands from** list, click the desired category.

3. In the **Commands** panel, click the desired command.

4. Click **Add**.

5. In the **Choose commands from** list, click **Macros**.

6. In the **Commands** panel, click the macro you want to run.

7. Click **Add**, and then cick **OK**.

To change the appearance of a Quick Access Toolbar button

1. On the **Quick Access Toolbar**, click the **Customize Quick Access Toolbar** button, and then click **More Commands**.

2. In the **Customize Quick Access Toolbar** command panel, click the command you want to change.

3. Click **Modify**.

4. Click the desired button design.

5. Click **OK** twice to close the **Modify Button** dialog box and the **Excel Options** dialog box.

To run a macro when a shape is clicked

1. Right-click the shape, and then click **Assign Macro**.

2. Click the macro you want to assign to the shape, and then click **OK**.

To run a macro when a workbook is opened

→ Name the macro *Auto_Open*.

14   Working with Other Microsoft Office System Programs

To link to another Microsoft Office system document

1. On the **Insert** tab, in the **Text** group, click the **Insert Object** button.

2. On the **Create from File** tab of the **Object** dialog box, click **Browse**.

3. Click the file to which you want to link, and then click **Insert**.

4. Select the **Link to file** check box, and then click **OK**.

To embed another document in a workbook

1. On the **Insert** tab, in the **Text** group, click **Object**.

2. On the **Create from File** tab of the **Object** dialog box, click **Browse**.

3. Click the file to which you want to link, and then click **Insert**.

4. Click **OK**.

To view a linked or embedded document

→ Double-click the document.

To create a hyperlink

1. On the **Insert** tab, in the **Links** group, click **Hyperlink**.

2. Click the type of hyperlink you want to create.

3. If necessary, use the controls in the **Look in** box to locate the file or location to which you want to link.

4. In the file list, click the hyperlink's target.

5. In the **Text to display** box, type the text you want displayed.

6. Click **OK**.

To edit a hyperlink

1. Right-click the cell that contains the hyperlink, and then click **Edit Hyperlink**.

2. Edit the values in the **Hyperlink** dialog box.

3. Click **OK**.

To delete a hyperlink

→ Right-click the cell that contains the hyperlink, and then click **Delete Hyperlink**.

To paste a chart into another document

1. Right-click the chart, and then click **Copy**.

2. Open the destination document.

3. Right-click the place you want to paste the chart, and then click **Paste**.

4. In the **Paste Options** list, click the desired option.

15   Collaborating with Colleagues

To turn on workbook sharing

1. On the **Review** tab, in the **Changes** group, click **Share Workbook**.

2. Select the **Allow changes by more than one use at the same time** check box.

3. Click **OK**.

To add a comment to a cell

1. Click the cell where you want the comment to appear.

2. On the **Review** tab, in the **Comments** group, click **New Comment**.

3. Type the comment text, and then click outside the body of the comment.

To edit a comment

1. Click the cell that contains the comment.

2. On the **Review** tab, in the **Comments** group, click **Edit Comment**.

3. Type the new comment text, and then click outside the body of the comment.

To delete a comment

1. Click the cell that contains the comment.

2. On the **Review** tab, in the **Comments** group, click **Delete Comment**.

To track changes made to a workbook

1. On the **Review** tab, in the **Changes** group, click **Track Changes**, and then in the list click **Highlight Changes**.
2. Select the **Track changes while editing. This also shares your workbook** check box.
3. Click **OK**.

To accept and reject changes

1. In the **Track Changes** list, click **Accept/Reject Changes**.
2. Click **OK**.
3. For each change, click **Accept** to accept the change, or click **Reject** to reject the change. You can also click **Accept All** or **Reject All**.

To record workbook changes on a History worksheet

1. In the **Track Changes** list, click **Highlight Changes**.
2. Select the **List changes on a new sheet** check box, and click **OK**.

To require a password to open a workbook

1. Click the **Microsoft Office Button**, and then click **Save As**.
2. Click the **Tools** button, and then click **General Options**.
3. Type a password in the **Password to open** box.
4. Type a different password in the **Password to modify** box.
5. In the **General Options** dialog box, click **OK**.
6. In the **Reenter password to proceed** box, type the first password, and then click **OK**.
7. In the **Reenter password to modify** box, type the second password, and then click **OK**.

To password protect a worksheet

1. On the **Review** tab, in the **Changes** group, click **Protect Sheet**.
2. In the **Password to unprotect sheet** box, type a password.
3. Clear the **Select locked cells** and **Select unlocked cells** check boxes, and then click **OK**.
4. In the **Reenter password to proceed** box, type the password you entered before, and then click **OK**.

To password protect a cell range

1. On the **Review** tab, in the **Changes** group, click **Allow Users to Edit Ranges**.
2. In the **Allow users to edit ranges** dialog box, click **New**.
3. In the **Title** box, type a title for the range.
4. In the **Range password** box, type a password, and then click **OK**.

To sign a workbook using a digital signature

1. Click the **Microsoft Office Button**, click **Prepare**, and then click **Add a Digital Signature**.
2. Click **OK** to clear the dialog box that appears.
3. In the **Purpose for signing this document** box, type a reason.
4. Verify that your certificate appears in the **Signing as** area of the dialog box, and then click **Sign**.
5. Click **OK**.

To publish a workbook to the Web

1. Click the **Microsoft Office Button**, and then click **Save As**.
2. In the **File name** box, type a name for the file.
3. In the **Save as type** list, click **Web Page**.
4. Click **Save**.
5. Click **Yes** to save the workbook as a Web file.

Chapter at a Glance

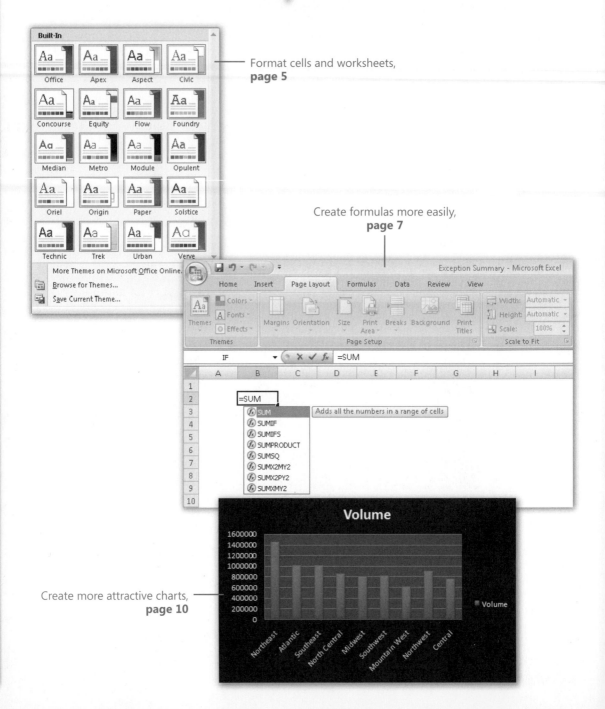

Format cells and worksheets,
page 5

Create formulas more easily,
page 7

Create more attractive charts,
page 10

1 What's New in Excel 2007?

In this chapter, you will become familiar with the Office Fluent user interface and the new Office file formats, and learn about new features of Excel 2007 that you can use to do the following:

✔ Manage larger data collections.

✔ Format cells and worksheets.

✔ Manage data tables more effectively.

✔ Create formulas more easily.

✔ Summarize data.

✔ Create powerful conditional formats.

✔ Create more attractive charts.

✔ Control printouts more carefully.

One of the first things you'll notice about Microsoft Office Excel 2007 is that the user interface has changed quite a bit. Earlier versions of Excel housed the program's more than 1,000 commands in a series of menus, toolbars, task panes, and dialog boxes. And, as it turns out, there were some functions that didn't appear by default on any of the menus or toolbars. In Excel 2007, there is only one place to look for the tools you need to use it: the user interface Ribbon at the top of the program window. The Microsoft Excel 2007 product team took the dozens of menus and toolbars and reorganized their contents onto the Ribbon tabs and galleries. If you've used Excel before, you'll need to spend only a little bit of time working with the new user interface to bring yourself back up to your usual proficiency. If you're new to Excel, you'll have a much easier time learning to use the program than you would have had with the previous user interface.

This chapter introduces many of the new features in Excel 2007: the new user interface, the improved formatting capabilities provided by galleries and minitoolbars, the new capabilities offered by data tables, the new color management scheme, and the improved charting engine. There are also new ways to manage the data in your workbooks. For example, you can create more flexible rules to have Excel 2007 format your data

1

based on its value, summarize your data by using new functions, and save your workbooks as documents in other useful file formats. All these improvements combine to make Excel 2007 an accessible, powerful program you can use to manage, analyze, and present your data effectively.

> **Important** There are no practice files for this chapter. See "Using the Companion CD" at the beginning of this book for more information.

Becoming Familiar with the New User Interface

After you enter your data into a worksheet, you can change the data appearance, summarize it, or sort it by using the commands on the user interface Ribbon. Unlike in previous versions of Excel, which made you hunt through a complex toolbar and menu system to find the commands you wanted, you can find everything you need at the top of the Excel 2007 program window.

The Excel 2007 user interface divides its commands into seven tabs: Home, Insert, Page Layout, Formulas, Data, Review, and View. The Home tab appears when you start Excel 2007.

> **Tip** If you work with macros or add-ins, you can add the Developer tab to the user interface. Click the Microsoft Office Button, click Excel Options, and on the Popular page of the Excel Options dialog box, click the Show Developer Tab In The Ribbon check box. Then click OK.

The Home tab contains a series of groups: Clipboard, Font, Alignment, Number, Styles, Cells, and Editing. Each group, in turn, hosts a series of controls that enable you to perform tasks related to that group (formatting fonts, setting cell alignment, creating number formats, and so on). Clicking a control with a drop-down arrow displays a menu that contains further options; if an option has an ellipsis (...) after the item name, clicking the item displays a dialog box. If a group has a dialog box associated with it, such as the Number group shown in the preceding graphic, you can display that dialog box by clicking the dialog box launcher at the lower-right corner of the group. (The dialog box launcher looks like a small box with an arrow pointing down and to the right.)

Managing Larger Data Collections

Many Excel users take advantage of the program's data summary and calculation capabilities to process large data collections. In Excel 2003 and earlier versions, you were limited to 65,536 rows and 256 columns of data in a worksheet. You could always spread larger data collections across multiple worksheets, but it took a lot of effort to make everything work correctly. You don't have that problem in Excel 2007. The Microsoft Excel 2007 product team expanded worksheets to include 16,384 columns and 1,048,576 rows of data, which should be sufficient for most of the projects you want to do in Excel 2007.

Excel 2007 also comes with more powerful and flexible techniques you can use to process your worksheet data. In Excel 2003, you could assign up to three conditional formats (rules that govern how Excel displays a value) to a cell. In Excel 2007, the only limit on the number of conditional formats you can create is your computer's memory.

The table below summarizes the expanded data storage and other capabilities found in Excel 2007.

Limit	Excel 2003	Excel 2007
Columns in a worksheet	256	16,384
Rows in a worksheet	65,536	1,048,576
Number of different colors allowed in a workbook	56	4.3 billion
Number of conditional format conditions applied to a cell	3	Limited by available memory
Number of sorting levels of a range or table	3	64
Number of items displayed in an AutoFilter list	1,024	32,768
Total number of characters displayed in a cell	1,024	32,768
Total number of characters per cell that Excel can print	1,024	32,768
Total number of unique cell styles in a workbook	4,000	65,536
Maximum length of a formula, in characters	1,024	8,192
Number of nested levels allowed in a formula	7	64
Maximum number of arguments in a formula	30	255
Number of characters that can be stored and displayed in a cell with a text format	255	32,768
Number of columns allowed in a PivotTable	255	16,384
Number of fields displayed in the PivotTable Field List task pane	255	16,384

Understanding the New Office File Formats

Starting with the 1997 release, all Microsoft Office programs have used a binary file format that computers (but not humans) can read. Excel 2007, Microsoft Office Word 2007, and Microsoft Office PowerPoint 2007 have new and improved file formats that, in addition to being somewhat readable, create much smaller files than the older binary format.

The new Microsoft Office Open XML Formats combine XML and file compression to create robust files that (on average) are about half the size of similar Excel 97–2003 files. You can open and save Excel 97–2003 files in Excel 2007, of course. If you want to open Excel 2007 files in Excel 2000, Excel 2002, or Excel 2003, you can install the Microsoft Office Compatibility Pack for Office Word 2007, Excel 2007, and Office PowerPoint 2007 file formats from *www.microsoft.com/downloads/*.

In addition to smaller file sizes, Office XML formats offer several other advantages:

- **Improved interoperability.** Because the new file formats use XML as their base, it is much easier for organizations to share and exchange data between the Microsoft Office system programs and other applications. The older binary file format was difficult to read and wasn't standards-based.

- **Enhanced customization.** The letter *X* in XML stands for *extensible*, which means that information professionals and developers can create custom document structures, or schema, that meet their organization's needs.

- **Improved automation.** The Excel 2007 file format is based on open standards, which means that any program written to process data based on those standards will work with Excel 2007. In other words, you don't need to write special routines or use another program in the Microsoft Office system to handle your Excel 2007 data programmatically.

- **Compartmentalizing information.** The new Microsoft Office system file format separates document data, macro code, and header information into separate containers, which Excel 2007 then combines into the file you see when you open your workbook. Separating macro code (automated program instructions) from your worksheet data improves security by identifying that a workbook contains a macro and enables you to prevent Excel 2007 from executing code that could harm your computer or steal valuable personal or business information.

You can save Excel 2007 files in the following Office XML file formats:

Extension	Description
.xlsx	Excel workbook
.xlsm	Excel macro-enabled workbook
.xlsb	Excel binary workbook
.xltx	Excel template
.xltxm	Excel macro-enabled template

If electronic recipients of your files will be using an earlier version of Excel and will not have access to the Office Compatibility Pack, you also have the options of saving files in earlier (Excel 97-2003) formats.

> **See Also** For more information about macro-enabled file formats, refer to "Introducing Macros" in Chapter 13, "Automating Repetitive Tasks by Using Macros."

Formatting Cells and Worksheets

Excel has always been a great program for analyzing numerical data, but even Excel 2003 came up a bit short in the presentation department. In Excel 2003 and earlier versions of the program, you could have a maximum of 56 different colors in your workbook. In addition, there was no easy way to ensure that your colors complemented the other colors in your workbook (unless you were a graphic designer and knew what you wanted going in).

Excel 2007 offers vast improvements over the color management and formatting options found in previous versions of the program. You can have as many different colors in a workbook as you like, for example, and you can assign a design theme to a workbook. Assigning a theme to a workbook offers you color choices that are part of a complementary whole, not just a dialog box with no guidance about which colors to choose. You can, of course, still select any color you want when you format your worksheet, define custom cell styles, and create your own themes. The preinstalled themes are there as guides, not prescriptions.

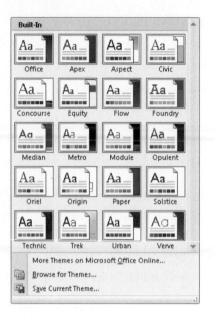

Managing Data Tables More Effectively

You'll often discover that it makes sense to arrange your Excel 2007 data as a table, in which each column contains a specific data element (such as an order number or the hours you worked on a given day), and each row contains data about a specific business object (such as the details of delivery number 1403).

Route	Deliveries	End Time
101	552	5:03 PM
102	480	4:15 PM
103	324	4:18 PM
104	492	3:56 PM
105	486	4:02 PM
106	277	5:30 PM
107	560	6:45 PM
108	413	4:31 PM
109	254	4:18 PM
110	595	5:49 PM
111	459	3:30 PM
112	338	4:14 PM
113	313	5:38 PM
114	458	4:19 PM
115	316	4:24 PM
116	284	5:45 PM
117	496	5:30 PM
118	413	4:08 PM
119	409	3:45 PM
120	533	3:50 PM
121	436	4:13 PM
122	408	5:11 PM
123	528	7:02 PM

In Excel 2007, tables enable you to enter and summarize your data efficiently. If you want to enter data in a new table row, all you have to do is type the data in the row below the table. After you press Tab or Enter after typing in the last cell's values, Excel 2007 expands the table to include your new data. You can also have Excel 2007 display a Totals row, which summarizes your table's data using a function you specify.

See Also For more information on how to change the appearance and summary operations of a data table, see "Defining a Table" in Chapter 3, "Working with Data and Data Tables."

Creating Formulas More Easily

Excel 2003 and earlier versions of the program provided two methods to find the name of a function to add to a formula: the help system and the Insert Function dialog box. Excel 2007 adds a new tool to your arsenal: Formula AutoComplete. Here's how it works: When you begin typing a formula into a cell, Excel 2007 examines what you're typing and then displays a list of functions and function arguments, such as named cell ranges or table columns that could be used in the formula.

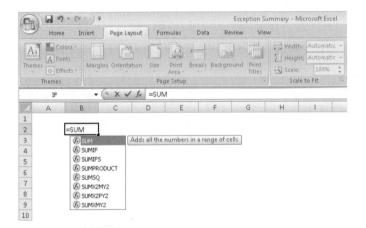

Formula AutoComplete offers lists of the following items as you create a formula:

- **Excel 2007 functions.** Typing the characters =*SUB* into a cell causes Excel 2007 to display a list with the functions *SUBSTITUTE* and *SUBTOTAL*. Clicking the desired function name adds that function to your formula without requiring you to finish typing the function's name.

- **User-defined functions.** Custom procedures created by a programmer and included in a workbook as macro code.

- **Formula arguments.** Some formulas accept a limited set of values for a function argument; Formula AutoComplete enables Excel 2007 to select from the list of acceptable values.

- **Defined names.** User-named cell ranges (for example, cells A2:A29 on the Sales worksheet could be named *February Sales*).

- **Table structure references.** A table structure reference denotes a table or part of a table. For example, if you create a table named Package Volume, typing the letter *P* in a formula prompts Excel 2007 to display the table name Package Volume as a possible entry.

Summarizing Data

The Microsoft Excel 2007 programming team encourages users to suggest new capabilities that might be included in the future versions of the program. One of the most common requests from corporations using Excel was to find the average value of cells where the value met certain criteria. For example, in a table summarizing daily sales by department, a formula could summarize sales in the Housewares department for days in which the sales total was more than $10,000.

The Excel 2007 team responded to those requests by creating five new formulas that enable you to summarize worksheet data that meets a given condition. Here are quick descriptions of the new functions and any existing functions to which they're related:

- *AVERAGEIF* enables you to find the average value of cells in a range for cells that meet a single criterion.

- *AVERAGEIFS* enables you to find the average value of cells in a range for cells that meet multiple criteria.

- *SUMIFS*, an extension of the *SUMIF* function, enables you to find the average value of cells in a range for cells that meet multiple criteria.

- *COUNTIFS*, an extension of the *COUNTIF* function, enables you to count the number of cells in a range that meet multiple criteria.

- *IFERROR*, an extension of the *IF* function, enables you to tell Excel 2007 what to do in case a cell's formula generates an error (as well as what to do if the formula works the way it's supposed to).

Creating Powerful Conditional Formats

Businesses often use Excel to track corporate spending and revenue. The actual figures are very important, of course, but it's also useful for managers to be able to glance at their data and determine whether the data exceeds expectations, falls within an acceptable range, or requires attention because the value falls below expectations. In versions prior to Excel 2007, you could create three conditions and define a format for each one. For example, you could create the following rules:

- If monthly sales are more than 10 percent ahead of sales during the same month in the previous year, display the value in green.

- If monthly sales are greater than or equal to sales during the same month in the previous year, display the value in yellow.

- If monthly sales are fewer than sales during the same month in the previous year, display the value in red.

In Excel 2007, you can have as many rules as you like, apply several rules to a single data value, choose to stop evaluating rules after a particular rule has been applied, and change the order in which the rules are evaluated without having to delete and re-create the rules you change. You can also apply several new types of conditional data formats: data bars, which create a horizontal bar across a cell to indicate how large the value is; color gradients, which change a cell's fill color to indicate how large the value is; and icon sets, which display one of three icons depending on the guidelines you establish.

Creating More Attractive Charts

Excel 2007 enables you to manage large amounts of numerical data effectively, but humans generally have a hard time determining patterns from that data if all they have to look at are the raw numbers. That's where charts come in. Charts summarize your data visually, which means that you and other decision-makers can quickly detect trends, determine high and low data points, and forecast future prospects using mathematical tools. The Excel charting engine and color palette haven't changed significantly since Excel 97, but Excel 2007 marks a tremendous step forward with more ways to create attractive and informative charts quickly.

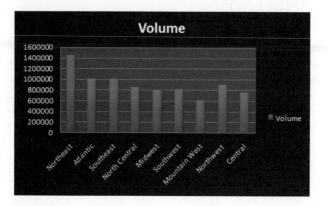

See Also   For more information about the new charting capabilities in Excel 2007, see Chapter 11, "Creating Charts and Graphics."

Controlling Printouts More Carefully

One of the Excel 2007 product group's goals for Excel 2007 was to enable you to create great-looking documents. Of course, to create these documents, you must know what your documents will look like when you print them. The Microsoft Excel team introduced the Page Break Preview view in Excel 97, which enabled you to see where one printed page ended and the next page began. Page Break Preview is somewhat limited from a printing control and layout perspective in that it displays your workbook's contents at an extremely small size. When you display a workbook in Page Layout view, you see exactly what your work will look like on the printed page. Page Layout view also enables you to change your workbook's margins, add and edit headers and footers, and edit your data.

Key Points

- Excel 2007 features a new user interface that enables you to discover the program's capabilities more easily.

- Excel 2007 greatly expands the size of the data collections you can manage in Excel and enables you to organize your data into tables.

- Excel 2007 offers new graphics, formatting, and charting capabilities, enabling you to create great-looking documents quickly.

- Excel 2007 offers powerful new functions to summarize your data and streamlines formula creation with Formula AutoComplete.

- Excel 2007 greatly enhances your ability to create conditional formats, which change the appearance of a cell's contents based on its value.

Chapter at a Glance

Create workbooks, **page 14**

Modify workbooks, **page 18**

Modify worksheets, **page 21**

Customize the Excel 2007 program window, **page 26**

2 Setting Up a Workbook

In this chapter, you will learn how to:

✔ Create workbooks.

✔ Modify workbooks.

✔ Modify worksheets.

✔ Customize the Excel 2007 program window.

When you start Microsoft Office Excel 2007, the program presents a blank workbook that contains three worksheets. You can add or delete worksheets, hide worksheets within the workbook without deleting them, and change the order of your worksheets within the workbook. You can also copy a worksheet to another workbook or move the worksheet without leaving a copy of the worksheet in the first workbook. If you and your colleagues work with a large number of documents, you can define property values to make your workbooks easier to find when you and your colleagues attempt to locate them by using the Windows search facility.

Another way to make Excel 2007 easier to use is by customizing the Excel 2007 program window to fit your work style. If you have several workbooks open at the same time, you can move between the workbook windows by using the new user interface. However, if you switch between workbooks frequently, you might find it easier to resize the workbooks so they don't take up the entire Excel 2007 window. In that case, you just need to click the title bar of the workbook you want to display.

The 2007 Microsoft Office system design team created the new user interface to reduce the number of places you have to look for commands; if you find that you use a command frequently, you can add it to the Quick Access Toolbar so it's never more than one click away.

In this chapter, you will learn how to create and modify workbooks, create and modify worksheets, make your workbooks easier to find, and customize the Excel 2007 program window.

See Also Do you need only a quick refresher on the topics in this chapter? See the Quick Reference section at the beginning of this book.

Important Before you can use the practice files in this chapter, you need to install them from the book's companion CD to their default location. See "Using the Companion CD" at the beginning of this book for more information.

Creating Workbooks

Every time you want to gather and store data that isn't closely related to any of your other existing data, you should create a new workbook. The default new workbook in Excel 2007 has three worksheets, although you can add more worksheets or delete existing worksheets if you want. Creating a new workbook is a straightforward process—you just click the Microsoft Office Button, click New, and identify the type of workbook you want to create.

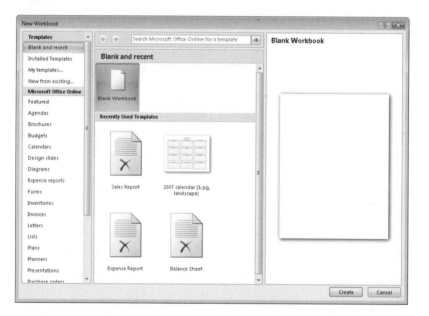

When you start Excel 2007, the program displays a new, blank workbook; you can begin to enter data in the worksheet's cells or open an existing workbook. In the exercises that follow, you'll work with some of the workbooks that have already been created for Consolidated Messenger. After you make any desired changes to a workbook, you should save the workbook to avoid losing your work.

When you save a file, you overwrite the previous copy of the file. If you have made changes that you want to save, but you want to keep a copy of the file as it was previously, you can use the Save As command to specify a name for the new file.

> **Tip** Readers frequently ask, "How often should I save my files?" It is good practice to save your changes every half hour or even every five minutes, but the best time to save a file is whenever you make a change that you would hate to have to make again.

You also can use the controls in the Save As dialog box to specify a different format for the new file and a different location in which to save the new version of the file. For example, Jenny Lysaker, the chief operating officer of Consolidated Messenger, might want to save an Excel file that tracks consulting expenses as an Excel 2003 file if she needs to share the file with a consulting firm that uses Excel 2003.

After you create a file, you can add additional information to make the file easier to find when you search for it using the Windows search facility. Each category of information, or *property*, stores specific information about your file. In Windows, you can search for files based on the file's author or title, or by keywords associated with the file. A file tracking the postal code destinations of all packages sent from a collection might have the keywords *postal*, *destination*, and *origin* associated with it.

To set values for your workbook's properties, click the Microsoft Office Button, point to Prepare, and click Properties to display the Document Properties panel on the user interface. The Standard version of the Document Properties panel has fields for the file's author, title, subject, keywords, category, and status, and any comments about the file. You can also create custom properties by clicking the Property Views And Options button, located just to the right of the Document Properties label, and then clicking Advanced Properties.

On the Custom tab of the Advanced Properties dialog box, you can click one of the existing custom categories or create your own by typing a new property name in the Name field, clicking the Type arrow and selecting a data type (for example, Text, Date, Number, Yes/No), selecting or typing a value in the Value field, and then clicking Add. If you want to delete an existing custom property, point to the Properties list, click the property you want to get rid of, and click Delete. After you finish making your changes, click the OK button. To hide the Document Properties panel, click the Close button in the upper-right corner of the panel.

In this exercise, you will create a new workbook, save the workbook with a new name, assign values to the workbook's standard properties, and create a custom property.

USE the *Exception Summary* workbook. This practice file is located in the *Documents\ Microsoft Press\Excel2007SBS\Creating* folder.
BE SURE TO start Excel 2007 before beginning this exercise.
OPEN the *Exception Summary* workbook.

Microsoft Office
Button

1. Click the **Microsoft Office Button**, and then click **Close**.

The *Exception Summary* workbook closes.

2. Click the **Microsoft Office Button**, and then click **New**.

The New Workbook dialog box opens.

3. Click **Blank Workbook**, and then click **Create**.

A new, blank workbook opens.

4. Click the **Microsoft Office Button**, and then click **Save As**.

The Save As dialog box opens.

Save As
« Documents ▸ Microsoft Press ▸   ▼ │ ✦ │ Search   ⌕
File name: Book2
Save as type: Excel Workbook
Authors: Curt   Tags: Add a tag
☐ Save Thumbnail
▾ Browse Folders   Tools ▾   Save   Cancel

5. Use the navigation controls to display the *Documents\Microsoft Press\ Excel2007SBS\Creating* folder. In the **File name** field, type Exceptions 2006.

6. Click the **Save** button.

Excel 2007 saves your work, and the Save As dialog box closes.

7. Click the **Microsoft Office Button**, click **Prepare**, and then click **Properties**.

The Document Properties panel appears.

8. In the **Keywords** field, type exceptions, regional, percentage.

9. In the **Category** field, type performance.

10. Click the **Property View and Options** button, and then click **Advanced Properties**.

The Exceptions 2006 Properties dialog box opens.

11. Click **Custom**.

The Custom tab appears.

12. In the **Name** field, type Performance.

13. In the **Value** field, type Exceptions.

Exceptions 2006 Properties	? ✕

General | Summary | Statistics | Contents | Custom

Name: Performance

Checked by
Client
Date completed
Department
Destination
Disposition

Add

Delete

Type: Text

Value: Exceptions   ☐ Link to content

Properties: | Name | Value | Type |
| --- | --- | --- |

OK   Cancel

14. Click the **Add** button, and then click **OK**.

The Exceptions 2006 Properties dialog box closes.

Save

15. On the **Quick Access Toolbar**, click the **Save** button to save your work.

CLOSE the Exceptions 2006 workbook.

Modifying Workbooks

Most of the time, you create a workbook to record information about a particular business activity, such as the number of packages that a regional distribution center handles or the average time of the last delivery on a route. Each worksheet within that workbook should thus represent a subdivision of that activity. To display a particular worksheet, just click the worksheet's tab on the tab bar (just below the grid of cells).

In the case of Consolidated Messenger, the workbook used to track daily package volumes could have a separate worksheet for each regional distribution center. New Excel 2007 workbooks contain three worksheets; because Consolidated Messenger uses nine regional distribution centers, you need to create six new ones. To create a new worksheet, click the Insert Worksheet button at the right edge of the tab bar.

When you create a worksheet, Excel 2007 assigns it a generic name such as Sheet4, Sheet5, or Sheet6. After you decide what type of data you want to store on a worksheet, you should change the default worksheet names to something more descriptive. For example, you could change the name of Sheet1 in the regional distribution center tracking workbook to *Northeast*. When you want to change a worksheet's name, double-click the worksheet's tab on the tab bar to highlight the worksheet name, type the new name, and press Enter.

Another way to work with more than one workbook is to copy a worksheet from another workbook to the current workbook. One circumstance in which you might consider copying worksheets to the current workbook is if you have a list of your current employees in another workbook. You can copy worksheets from another workbook by right-clicking the tab of the sheet you want to copy and, on the shortcut menu that appears, clicking Move Or Copy to display the Move Or Copy dialog box.

> **Tip** Selecting the Create A Copy check box leaves the copied worksheet in its original workbook, whereas clearing the check box causes Excel 2007 to delete the worksheet from its original workbook.

After the worksheets are in the target workbook, you can change their order to make the data easier to locate within the workbook. To change a worksheet's location in the workbook, you drag its sheet tab to the desired location on the tab bar. If you want a worksheet to stand out in a workbook, you can right-click its sheet tab and use the menu that appears to change the tab's color. At the other end of the spectrum, you can hide the active worksheet by right-clicking the worksheet's tab on the tab bar and clicking Hide on the context menu that appears. When you want Excel 2007 to redisplay the worksheet, right-click any visible sheet tab, and click Unhide. In the Unhide dialog box, click the sheet you want to display, and click OK.

To differentiate a worksheet from others, or to visually indicate groups or categories of worksheets in a multiple-worksheet workbook, you can easily change the color of a worksheet tab. To do so, right-click the tab, point to Tab Color, and then click the color you want.

> **Tip** If you copy a worksheet to another workbook, and the destination workbook has the same theme applied as the active workbook, the worksheet retains its tab color. If the destination workbook has another theme applied, the worksheet's tab color changes to reflect that theme.

If you determine that you no longer need a particular worksheet, such as one you created to store some figures temporarily, you can delete the worksheet quickly. To do so, right-click its sheet tab, and then click Delete.

In this exercise, you will insert and rename a worksheet, change a worksheet's position in a workbook, hide and unhide a worksheet, copy a worksheet to another workbook, change a worksheet's tab color, and delete a worksheet.

> **USE** the *Exception Summary* workbook. This practice file is located in the *Documents\ Microsoft Press\Excel2007SBS\Creating* folder.
> **OPEN** the *Exception Summary* workbook.

Insert Worksheet

1. On the tab bar, click the **Insert Worksheet** button.

   A new worksheet appears.

2. Right-click the new worksheet's sheet tab, and then click **Rename**.

   Excel 2007 highlights the new worksheet's name.

3. Type 2007, and then press Enter.

4. On the tab bar, right-click the **Sheet1** sheet tab, and then click **Rename**.

5. Type 2006, and then press Enter.

6. Right-click the **2006** sheet tab, point to **Tab Color**, and then, in the **Standard Colors** section of the color palette, click a green square.

   Excel 2007 changes the 2006 sheet tab to green.

7. On the tab bar, drag the **2007** sheet tab to the left of the **Scratch Pad** sheet tab.

8. Right-click the **2007** sheet tab, and then click **Hide**.

   Excel 2007 hides the 2007 worksheet.

9. Right-click the **2006** sheet tab, and then click **Move or Copy**.

   The Move Or Copy dialog box opens.

   ![Move or Copy dialog box. Move selected sheets. To book: Exception Summary.xlsx. Before sheet: 2006 (highlighted), Scratch Pad, (move to end). Create a copy checkbox. OK, Cancel buttons.]

10. Click the **To book** arrow, and then in the list, click **(new book)**.

11. Select the **Create a copy** check box.

12. Click **OK**.

    A new workbook appears, containing only the worksheet you copied into it.

Save

13. On the **Quick Access Toolbar**, click the **Save** button.

    The Save As dialog box opens.

14. In the **File name** field, type **2006 Archive**, and then press Enter.

    Excel 2007 saves the workbook, and the Save As dialog box closes.

15. On the **View** tab, click the **Switch Windows** button, and then click **Exception Summary**.

    The *Exception Summary* workbook appears.

16. On the tab bar, right-click the **Scratch Pad** sheet tab, and then click **Delete**.

    The Scratch Pad worksheet disappears.

17. Right-click the **2006** sheet tab, and then click **Unhide**.

The Unhide dialog box opens.

18. Click **2007**, and then click **OK**.

The Unhide dialog box closes, and the 2007 worksheet appears in the workbook.

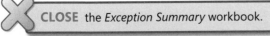

CLOSE the *Exception Summary* workbook.

Modifying Worksheets

After you put up the signposts that make your data easy to find, you can take other steps to make the data in your workbooks easier to work with. For instance, you can change the width of a column or the height of a row in a worksheet by dragging the column or row's border to the desired position. Increasing a column's width or a row's height increases the space between cell contents, making it easier to select a cell's data without inadvertently selecting data from other cells as well.

> **Tip** You can apply the same change to more than one row or column by selecting the rows or columns you want to change and then dragging the border of one of the selected rows or columns to the desired location. When you release the mouse button, all the selected rows or columns change to the new height or width.

Modifying column width and row height can make a workbook's contents easier to work with, but you can also insert a row or column between the edge of a worksheet and the cells that contain the data to accomplish this. Adding space between the edge of a worksheet and cells, or perhaps between a label and the data to which it refers, makes the workbook's contents less crowded and easier to work with. You insert rows by clicking a cell and clicking the Home tab. Then, in the Cells group, in the Insert list, click Insert Sheet Rows. Excel 2007 inserts a row above the row that contains the active cell. You insert a column in much the same way by choosing Insert Sheet Columns from the Insert button's drop-down list. When you do this, Excel 2007 inserts a column to the left of the active cell.

When you insert a row, column, or cell in a worksheet with existing formatting, the Insert Options button appears. Clicking the Insert Options button displays a list of choices you can make about how the inserted row or column should be formatted. The following table summarizes your options.

Option	Action
Format Same As Above	Applies the format of the row above the inserted row to the new row
Format Same As Below	Applies the format of the row below the inserted row to the new row
Format Same As Left	Applies the format of the column to the left of the inserted column to the new column
Format Same As Right	Applies the format of the column to the right of the inserted column to the new column
Clear Formatting	Applies the default format to the new row or column

If you want to delete a row or column, right-click the row or column head and then, on the shortcut menu that appears, click Delete. You can temporarily hide a number of rows or columns by selecting those rows or columns and then, on the Home tab, in the Cells group, clicking the Format button, pointing to Hide & Unhide, and then clicking either Hide Rows or Hide Columns. The rows or columns you selected disappear, but they aren't gone for good, as they would be if you'd used Delete. Instead, they have just been removed from the display until you call them back. To return the hidden rows to the display, on the Home tab, in the Cells group, click the Format button, point to Hide & Unhide, and then click either Unhide Rows or Unhide Columns.

Likewise, you can insert individual cells into a worksheet. To insert a cell, click the cell that is currently in the position where you want the new cell to appear. On the Home tab, in the Cells group, in the Insert list, click Insert Cells to display the Insert dialog box. In the Insert dialog box, you can choose whether to shift the cells surrounding the inserted cell down (if your data is arranged as a column) or to the right (if your data is arranged as a row). When you click OK, the new cell appears, and the contents of affected cells shift down or to the right, as appropriate. In a similar vein, if you want to delete a block of cells, select the cells, and on the Home tab, in the Cells group, in the Delete list, click Delete Cells to display the Delete dialog box—complete with options that enable you to choose how to shift the position of the cells around the deleted cells.

> **Tip** The Insert dialog box also includes options you can click to insert a new row or column; the Delete dialog box has similar options for deleting an entire row or column.

If you want to move the data in a group of cells to another location in your worksheet, select the cells you want to move and point to the selection's border. When the mouse pointer changes to a four-way arrow, you can drag the selected cells to the desired location on the worksheet. If the destination cells contain data, Excel 2007 displays a dialog box asking if you want to overwrite the destination cells' contents. If you want to replace the existing values, click the OK button. If you don't want to overwrite the existing values, click the Cancel button and insert the required number of cells to accommodate the data you want to move.

In this exercise, you will insert a column and row into a worksheet, specify insert options, hide a column, insert a cell into a worksheet, delete a cell from a worksheet, and move a group of cells within the worksheet.

USE the *Route Volume* workbook. This practice file is located in the *Documents\Microsoft Press\Excel2007SBS\Creating* folder.
OPEN the *Route Volume* workbook.

1. On the May 12 worksheet, select cell A1.

2. On the **Home** tab, in the **Cells** group, click the **Insert** arrow, and then in the list, click **Insert Sheet Columns**.

   A new column A appears.

3. In the **Insert** list, click **Insert Sheet Rows**.

   A new row 1 appears.

4. On the **Home** tab, in the **Editing** group, click the arrow next to the **Clear** button. Click **Clear Formats**.

   Excel 2007 removes the formatting from the new row 1.

5. Right-click the column header of column E, and then click **Hide**.

   Column E disappears.

Delete

6. On the tab bar, click the **May 13** sheet tab.

   The worksheet named *May 13* appears.

7. Click cell B6.

8. On the **Home** tab, in the **Cells** group, click the **Delete** arrow, and then in the list, click **Delete Cells**.

   The Delete dialog box opens.

9. If necessary, click **Shift cells up**, and then click **OK**.

   The Delete dialog box closes and Excel 2007 deletes cell B6, moving the cells below it up to fill in the gap.

10. Click cell C6.

11. In the **Cells** group, in the **Insert** list, click **Insert Cells**.

    The Insert dialog box opens.

12. If necessary, click **Shift cells down**, and then click **OK**.

    The Insert dialog box closes, and Excel 2007 creates a new cell C6, moving cells C6:C11 down to accommodate the inserted cell.

13. In cell C6, type 4499, and then press Enter .

14. Select cells E13:F13.

15. Point to the border of the selected cells. When your mouse pointer changes to a four-pointed arrow, drag the selected cells to cells B13:C13.

    The dragged cells replace cells C13:D13.

CLOSE the *Route Volume* workbook.

Customizing the Excel 2007 Program Window

How you use Excel 2007 depends on your personal working style and the type of data collections you manage. The Excel 2007 product team interviews customers, observes how differing organizations use the program, and sets up the user interface so that you don't need to change it to work effectively. If you do find yourself wishing that you could change the Excel 2007 program window, including the user interface, you can. You can change how Excel 2007 displays your worksheets, zoom in on worksheet data, and add frequently used commands to the Quick Access Toolbar.

Zooming In on a Worksheet

One way to make Excel 2007 easier to work with is to change the program's zoom level. Just as you can "zoom in" with a camera to increase the size of an object in the camera's viewer, you can use the Excel 2007 zoom setting to change the size of objects within the Excel 2007 program window. For example, if Peter Villadsen, the Consolidated Messenger European Distribution Center Manager, displayed a worksheet that summarized his distribution center's package volume by month, he could click the View tab and then, in the Zoom group, click the Zoom button to display the Zoom dialog box. The Zoom dialog box contains controls that enable him to select a preset magnification level or to type in a custom magnification level. He could also use the Zoom control in the lower-right corner of the Excel 2007 window.

Zoom out ┐   ┌ Zoom in

Clicking the Zoom In control increases the size of items in the program window by 10 percent, whereas clicking the Zoom Out control decreases the size of items in the program window by 10 percent. If you want more fine-grained control of your zoom level, you can use the slider control to select a specific zoom level.

The Zoom group on the View tab also contains the Zoom To Selection button, which fills the program window with the contents of any selected cells, up to the program's maximum zoom level of 400 percent.

> **Tip** The minimum zoom level in Excel 2007 is 10 percent.

Arranging Multiple Workbook Windows

As you work with Excel 2007, you will probably need to have more than one workbook open at a time. For example, you could open a workbook that contains customer contact information and copy it into another workbook to be used as the source data for a mass mailing you create in Microsoft Office Word 2007. When you have multiple workbooks open simultaneously, you can switch between them by clicking the View tab and then, in the Window group, clicking the Switch Windows button and clicking the name of the workbook you want to view.

You can arrange your workbooks within the Excel 2007 window so that most of the active workbook is shown, but the others are easily accessible by clicking the View tab and then, in the Window group, clicking the Arrange All button. Then, in the Arrange Windows dialog box, click Cascade.

Many Excel 2007 workbooks contain formulas on one worksheet that derive their value from data on another worksheet, which means you need to change between two worksheets every time you want to see how modifying your data changes the formula's result. However, you can display two copies of the same workbook, displaying the worksheet that contains the data in the original window and displaying the worksheet with the formula in the new window. When you change the data in the original copy of the workbook, Excel 2007 updates the formula result in a new window. To display two copies of the same workbook, open the desired workbook and then, on the View tab's Window group, click New Window. Excel 2007 opens a second copy of the workbook. If the original workbook's name is *Exception Summary*, Excel 2007 displays the name *Exception Summary:1* on the original workbook's title bar and *Exception Summary:2* on the second workbook's title bar.

Adding Buttons to the Quick Access Toolbar

As you continue to work with Excel 2007, you might discover that you use certain commands much more frequently than others. If your workbooks draw data from external sources, you might find yourself displaying the Data tab and then, in the Connections group, clicking the Refresh All button much more often than the program's designers might have expected. You can make any button accessible with one click by adding the button to the Quick Access Toolbar, located just to the right of the Microsoft Office Button in the upper-left corner of the Excel 2007 program window.

To add a button to the Quick Access Toolbar, click the Microsoft Office Button, and click Excel Options. In the Excel Options dialog box, display the Customize page, and then in the Choose Commands From list, click the category from which you want to select the control to add. Excel 2007 displays the available commands in the list box below the Choose Commands From field. Click the control you want, and then click the Add button. You can change a button's position on the Quick Access Toolbar by clicking its name in the lower-right pane and then clicking either the Move Up or Move Down button. To remove a button from the Quick Access Toolbar, click the button's name, and then click the Remove button. When you're done making your changes, click the OK button.

You can also choose whether your Quick Access Toolbar change affects all your workbooks or just the active workbook. To control how Excel 2007 applies your change, in the Customize Quick Access Toolbar list, click either For All Documents to apply the change to all of your workbooks or For Workbook to apply the change to the active workbook only.

Maximizing the Usable Space

You can increase the amount of space available inside the program window by hiding the Ribbon, the formula bar, or the row and column labels.

To hide the Ribbon, double-click the active tab label. The tab labels remain visible at the top of the program window, but the tab content is hidden. To temporarily redisplay the Ribbon, click the tab label you want. Then click any button on the tab, or click away from the tab, to rehide it. To permanently redisplay the Ribbon, double-click any tab label.

To hide the formula bar, clear the Formula Bar check box in the Show/Hide group on the View tab. To hide the row and column labels, clear the Headings check box in the Show/Hide group on the View tab.

In this exercise, you will change your worksheet's zoom level, zoom in to emphasize a selected cell range, switch between multiple open workbooks, cascade multiple open workbooks within the Excel 2007 program window, and add a button to the Quick Access Toolbar.

> **USE** the *Route Volume* and *Exception Summary* workbooks. These practice files are located in the *Documents\Microsoft Press\Excel2007SBS\Creating* folder.
>
> **OPEN** the *Route Volume* workbook and the *Exception Summary* workbook.

1. In the *Exception Summary* workbook, display the 2006 worksheet.

2. In the lower-right corner of the Excel 2007 window, click the **Zoom In** control five times.

   The worksheet's zoom level changes to 150%.

3. Select cells B2:C11.

Zoom to Selection

4. On the **View** tab, in the **Zoom** group, click the **Zoom to Selection** button.

   Excel 2007 displays the selected cells so they fill the program window.

	A	B	C	D
2		**Region**	**2006 Exceptions**	
3		Northeast	0.0021%	
4		Atlantic	0.0025%	
5		Southeast	0.0026%	
6		North Central	0.0026%	
7		Midwest	0.0020%	
8		Southwest	0.0018%	
9		Mountain West	0.0002%	
10		Northwest	0.0004%	
11		Central	0.0011%	

Zoom

5. On the **View** tab, in the **Zoom** group, click the **Zoom** button.

   The Zoom dialog box opens.

6. Click **100%**, and then click **OK**.

The worksheet returns to its default zoom level.

7. On the **View** tab, in the **Window** group, click the **Switch Windows** button, and then click **Route Volume**.

The *Route Volume* workbook appears.

8. On the **View** tab, in the **Window** group, click the **Arrange All** button.

The Arrange Windows dialog box opens.

9. Click **Cascade**, and then click **OK**.

Excel 2007 cascades the open workbook windows within the Excel 2007 program window.

Microsoft Office
Button

10. Click the **Microsoft Office Button**, and then click **Excel Options**.

The Excel Options dialog box opens.

11. Click **Customize**.

The Customize tab appears.

12. Click the **Choose commands from** arrow, and then in the list, click **Review Tab**.

The commands in the Review Tab category appear in the command list.

13. Click the **Spelling** command, and then click **Add**.

14. Click **OK**.

Excel 2007 adds the Spelling command to the Quick Access Toolbar.

> **CLOSE** all open workbooks. If you are not continuing directly to the next chapter, exit Excel.

Key Points

- Save your work whenever you do something you'd hate to have to do again.

- Assigning values to a workbook's properties makes it easier to find your workbook using the Windows search facility.

- Be sure to give your worksheets descriptive names.

- If you want to use a worksheet's data in another workbook, you can send a copy of the worksheet to that other workbook without deleting the original worksheet.

- You can delete a worksheet you no longer need, but you can also hide a worksheet in the workbook. When you need the data on the worksheet, you can unhide it.

- You can save yourself a lot of bothersome cutting and pasting by inserting and deleting worksheet cells, columns, and rows.

- Customize your Excel 2007 program window by changing how it displays your workbooks, zooming in on data, and adding frequently used buttons to the Quick Access Toolbar.

Chapter at a Glance

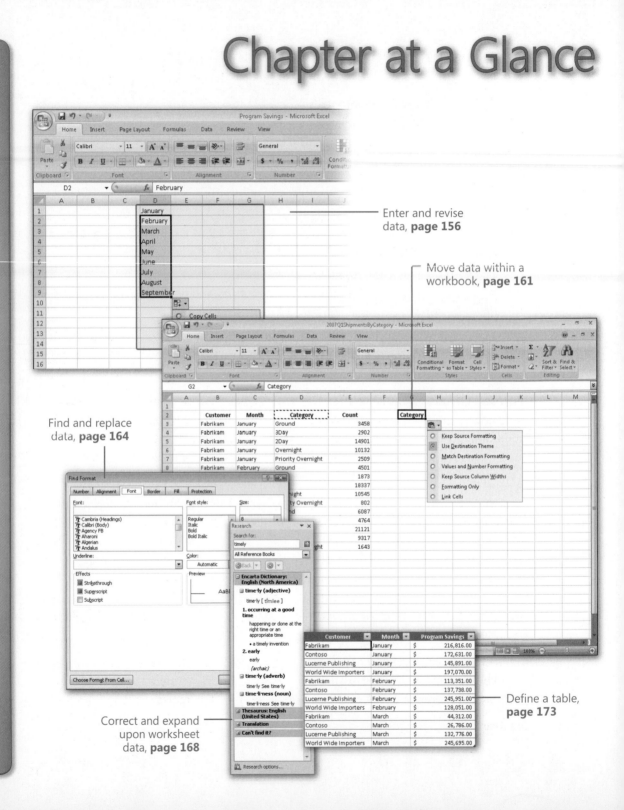

Enter and revise data, **page 156**

Move data within a workbook, **page 161**

Find and replace data, **page 164**

Correct and expand upon worksheet data, **page 168**

Define a table, **page 173**

3 Working with Data and Data Tables

In this chapter, you will learn to:

✔ Enter and revise data.

✔ Move data within a workbook.

✔ Find and replace data.

✔ Correct and expand upon worksheet data.

✔ Define a table.

Microsoft Office Excel 2007 enables you to visualize and present information effectively using charts, graphics, and formatting, but the data is the most important part of any workbook. By learning to enter data efficiently, you will make fewer data entry errors and give yourself more time to analyze your data so you can make decisions about your organization's performance and direction.

Excel 2007 provides a wide variety of tools you can use to enter and manage worksheet data effectively. For example, Excel 2007 enables you to organize your data into tables, which enables you to analyze and store your data quickly and easily. Excel 2007 also enables you to enter a data series quickly; repeat one or more values; or control how Excel 2007 formats cells, columns, and rows moved from one part of a worksheet to another. And you can do so with a minimum of effort. Excel 2007 also enables you to check the spelling of worksheet text, look up alternative words by using the Thesaurus, and translate words to foreign languages.

In this chapter, you will learn how to enter and revise Excel 2007 data, move data within a workbook, find and replace existing data, use proofing and reference tools to enhance your data, and organize your data by using Excel 2007 data tables.

See Also Do you need only a quick refresher on the topics in this chapter? See the Quick Reference section at the beginning of this book.

> **Important** Before you can use the practice sites in this chapter, you need to install them from the book's companion CD to their default location. See "Using the Companion CD" at the beginning of this book for more information.

Entering and Revising Data

After you create a workbook, you can begin entering data. The simplest way to enter data is to click a cell and type a value, which is a method that works very well when you're entering a few pieces of data, but it is less than ideal when you're entering long sequences or series of values. For example, Craig Dewar, the VP of Marketing for Consolidated Messenger, might want to create a worksheet listing the monthly program savings that large customers can enjoy if they sign exclusive delivery contracts with Consolidated Messenger. To record those numbers, he would need to create a worksheet with the following layout.

	Customer	Month	Program Savings
	Fabrikam	January	$ 216,816.00
	Contoso	January	$ 172,631.00
	Lucerne Publishing	January	$ 145,891.00
	World Wide Importers	January	$ 197,070.00
	Fabrikam	February	$ 113,351.00
	Contoso	February	$ 137,738.00
	Lucerne Publishing	February	$ 245,951.00
	World Wide Importers	February	$ 128,051.00
	Fabrikam	March	$ 44,312.00
	Contoso	March	$ 26,786.00
	Lucerne Publishing	March	$ 132,776.00
	World Wide Importers	March	$ 245,695.00

Repeatedly entering the sequence January, February, March, and so on can be handled by copying and pasting the first occurrence of the sequence, but there's an easier way to do it: use *AutoFill*. With AutoFill, you enter the first element in a recognized series, grab the *fill handle* at the lower-right corner of the cell, and drag the fill handle until the series extends far enough to accommodate your data. A similar tool, *FillSeries*, enables you to enter two values in a series and use the fill handle to extend the series in your worksheet. For example, if you want to create a series starting at 2 and increasing by 2, you can put *2* in the first cell and *4* in the second cell, select both cells, and then use the fill handle to extend the series to your desired end value.

You do have some control over how Excel 2007 extends the values in a series when you drag the fill handle. For example, if you drag the fill handle up (or to the left), Excel 2007 extends the series to include previous values. If you type *January* in a cell and then drag that cell's fill handle up (or to the left), Excel 2007 places *December* in the first cell, *November* in the second cell, and so on.

Another way to control how Excel 2007 extends a data series is by holding down the Ctrl key while you drag the fill handle. For example, if you select a cell that contains the value *January* and then drag the fill handle down, Excel 2007 extends the series by placing *February* in the next cell, *March* in the cell after that, and so on. If you hold down the Ctrl key, however, Excel 2007 repeats the value *January* in each cell you add to the series.

> **Tip** Be sure to experiment with how the fill handle extends your series and how pressing the Ctrl key changes that behavior. Using the fill handle can save you a lot of time entering data.

Other data entry techniques you'll use in this section are *AutoComplete*, which detects when a value you're entering is similar to previously entered values; *Pick From Drop-down List*, which enables you to choose a value from existing values in a column; and Ctrl+Enter, which enables you to enter a value in multiple cells simultaneously.

> **Troubleshooting** If an AutoComplete suggestion doesn't appear as you begin typing a cell value, the option might be turned off. To turn on AutoComplete, click the Microsoft Office Button, and then click Excel Options. In the Excel Options dialog box, display the Advanced page. In the Editing Options section of the page, select the Enable AutoComplete For Cell Values check box, and then click OK.

The following table summarizes these data entry techniques.

Method	Action
AutoFill	Enter the first value in a recognized series and use the fill handle to extend the series.
FillSeries	Enter the first two values in a series and use the fill handle to extend the series.
AutoComplete	Type the first few letters in a cell, and if a similar value exists in the same column, Excel 2007 suggests the existing value.
Pick From Drop-Down List	Right-click a cell, and then click Pick From Drop-Down List. A list of existing values in the cell's column appears. Click the value you want to enter into the cell.
Ctrl+Enter	Select a range of cells to contain the same data, type the data in the active cell, and press Ctrl+Enter.

Another handy feature in the current version of Excel 2007 is the Auto Fill Options button that appears next to data you add to a worksheet by using AutoFill.

Clicking the Auto Fill Options button displays a list of actions Excel 2007 can take regarding the cells affected by your fill operation. The options in the list are summarized in the following table.

Option	Action
Copy Cells	Copies the contents of the selected cells to the cells indicated by the Fill operation
Fill Series	Fills the cells indicated by the Fill operation with the next items in the series
Fill Formatting Only	Copies the format of the selected cell to the cells indicated by the Fill operation, but does not place any values in the target cells
Fill Without Formatting	Fills the cells indicated by the Fill operation with the next items in the series, but ignores any formatting applied to the source cells
Fill Days, Weekdays, and so on	Changes according to the series you extend. For example, if you extend the cells *Wed*, *Thu*, and *Fri*, Excel 2007 presents two options, Fill Days and Fill Weekdays, and enables you to select which one you intended. If you do not use a recognized sequence, the option does not appear

In this exercise, you will enter data by multiple methods, and control how Excel 2007 formats an extended data series.

USE the *Series* workbook. This practice file is located in the *Documents\Microsoft Press\Excel2007SBS\Data* folder.

BE SURE TO start Excel 2007 before beginning this exercise.

OPEN the *Series* workbook.

1. On the Monthly worksheet, select cell B3, and then drag the fill handle down until it covers cells B3:B7.

Excel 2007 repeats the value *Fabrikam* in cells B4:B7.

2. Select cell C3, hold down the [Ctrl] key, and drag the fill handle down until it covers cells C3:C7.

Excel 2007 repeats the value *January* in cells C4:C7.

3. Select cell B8, and then type the letter F.

Excel 2007 displays the characters *abrikam* in reverse video.

4. Press [Tab] to accept the value *Fabrikam* for the cell.

5. In cell **C8**, type February.

6. Right-click cell **D8**, and then click **Pick From Drop-down List**.

   A list of values in column D appears below cell D8.

7. From the list that appeared, click **2Day**.

   The value *2Day* appears in cell D8.

8. In cell E8, type 11802.14, and then press **Tab** or **Enter**.

   The value *$11,802.14* appears in cell E8.

9. Select cell B2, and then drag the fill handle so that it covers cells C2:E2.

   Excel 2007 replaces the values in cells C2:E2 with the value *Customer*.

Auto Fill Options

10. Click the **Auto Fill Options** button, and then click **Fill Formatting Only**.

    Excel 2007 restores the original values in cells C2:E2 but applies the formatting of cell B2 to those cells.

CLOSE the *Series* workbook.

Moving Data Within a Workbook

You can move to a specific cell in lots of ways, but the most direct method is to click the cell to which you want to move. The cell you click will be outlined in black, and its contents, if any, will appear in the formula bar. When a cell is outlined, it is the *active cell*, meaning that you can modify its contents. You use a similar method to select multiple cells (referred to as a *cell range*)—just click the first cell in the range and drag the mouse pointer over the remaining cells you want to select. After you select the cell or cells you want to work with, you can cut, copy, delete, or change the format of the contents of the cell or cells. For instance, Gregory Weber, the Northwestern Distribution Center Manager, might want to copy the cells that contain a set of column labels to a new page that summarizes similar data.

> **Important** If you select a group of cells, the first cell you click is designated the active cell.

You're not limited to selecting cells individually or as part of a range. For example, you might need to move a column of price data one column to the right to make room for a column of headings that indicate to which service category (ground, three-day express, two-day express, overnight, or priority overnight) a set of numbers belongs. To move an entire column (or entire columns) of data at a time, you click the column's header, located at the top of the worksheet. Clicking a column header highlights every cell in that column and enables you to copy or cut the column and paste it elsewhere in the workbook.

The Paste Options button appears next to data you copy from a cell and paste into another cell. Clicking the Paste Options button displays a list of actions that Excel 2007 can take regarding the pasted cells.

The options in the list are summarized in the following table.

Option	Action
Use Destination Theme	Pastes the contents of the Clipboard (which holds the last information selected via Cut or Copy) into the target cells and formats the data using the theme applied to the target workbook
Match Destination Formatting	Pastes the contents of the Clipboard into the target cells and formats the data using the existing format in the target cells, regardless of the workbook's theme
Keep Source Formatting	Pastes a column of cells into the target column; applies the format of the copied column to the new column
Values Only	Pastes the values from the copied column into the destination column without applying any formatting
Values And Number Formatting	Pastes the contents of the Clipboard into the target cells, keeping any numeric formats
Values And Source Formatting	Pastes the contents of the Clipboard into the target cells, retaining all the source cells' formatting
Keep Source Column Widths	Pastes the contents of the Clipboard into the target cells and resizes the columns of the target cells to match the widths of the columns of the source cells
Formatting Only	Applies the format of the source cells to the target cells, but does not copy the contents of the source cells

> **Troubleshooting** If the Paste Options button doesn't appear, you can turn the feature on by clicking the Microsoft Office Button and then clicking Excel Options to display the Excel Options dialog box. In the Excel Options dialog box, display the Advanced page and then, in the Cut, Copy, And Paste section, select the Show Paste Options Buttons check box. Click OK to close the dialog box and save your setting.

After cutting or copying data to the Clipboard, you can access additional paste options from the Paste list and from the Paste Special dialog box, which you display by clicking Paste Special in the Paste list.

In the Paste Special dialog box, you can specify the aspect of the Clipboard contents you want to paste, restricting the pasted data to values, formats, comments, and so on. You can perform mathematical operations involving the cut or copied data and the existing data in the cells you paste the content into. You can transpose data—change rows to columns and columns to rows—when you paste it by clicking Transpose in the Paste list, or by selecting the Transpose check box in the Paste Special dialog box.

In this exercise, you will copy a set of column headers to another worksheet, move a column of data within a worksheet, and select paste options for copied data.

> **USE** the *2007Q1ShipmentsByCategory* workbook. This practice file is located in the *Documents\Microsoft Press\Excel2007SBS\Data* folder.
>
> **OPEN** the *2007Q1ShipmentsByCategory* workbook.

1. On the **Count** worksheet, select cells B2:D2.

2. On the **Home** tab, in the **Clipboard** group, click the **Copy** button.

Copy

Excel 2007 copies the contents of cells B2:D2 to the Clipboard.

3. Create a worksheet named Sales, and display it.

4. Select cell B2.

Paste

5. On the **Home** tab, in the **Clipboard** group, click **Paste**.

   Excel 2007 pastes the header values into cells B2:D2.

6. Click the **Paste Options** smart tag, and then click **Keep Source Formatting**.

   Excel 2007 retains the cells' original formatting.

7. Right-click the column header of column I, and then click **Cut**.

   Excel 2007 outlines column I with a marquee.

8. Right-click the header of column E, and then click **Paste**.

   Excel 2007 pastes the contents of column I into column E.

CLOSE the *2007Q1ShipmentsByCategory* workbook.

Finding and Replacing Data

Excel 2007 worksheets can contain more than one million rows of data, so it's unlikely that you would have the time to move through a worksheet a row at a time to locate the data you want to find. You can locate specific data on an Excel 2007 worksheet by using the Find And Replace dialog box, which has two tabs (one named Find; the other named Replace) that enable you to search for cells that contain particular values. Using the controls on the Find tab finds the data you specify; using the controls on the Replace tab enables you to substitute one value for another. As an example, one of Consolidated Messenger's customers might change the company name. If that's the case, you can change every instance of the old name to the new name.

When you need more control over the data that you find and replace, such as if you want to find cells in which the entire cell value matches the value you're searching for, you can click the Options button to expand the Find And Replace dialog box.

One way you can use the extra options in the Find And Replace dialog box is to identify data that requires review using a specific format. As an example, Consolidated Messenger VP of Marketing Craig Dewar could make corporate sales plans based on a projected budget for the next year. After the executive board finalizes the numbers, he could use Find Format in the Find And Replace dialog box to locate the old prices and then change them by hand.

To change a value by hand, select the cell, and then either type a new value in the cell or, in the formula bar, select the value you want to replace and type the new value.

The following table summarizes the Find And Replace dialog box controls' functions.

Control	Function
Find What field	Contains the value you want to find or replace
Find All button	Selects every cell that contains the value in the Find What field
Find Next button	Selects the next cell that contains the value in the Find What field
Replace With field	Contains the value to overwrite the value in the Find What field
Replace All button	Replaces every instance of the value in the Find What field with the value in the Replace With field
Replace button	Replaces the next occurrence of the value in the Find What field and highlights the next cell that contains that value
Options button	Expands the Find And Replace dialog box to display additional capabilities
Format button	Displays the Find Format dialog box, which you can use to specify the format of values to be found or to replace found values
Within list box	Enables you to select whether to search the active worksheet or the entire workbook
Search list box	Enables you to select whether to search by rows or by columns
Look In list box	Enables you to select whether to search cell formulas or values
Match Case check box	When checked, requires that all matches have the same capitalization as the text in the Find What field (for example, *cat* doesn't match *Cat*)
Match Entire Cell Contents check box	Requires that the cell contain exactly the same value as in the Find What field (for example, *Cat* doesn't match *Catherine*)
Close button	Closes the Find And Replace dialog box

In this exercise, you will find a specific value in a worksheet, replace every occurrence of a company name in a worksheet, and find a cell with a particular formatting.

> **USE** the *Average Deliveries* workbook. This practice file is located in the *Documents\ Microsoft Press\Excel2007SBS\Data* folder.
>
> **OPEN** the *Average Deliveries* workbook.

1. If necessary, click the **Time Summary** sheet tab.

   The Time Summary worksheet appears.

Find & Select

2. On the **Home** tab, in the **Editing** group, click **Find & Select**, and then click **Find**.

   The Find And Replace dialog box opens with the Find tab displayed.

3. In the **Find what** field, type 114.

4. Click **Find Next**.

   Excel 2007 highlights cell B16, which contains the value *114*.

Route	Deliveries	End Time
101	552	5:03 PM
102	480	4:15 PM
103	324	4:18 PM
104	492	3:56 PM
105	486	4:02 PM
106	277	5:30 PM
107	560	6:45 PM
108	413	4:31 PM
109	254	4:18 PM
110	595	5:49 PM
111	459	3:30 PM
112	338	4:14 PM
113	313	5:38 PM
114	458	4:19 PM
115	316	4:24 PM
116	284	5:45 PM
117	496	5:30 PM
118	413	4:08 PM
119	409	3:45 PM
120	533	3:50 PM
121	436	4:13 PM
122	408	5:11 PM
123	528	7:02 PM
124	554	4:32 PM
125	598	5:00 PM

5. Delete the value in the **Find what** field, and then click the **Options** button.

   The Find And Replace dialog box expands to display additional search options.

6. Click **Format**.

   The Find Format dialog box opens.

7. Click the **Font** tab.

   The Font tab appears.

8. In the **Font style** list, click **Italic**.

9. Click **OK**.

   The Find Format dialog box closes.

10. Click **Find Next**.

    Excel 2007 highlights cell D25.

11. Click **Close**.

    The Find And Replace dialog box closes.

12. On the tab bar, click the **Customer Summary** sheet tab.

    The Customer Summary worksheet appears.

13. On the **Home** tab, in the **Editing** group, click **Find & Select**, and then click **Replace**.

    The Find And Replace dialog box opens with the Replace tab displayed.

14. Click the **Format** arrow to the right of the **Find what** field, and then in the list, click **Clear Find Format**.

    The format displayed next to the Find What field disappears.

15. In the **Find what** field, type Contoso.

16. In the **Replace with** field, type Northwind Traders.

17. Click **Replace All**.

18. Click **OK** to clear the message box that appears, indicating that Excel 2007 made three replacements.

19. Click **Close**.

    The Find And Replace dialog box closes.

CLOSE the *Average Deliveries* workbook.

Correcting and Expanding Upon Worksheet Data

After you enter your data, you should take the time to check and correct it. You do need to verify visually that each piece of numeric data is correct, but you can make sure that the text is spelled correctly by using the Excel 2007 spelling checker. When the spelling checker encounters a word it doesn't recognize, it highlights the word and offers suggestions representing its best guess of the correct word. You can then edit the word directly, pick the proper word from the list of suggestions, or have the spelling checker ignore the misspelling. You can also use the spelling checker to add new words to a custom dictionary so that Excel 2007 will recognize them later, saving you time by not requiring you to identify the words as correct every time they occur in your worksheets. After you make a change, you can remove the change as long as you haven't closed the workbook in which you made the change. To undo a change, click the Undo button on the Quick Access Toolbar. If you decide you want to keep a change, you can use the Redo command to restore it.

If you're not sure of your word choice or if you use a word that is almost but not quite right for your meaning, you can check for alternative words by using the Thesaurus. A number of other research tools are also available, such as the Microsoft Encarta encyclopedia, which you can refer to as you create your workbook. To display those tools, on the Review tab, in the Proofing group, click Research to display the Research task pane.

Finally, if you want to translate a word from one language to another, you can do so by selecting the cell that contains the value you want to translate, by displaying the Review tab, and then, in the Proofing group, by clicking Translate. The Research task pane appears (or changes if it's already open) and displays controls you can use to select the original and destination languages.

Research ▾ ×
Search for:
timely ▸
Translation ▾
◉Back ▾   ◉ ▾
⊟ **Translation** ▲
Translate a word or sentence.
From
English (United States) ▾
To
French (France) ▾
Translation options...
⊟ **Bilingual Dictionary**
⊟ **timely**
['taɪmlɪ] *adjective* opportun
⊟ **Can't find it?**
Try one of these alternatives or see Help for hints on refining your search.
Other places to search
Search for 'timely' in:
📖 All Reference Books
📖 All Research Sites
▾
📖 Research options...

> **Important** Excel 2007 translates a sentence by using word substitutions, which means that the translation routine doesn't always pick the best word for a given context. The translated sentence might not capture your exact meaning.

In this exercise, you will check a worksheet's spelling, add two new terms to a dictionary, undo a change, search for an alternative word using the Thesaurus, and translate a word to French.

> **USE** the *Service Levels* workbook. This practice file is located in the *Documents\ Microsoft Press\Excel2007SBS\Data* folder.
>
> **OPEN** the *Service Levels* workbook.

ABC
✓
Spelling

1. On the **Review** tab, in the **Proofing** group, click **Spelling**.

   The Spelling dialog box opens with the misspelled word displayed in the Not In Dictionary field.

Spelling: English (United States)	? ✕

   Not in Dictionary:

   shiped   Ignore Once

                                                   Ignore All

                                                   Add to Dictionary

   Suggestions:

   shipped   Change
   shaped
   shied   Change All
   sniped
   shined   AutoCorrect
   swiped

   Dictionary language: English (United States) ▾

   Options...   Undo Last   Cancel

2. Verify that the word *shipped* is highlighted in the **Suggestions** pane, and then click **Change**.

   Excel 2007 corrects the word and displays the next questioned word: *withn*.

3. Click **Change**.

   Excel corrects the word and displays the next questioned word: *TwoDay*.

4. Click **Add to Dictionary**.

   Excel 2007 adds the word to the dictionary and displays the next questioned word: *ThreeDay*.

5. Click **Add to Dictionary**.

   Excel 2007 adds the word to the dictionary.

6. Click **Close**.

   The Spelling dialog box closes, and a message box appears, indicating that the spell check is complete for the selected items.

7. Click **OK** to close the message box.

8. Click cell B6.

Thesaurus

9. On the **Review** tab, in the **Proofing** group, click **Thesaurus**.

   The Research task pane appears and displays a list of synonyms and antonyms for the word *Overnight*.

Translate

10. On the **Review** tab, in the **Proofing** group, click **Translate**.

    The Research task pane displays the translation tools.

11. If necessary, in the **From** list, click **English (United States)**.

12. In the **To** list, click **French (France)**.

    The Research task pane displays French words that mean *overnight*.

CLOSE the *Service Levels* workbook.

Defining a Table

Excel has always enabled you to manage lists of data effectively, enabling you to sort your worksheet data based on the values in one or more columns, limit the data displayed by using criteria (for example, show only those routes with fewer than 100 stops), and create formulas that summarize the values in visible (that is, unfiltered) cells. Customer feedback indicated that many Excel 2007 users wanted a more robust structure within Excel 2007 that enabled users to perform those operations and more. Excel 2003 included a structure called a *data list* that has evolved into the *table* in Excel 2007.

Customer ▼	Month ▼	Program Savings ▼
Fabrikam	January	$ 216,816.00
Contoso	January	$ 172,631.00
Lucerne Publishing	January	$ 145,891.00
World Wide Importers	January	$ 197,070.00
Fabrikam	February	$ 113,351.00
Contoso	February	$ 137,738.00
Lucerne Publishing	February	$ 245,951.00
World Wide Importers	February	$ 128,051.00
Fabrikam	March	$ 44,312.00
Contoso	March	$ 26,786.00
Lucerne Publishing	March	$ 132,776.00
World Wide Importers	March	$ 245,695.00

To create a data table (also referred to as an *Excel table*), type a series of column headers in adjacent cells, and then type a row of data below the headers. Select the headers and data, and on the Home tab, in the Styles group, click Format As Table. Then, from the gallery that appears, click the style you want to apply to the table. When the Format As Table dialog box opens, verify that the cells in the Where Is The Data For Your Table? field reflect your current selection and that the My Table Has Headers check box is selected, and then click OK.

Excel 2007 can also create a table from an existing data list as long as your data has a differently formatted header row, the list has no blank rows or columns within the data, and there is no extraneous data in cells immediately below or next to the list.

When you want to add data to a table, select a cell in the row immediately below the last row in the table or a cell in the column immediately to the right of the table, and then type a value into the cell. After you enter the value and move out of the cell, the AutoCorrect Options smart tag appears. If you didn't mean to include the data in the table, you can click Undo Table AutoExpansion to exclude the cells from the table. If you never want Excel 2007 to include adjacent data in a table, click Stop Automatically Expanding Tables.

> **Tip** To stop Table AutoExpansion before it starts, click the Microsoft Office Button, and then click Excel Options. In the Excel Options dialog box, click Proofing, and then click the AutoCorrect Options button to display the AutoCorrect dialog box. Click the AutoFormat As You Type tab, clear the Include New Rows And Columns In Table check box, and then click OK twice.

You can add rows and columns to a table, or remove them from a table, by dragging the resize handle at the table's lower-right corner. If your table's headers contain a recognizable series of values (such as *Region1*, *Region2*, and *Region3*), and you drag the resize handle to create a fourth column, Excel 2007 creates the column with the label *Region4*—the next value in the series.

Tables often contain data you can summarize by calculating a sum or average, or by finding the maximum or minimum value in a column. To summarize one or more columns of data, you can add a Total row to your table.

Contoso	March	$	26,786.00
Lucerne Publishing	March	$	132,776.00
World Wide Importers	March	$	245,695.00
Total		$	**1,807,068.00**

When you add the Total row, Excel 2007 creates a formula that calculates the sum of the values in the rightmost table column. To change that summary operation or to add a summary operation to any other cell in the Total row, click the cell, click the arrow that appears, and then click the summary operation you want to apply. Clicking the More Functions item displays the Insert Function dialog box, from which you can select any of the functions in Excel 2007.

Much as it does when you create a new worksheet, Excel 2007 gives your tables generic names such as *Table1* and *Table2*. You can change a table name to something easier to recognize by clicking any cell in the table, clicking the Design contextual tab, and then, in the Properties group, editing the value in the Table Name field. Changing a table name might not seem important, but it helps make formulas that summarize table data much easier to understand. You should make a habit of renaming your tables so you can recognize the data they contain.

See Also For more information about using the Insert Function dialog box and about referring to tables in formulas, see "Creating Formulas to Calculate Values" in Chapter 4, "Performing Calculations on Data."

If for any reason you want to convert your table back to a normal range of cells, click any cell in the table and then, on the Table Tools contextual tab, in the Tools group, click Convert To Range. When Excel 2007 displays a message box asking if you're sure you want to convert the table to a range, click OK.

In this exercise, you will create a data table from existing data, add data to a table, add a Total row, change the Total row's summary operation, and rename the table.

> **USE** the *Driver Sort Times* workbook. This practice file is located in the *Documents\ Microsoft Press\Excel2007SBS\Data* folder.
>
> **OPEN** the *Driver Sort Times* workbook.

1. Select cell B2.

2. On the **Home** tab, in the **Styles** group, click **Format as Table**, and then select a table style.

   The Format As Table dialog box opens.

3. Verify that the range *=$B$2:$C$17* appears in the **Where is the data for your table?** field and that the **My table has headers** check box is selected, and then click **OK**.

    Excel 2007 creates a table from your data and displays the Design contextual tab.

4. In cell B18, type D116, press [Tab], type 100 in cell C18, and then press [Enter].

    Excel 2007 includes the data in your table.

5. Select a cell in the table. Then on the **Design** contextual tab, in the **Table Style Options** group, select the **Total Row** check box.

    A Total row appears in your table.

6. Select cell C19, click the arrow that appears at the right edge of the cell, and then click **Average**.

    Excel 2007 changes the summary operation to Average.

Drive ▾	Sorting Minutes ▾
D101	102
D102	162
D103	165
D104	91
D105	103
D106	127
D107	112
D108	137
D109	102
D110	147
D111	163
D112	109
D113	91
D114	107
D115	93
D116	100
Total	119.4375 ▾

7. On the **Design** contextual tab, in the **Properties** group, type the value SortingSample01 in the **Table Name** field, and then press [Enter].

    Excel 2007 renames your table.

Save

8. On the **Quick Access Toolbar**, click the **Save** button to save your work.

> **CLOSE** the *Driver Sort Times* workbook. If you are not continuing directly to the next chapter, exit Excel.

Key Points

- You can enter a series of data quickly by entering one or more values in adjacent cells, selecting the cells, and then dragging the fill handle. To change how dragging the fill handle extends a data series, hold down the Ctrl key.

- Dragging a fill handle displays the Auto Fill Options button, which enables you to specify whether to copy the selected cells' values, extend a recognized series, or apply the selected cells' formatting to the new cells.

- Excel 2007 enables you to enter data by using a drop-down list, AutoComplete, and Ctrl+Enter. You should experiment with these techniques and use the one that best fits your circumstances.

- When you copy (or cut) and paste cells, columns, or rows, Excel 2007 displays the Paste Options smart tag. You can use its controls to determine which elements of the cut or copied elements Excel 2007 applies when they are pasted back into the worksheet.

- By using the options in the Paste Special dialog box, you can paste only specific aspects of cut or copied data, perform mathematical operations, transpose data, or delete blank cells when pasting.

- You can find and replace data within a worksheet by searching for specific values or by searching for cells that have a particular format applied.

- Excel 2007 provides a variety of powerful proofing and research tools, enabling you to check your workbook's spelling, find alternative words using the Thesaurus, and translate words between languages.

- Data tables, which are new in Excel 2007, enable you to organize and summarize your data effectively.

Chapter at a Glance

Name groups
of data,
page 60

Create formulas to
calculate values,
page 64

Summarize data
that meets specific
conditions, **page 71**

Find and correct
errors in calculations,
page 75

4 Performing Calculations on Data

In this chapter, you will learn to:

- ✔ Name groups of data.
- ✔ Create formulas to calculate values.
- ✔ Summarize data that meets specific conditions.
- ✔ Find and correct errors in calculations.

Microsoft Office Excel 2007 workbooks give you a handy place to store and organize your data, but you can also do a lot more with your data in Excel 2007. One important task you can perform is to calculate totals for the values in a series of related cells. You can also use Excel 2007 to find out other information about the data you select, such as the maximum or minimum value in a group of cells. By finding the maximum or minimum value in a group, you can identify your best salesperson, product categories you might need to pay more attention to, or suppliers that consistently give you the best deal. Regardless of your bookkeeping needs, Excel 2007 gives you the ability to find the information you want. And if you should make an error, you can find the cause and correct it quickly.

Many times, you can't access the information you want without referencing more than one cell, and it's also often true that you'll use the data in the same group of cells for more than one calculation. Excel 2007 makes it easy to reference a number of cells at once, enabling you to define your calculations quickly.

In this chapter, you'll learn how to streamline references to groups of data on your worksheets and how to create and correct formulas that summarize Consolidated Messenger's business operations.

See Also Do you need only a quick refresher on the topics in this chapter? See the Quick Reference section at the beginning of this book.

Important Before you can use the practice files in this chapter, you need to install them from the book's companion CD to their default location. See "Using the Companion CD" at the beginning of this book for more information.

Naming Groups of Data

When you work with large amounts of data, it's often useful to identify groups of cells that contain related data. For example, you can create a worksheet in which cells C4:I4 hold the number of packages Consolidated Messenger's Northeast processing facility handled from 5:00 P.M. to 12:00 A.M. on the previous day.

	5:00 PM	6:00 PM	7:00 PM	8:00 PM	9:00 PM	10:00 PM	11:00 PM
Northeast	10208	13889	17570	21251	24932	28613	32294
Atlantic	8472	9013	9554	10095	10636	11177	11718
Southeast	7328	8108	8888	9668	10448	11228	12008
North Central	6974	8160	9346	10532	11718	12904	14090
Midwest	9558	10902	12246	13590	14934	16278	17622
Southwest	7436	8223	9010	9797	10584	11371	12158
Mountain West	4631	5230	5829	6428	7027	7626	8225
Northwest	9105	10346	11587	12828	14069	15310	16551
Central	5704	6300	6896	7492	8088	8684	9280

Instead of specifying the cells individually every time you want to use the data they contain, you can define those cells as a *range* (also called a *named range*). For instance, you can group the items from the preceding graphic into a range named NortheastLastDay.

Whenever you want to use the contents of that range in a calculation, you can simply use the name of the range instead of specifying each cell individually.

> **Tip** Yes, you could just name the range *Northeast*, but if you use the range's values in a formula in another worksheet, the more descriptive range name tells you and your colleagues exactly what data is used in the calculation.

To create a named range, select the cells you want to include in your range, click the Formulas tab, and then, in the Defined Names group, click Define Name to display the New Name dialog box. In the New Name dialog box, type a name in the Name field, verify that the cells you selected appear in the Refers To field, and then click OK. You can also add a comment about the field in the Comment field and select whether you want to make the name available for formulas in the entire workbook or just on an individual worksheet.

If the cells you want to define as a named range have a label you want to use as the range's name, you can display the Formulas tab and then, in the Defined Names group, click Create From Selection to display the Create Names From Selection dialog box. In the Create Names From Selection dialog box, select the check box that represents the label's position in relation to the data cells, and then click OK.

A final way to create a named range is to select the cells you want in the range, click in the Name box next to the formula box, and then type the name for the range. You can display the ranges available in a workbook by clicking the Name arrow.

To manage the named ranges in a workbook, display the Formulas tab, and then, in the Defined Names group, click Name Manager to display the Name Manager dialog box.

When you click a named range, Excel 2007 displays the cells it encompasses in the Refers To field. Clicking the Edit button displays the Edit Name dialog box, which is a version of the New Name dialog box, enabling you to change a named range's definition; for example, by adding a column. You can delete a named range (the range, not the data) by clicking it, clicking the Delete button, and then clicking OK in the confirmation dialog box that opens.

> **Important** If your workbook contains a lot of named ranges, you can click the Filter button in the Name Manager dialog box and select a criterion to limit the names displayed in the Name Manager dialog box.

In this exercise, you will create named ranges to streamline references to groups of cells.

> **USE** the *VehicleMiles* workbook. This practice file is located in the *Documents\Microsoft Press\Excel2007SBS\Formulas* folder.
> **BE SURE TO** start Excel 2007 before beginning this exercise.
> **OPEN** the *VehicleMiles* workbook.

1. Select cells C4:G4.

2. In the **Name** box at the left end of the formula bar, type V101LastWeek, and then press ⌷Enter⌷.

   Excel 2007 creates a named range named *V101LastWeek*.

Name Manager

3. On the **Formulas** tab, in the **Defined Names** group, click **Name Manager**.

   The Name Manager dialog box opens.

4. Click the **V101LastWeek** name.

   The cell range to which the V101LastWeek name refers appears in the Refers To box at the bottom of the Name Manager dialog box.

5. Edit the cell range in the **Refers to** box to =MilesLastWeek!$C$4:$H$4 (change the *G* to an *H*), and then click the check mark button to the left of the box.

   Excel 2007 changes the named range's definition.

6. Click **Close**.

   The Name Manager dialog box closes.

7. Select the cell range C5:H5.

Define Name ▾

8. On the **Formulas** tab, in the **Defined Names** group, click **Define Name**.

   The New Name dialog box opens.

9. In the **Name** field, type V102LastWeek.

10. Verify that the definition in the **Refers to** field is =MilesLastWeek!$C$5:$H$5.

11. Click **OK**.

   Excel 2007 creates the name and closes the New Name dialog box.

CLOSE the *VehicleMiles* workbook.

Creating Formulas to Calculate Values

After you add your data to a worksheet and define ranges to simplify data references, you can create a formula, or an expression that performs calculations on your data. For example, you can calculate the total cost of a customer's shipments, figure the average number of packages for all Wednesdays in the month of January, or find the highest and lowest daily package volumes for a week, month, or year.

To write an Excel 2007 formula, you begin the cell's contents with an equal (=) sign; when Excel 2007 sees it, it knows that the expression following it should be interpreted as a calculation, not text. After the equal sign, type the formula. For example, you can find the sum of the numbers in cells C2 and C3 using the formula *=C2+C3*. After you have entered a formula into a cell, you can revise it by clicking the cell and then editing the formula in the formula box. For example, you can change the preceding formula to *=C3-C2*, which calculates the difference between the contents of cells C2 and C3.

> **Troubleshooting**   If Excel 2007 treats your formula as text, make sure that you haven't accidentally put a space before the equal sign. Remember, the equal sign must be the first character!

Typing the cell references for 15 or 20 cells in a calculation would be tedious, but Excel 2007 makes it easy to handle complex calculations. To create a new calculation, click the Formulas tab, and then in the Function Library group, click Insert Function. The Insert Function dialog box opens, with a list of functions, or predefined formulas, from which you can choose.

The following table describes some of the most useful functions in the list.

Function	Description
SUM	Finds the sum of the numbers in the specified cells
AVERAGE	Finds the average of the numbers in the specified cells
COUNT	Finds the number of entries in the specified cells
MAX	Finds the largest value in the specified cells
MIN	Finds the smallest value in the specified cells

Two other functions you might use are the *NOW()* and *PMT()* functions. The *NOW()* function returns the time the workbook was last opened, so the value will change every time the workbook is opened. The proper form for this function is *=NOW()*. To update the value to the current date and time, just save your work, close the workbook, and then reopen it.

The *PMT()* function is a bit more complex. It calculates payments due on a loan, assuming a constant interest rate and constant payments. To perform its calculations, the *PMT()* function requires an interest rate, the number of months of payments, and the starting balance. The elements to be entered into the function are called *arguments* and must be entered in a certain order. That order is written *PMT(rate, nper, pv, fv, type)*. The following table summarizes the arguments in the *PMT()* function.

Argument	Description
rate	The interest rate, to be divided by 12 for a loan with monthly payments
nper	The total number of payments for the loan
pv	The amount loaned (pv is short for present value, or principal)
fv	The amount to be left over at the end of the payment cycle (usually left blank, which indicates 0)
type	0 or 1, indicating whether payments are made at the beginning or at the end of the month (usually left blank, which indicates 0, or the end of the month)

If Consolidated Messenger wanted to borrow $2,000,000 at a 6 percent interest rate and pay the loan back over 24 months, you could use the *PMT()* function to figure out the monthly payments. In this case, the function would be written *=PMT(6%/12, 24, 2000000)*, which calculates a monthly payment of $88,641.22.

You can also use the names of any ranges you defined to supply values for a formula. For example, if the named range NortheastLastDay refers to cells C4:I4, you can calculate the average of cells C4:I4 with the formula *=AVERAGE(NortheastLastDay)*. In previous versions of Excel, you had to type the name into your formula by hand. Excel 2007 enables you to add functions, named ranges, and table references to your formulas more efficiently by using the new *Formula AutoComplete* capability. Just as AutoComplete offers to fill in a cell's text value when Excel 2007 recognizes that the value you're typing matches a previous entry, Formula AutoComplete offers to fill in a function, named range, or table reference while you create a formula.

As an example, consider a worksheet that contains a two-column table named Exceptions. The first column is labeled Route; the second is labeled Count.

Route	Count
101	7
102	0
103	4
104	6
105	18
106	12
107	3
108	3
109	8
110	9
111	8
112	18
113	12
114	16
115	12
116	9
117	10
118	6
119	10
120	4

You refer to a table by typing the table name, followed by the column or row name in square brackets. For example, the table reference *Exceptions[Count]* would refer to the Count column in the Exceptions table.

To create a formula that finds the total number of exceptions by using the *SUM* function, you begin by typing *=SU*. When you type the letter *S*, Formula AutoComplete lists functions that begin with the letter *S*; when you type the letter *U*, Excel 2007 narrows the list down to the functions that start with the letters *SU*.

To add the *SUM* function (followed by an opening parenthesis) to the formula, click *SUM* and then press Tab. To begin adding the table column reference, type the letter *E*. Excel 2007 displays a list of available functions, tables, and named ranges that start with the letter *E*. Click Exceptions, and press Tab to add the table reference to the formula. Then, because you want to summarize the values in the table's Count column, type *[Count]* to create the formula *=SUM(Exceptions[Count])*.

If you want to include a series of contiguous cells in a formula, but you haven't defined the cells as a named range, you can click the first cell in the range and drag to the last cell. If the cells aren't contiguous, hold down the Ctrl key and click the cells to be included. In both cases, when you release the mouse button, the references of the cells you selected appear in the formula.

After you create a formula, you can copy it and paste it into another cell. When you do, Excel 2007 tries to change the formula so that it works in the new cells. For instance, suppose that you have a worksheet in which cell D8 contains the formula *=SUM(C2:C6)*. Clicking cell D8, copying the cell's contents, and then pasting the result into cell D16 writes *=SUM(C10:C14)* into cell D16. Excel 2007 has reinterpreted the formula so that it fits the surrounding cells! Excel 2007 knows it can reinterpret the cells used in the formula because the formula uses a *relative reference*, or a reference that can change if the formula is copied to another cell. Relative references are written with just the cell row and column (for example, C14). If you want a cell reference to remain constant when the formula using it is copied to another cell, you can use an absolute reference. To write a cell reference as an absolute reference, type *$* before the row name and the column number. If you want the formula in cell D16 to show the sum of values in cells C10 through C14 regardless of the cell into which it is pasted, you can write the formula as *=SUM($C$10:$C$14)*.

Tip If you copy a formula from the formula box, use absolute references or use only named ranges in your formula. Excel 2007 doesn't change the cell references when you copy your formula to another cell.

One quick way to change a cell reference from relative to absolute is to select the cell reference in the formula box and then press F4. Pressing F4 cycles a cell reference through the four possible types of references:

● Relative columns and rows (for example, *C4*)

● Absolute columns and rows (for example, *$C$4*)

● Relative columns and absolute rows (for example, *C$4*)

● Absolute columns and relative rows (for example, *$C4*)

In this exercise, you will create a formula manually, revise it to include additional cells, create a formula that contains a table reference, create a formula with relative references, and change the formula so it contains absolute references.

> **USE** the *ITExpenses* workbook. This practice file is located in the *Documents\Microsoft Press\Excel2007SBS\Formulas* folder.
>
> **OPEN** the *ITExpenses* workbook.

1. If necessary, display the **Summary** worksheet. Then, in cell F9, type =C4, and press ⎶Enter⎶.

   The value *$385,671.00* appears in cell F9.

2. Select cell F9, and then in the formula box, erase the existing formula and type =SU.

   Formula AutoComplete displays a list of possible functions to use in the formula.

3. In the **Formula AutoComplete** list, click **SUM**, and then press ⎶Tab⎶.

   Excel 2007 changes the contents of the formula bar to *=SUM(*.

4. Select the cell range C3:C8, type a right parenthesis (the *)* character) to make the formula bar's contents *=SUM(C3:C8)*, and then press ⎶Enter⎶.

   The value *$2,562,966.00* appears in cell F9.

5. In cell F10, type =SUM(C4:C5), and then press ⎶Enter⎶.

6. Select cell **F10**, and then in the formula box, select the cell reference **C4**, and press ⎶F4⎶.

   Excel 2007 changes the cell reference to *$C$4*.

7. In the formula box, select the cell reference **C5**, press ⎶F4⎶, and then press ⎶Enter⎶.

   Excel 2007 changes the cell reference to *$C$5*.

8. On the tab bar, click the **JuneLabor** sheet tab.

The JuneLabor worksheet opens.

9. In cell F13, type =SUM(J.

Excel 2007 displays JuneSummary, the name of the table in the JuneLabor worksheet.

10. Press Tab.

Excel 2007 extends the formula to read =SUM(JuneSummary.

11. Type [, and then in the **Formula AutoComplete** list, click **[Labor Expense]**, and press Tab.

Excel 2007 extends the formula to read =SUM(JuneSummary[Labor Expense.

12. Type]) to complete the formula, and then press Enter.

The value $637,051.00 appears in cell F13.

CLOSE the *ITExpenses* workbook.

Summarizing Data That Meets Specific Conditions

Another use for formulas is to display messages when certain conditions are met. For instance, Consolidated Messenger's VP of Marketing, Craig Dewar, might have agreed to examine the rates charged to corporate customers who were billed for more than $100,000 during a calendar year. This kind of formula is called a *conditional formula*, and it uses the *IF* function. To create a conditional formula, you click the cell to hold the formula and open the Insert Function dialog box. From within the dialog box, click *IF* in the list of available functions, and then click OK. The Function Arguments dialog box opens.

When you work with an *IF* function, the Function Arguments dialog box has three boxes: Logical_test, Value_if_true, and Value_if_false. The Logical_test box holds the condition you want to check. If the customer's year-to-date shipping bill appears in cell G8, the expression would be G8>100000.

Now you need to have Excel 2007 display messages that indicate whether Craig Dewar should evaluate the account for a possible rate adjustment. To have Excel 2007 print a message from an *IF* function, you enclose the message in quotes in the Value_if_true or Value_if_false box. In this case, you would type *"High-volume shipper—evaluate for rate decrease."* in the Value_if_true box and *"Does not qualify at this time."* in the Value_if_false box.

Excel 2007 also includes five new conditional functions with which you can summarize your data:

- *IFERROR*, which displays one value if a formula results in an error; another if it doesn't
- *AVERAGEIF*, which finds the average of values within a cell range that meet a given criterion

- *AVERAGEIFS*, which finds the average of values within a cell range that meet multiple criteria

- *SUMIFS*, which finds the sum of values in a range that meet multiple criteria

- *COUNTIFS*, which counts the number of cells in a range that meet multiple criteria

The *IFERROR* function enables you to display a custom error message instead of relying on the default Excel 2007 error messages to explain what happened. One example of an *IFERROR* formula is if you want to look up the CustomerID value from cell G8 in the Customers table by using the *VLOOKUP* function. One way to create such a formula is =IFERROR(VLOOKUP(G8,Customers,2,false),"Customer not found"). If the function finds a match for the CustomerID in cell G8, it displays the customer's name; if it doesn't find a match, it displays the text *Customer not found*.

See Also for more information about the VLOOKUP function, see "Looking Up Information in a Data List" in Chapter 7, "Reordering and Summarizing Data."

The *AVERAGEIF* function is a variation on the existing *COUNTIF* and *SUMIF* functions. To create a formula using the *AVERAGEIF* function, you define the range to be examined, the criteria, and, if required, the range from which to draw the values. As an example, consider the following worksheet, which lists each customer's ID number, name, state, and total monthly shipping bill.

If you want to find the average order of customers from Washington State (abbreviated in the worksheet as WA), you can create the formula *=AVERAGEIF(D3:D6,"=WA", E3:E6)*.

The *AVERAGEIFS*, *SUMIFS*, and *COUNTIFS* functions extend the capabilities of the *AVERAGEIF*, *SUMIF*, and *COUNTIF* functions to allow for multiple criteria. If you want to find the sum of all orders of at least $100,000 placed by companies in Washington, you can create the formula *=SUMIFS(E3:E6, D3:D6, "=WA", E3:E6, ">=100000")*.

The *AVERAGEIFS* and *SUMIFS* functions start with a data range that contains values that the formula summarizes; you then list the data ranges and the criteria to apply to that range. In generic terms, the syntax runs *=AVERAGEIFS(data_range, criteria_range1, criteria1[,criteria_range2, criteria2...])*. The part of the syntax in square brackets is optional, so an *AVERAGEIFS* or *SUMIFS* formula that contains a single criterion works. The *COUNTIFS* function, which doesn't perform any calculations, doesn't need a data range—you just provide the criteria ranges and criteria. For example, you could find the number of customers from Washington billed at least $100,000 by using the formula *=COUNTIFS(D3:D6, "=WA", E3:E6, ">=100000")*.

In this exercise, you will create a conditional formula that displays a message if a condition is true, find the average of worksheet values that meet one criterion, and find the sum of worksheet values that meet two criteria.

> **USE** the *PackagingCosts* workbook. This practice file is located in the *Documents\Microsoft Press\Excel2007SBS\Formulas* folder.
>
> **OPEN** the *PackagingCosts* workbook.

1. In cell G3, type the formula =IF(F3>=35000,"Request discount","No discount available"), and press ⌷Enter⌷.

   Excel 2007 accepts the formula, which displays *Request discount* if the value in cell F3 is at least 35,000 and displays *No discount available* if not. The value *Request discount* appears in cell G3.

2. Click cell G3, and drag the fill handle down until it covers cell G14.

Excel 2007 copies the formula in cell G3 to cells G4:G14, adjusting the formula to reflect the cells' addresses. The results of the copied formulas appear in cells G4:G14.

	Code	Type	Size	Destination	Expense	Potential Discount		Average Box Cost
3	PKG0001	Box	Small	Domestic	$ 44,816.00	Request discount		
4	PKG0002	Box	Medium	Domestic	$ 57,715.00	Request discount		
5	PKG0003	Box	Large	Domestic	$ 51,965.00	Request discount		International Envelope Cost
6	PKG0004	Box	Small	International	$ 31,813.00	No discount available		
7	PKG0005	Box	Medium	International	$ 52,830.00	Request discount		
8	PKG0006	Box	Large	International	$ 37,476.00	Request discount		
9	PKG0007	Envelope	Small	Domestic	$ 22,793.00	No discount available		
10	PKG0008	Envelope	Medium	Domestic	$ 21,056.00	No discount available		
11	PKG0009	Envelope	Large	Domestic	$ 20,488.00	No discount available		
12	PKG0010	Envelope	Small	International	$ 10,189.00	No discount available		
13	PKG0011	Envelope	Medium	International	$ 18,309.00	No discount available		
14	PKG0012	Envelope	Large	International	$ 17,255.00	No discount available		

G14 fx =IF(F14>=35000,"Request discount","No discount available")

3. In cell I3, type the formula =AVERAGEIF(C3:C14, "=Box", F3:F14), and press Enter.

   The value *$46,102.50*, which represents the average cost per category of boxes, appears in cell I3.

4. In cell I6, type =SUMIFS(F3:F14, C3:C14, "=Envelope", E3:E14, "=International").

   The value *$45,753.00*, which represents the total cost of all envelopes used for international shipments, appears in cell I6.

I6 fx =SUMIFS(F3:F14,C3:C14,"Envelope",E3:E14,"=International")

	Code	Type	Size	Destination	Expense	Potential Discount		Average Box Cost
3	PKG0001	Box	Small	Domestic	$ 44,816.00	Request discount		$ 46,102.50
4	PKG0002	Box	Medium	Domestic	$ 57,715.00	Request discount		
5	PKG0003	Box	Large	Domestic	$ 51,965.00	Request discount		International Envelope Cost
6	PKG0004	Box	Small	International	$ 31,813.00	No discount available		$ 45,753.00
7	PKG0005	Box	Medium	International	$ 52,830.00	Request discount		
8	PKG0006	Box	Large	International	$ 37,476.00	Request discount		
9	PKG0007	Envelope	Small	Domestic	$ 22,793.00	No discount available		
10	PKG0008	Envelope	Medium	Domestic	$ 21,056.00	No discount available		
11	PKG0009	Envelope	Large	Domestic	$ 20,488.00	No discount available		
12	PKG0010	Envelope	Small	International	$ 10,189.00	No discount available		

CLOSE the *PackagingCosts* workbook.

Finding and Correcting Errors in Calculations

Including calculations in a worksheet gives you valuable answers to questions about your data. As is always true, however, it is possible for errors to creep into your formulas. Excel 2007 makes it easy to find the source of errors in your formulas by identifying the cells used in a given calculation and describing any errors that have occurred. The process of examining a worksheet for errors in formulas is referred to as *auditing*.

Excel 2007 identifies errors in several ways. The first way is to fill the cell holding the formula generating the error with an *error code*. In the following graphic, cell F13 has the error code *#NAME?*.

When a cell with an erroneous formula is the active cell, an Error button appears next to it. You can click the arrow to the right of the button to display a menu with options that provide information about the error and offer to help you fix it.

The following table lists the most common error codes and what they mean.

Error code	Description
#####	The column isn't wide enough to display the value.
#VALUE!	The formula has the wrong type of argument (such as text in which a *TRUE* or *FALSE* value is required).
#NAME?	The formula contains text that Excel 2007 doesn't recognize (such as an unknown named range).
#REF!	The formula refers to a cell that doesn't exist (which can happen whenever cells are deleted).
#DIV/0!	The formula attempts to divide by zero.

Another technique you can use to find the source of formula errors is to ensure that the appropriate cells are providing values for the formula. For example, you might want to calculate the total number of deliveries for a service level, but you could accidentally create a formula referring to the service levels' names instead of their quantities. You can identify what kind of error has appeared by having Excel 2007 trace a cell's *precedents*, which are the cells with values used in the active cell's formula. Excel 2007 identifies a cell's precedents by drawing a blue tracer arrow from the precedent to the active cell.

You can also audit your worksheet by identifying cells with formulas that use a value from a given cell. For example, you might use one region's daily package total in a formula that calculates the average number of packages delivered per region on a given day. Cells that use another cell's value in their calculations are known as *dependents*, meaning that they depend on the value in the other cell to derive their own value. As with tracing precedents, you can click the Formulas tab, and then in the Formula Auditing group, click Trace Dependents to have Excel 2007 draw blue arrows from the active cell to those cells that have calculations based on that value.

If the cells identified by the tracer arrows aren't the correct cells, you can hide the arrows and correct the formula. To hide the tracer arrows on a worksheet, display the Formulas tab, and then in the Formula Auditing group, click Remove Arrows.

If you prefer to have the elements of a formula error presented as text in a dialog box, you can use the Error Checking dialog box (which you can display by displaying the Formulas tab, and then in the Formula Auditing group, clicking the Error Checking button) to view the error and the formula in the cell in which the error occurs. You can also use the controls in the Error Checking dialog box to move through the formula one step at a time, to choose to ignore the error, or to move to the next or the previous error. If you click the Options button in the dialog box, you can also use the controls in the Excel Options dialog box to change how Excel 2007 determines what is an error and what isn't.

> **Tip** You can have the Error Checking tool ignore formulas that don't use every cell in a region (such as a row or column). If you clear the Formulas that omit cells in a region check box, you can create formulas that don't add up every value in a row or column (or rectangle) without Excel 2007 marking them as an error.

For times when you just want to display the results of each step of a formula and don't need the full power of the Error Checking tool, you can use the Evaluate Formula dialog box to move through each element of the formula. To display the Evaluate Formula dialog box, you display the Formulas tab and then, in the Formula Auditing group, click the Evaluate Formula button. The Evaluate Formula dialog box is much more useful for examining formulas that don't produce an error but aren't generating the result you expect.

Finally, you can monitor the value in a cell regardless of where in your workbook you are by opening a Watch Window that displays the value in the cell. For example, if one of your formulas uses values from cells in other worksheets or even other workbooks, you can set a watch on the cell that contains the formula and then change the values in the other cells. To set a watch, click the cell you want to monitor, and then on the Formulas tab, in the Formula Auditing group, click Watch Window. Click Add Watch to have Excel 2007 monitor the selected cell.

As soon as you type in the new value, the Watch Window displays the new result of the formula. When you're done watching the formula, select the watch, click Delete Watch, and close the Watch Window.

In this exercise, you will use the formula-auditing capabilities in Excel 2007 to identify and correct errors in a formula.

USE the *ConveyerBid* workbook. This practice file is located in the *Documents\ Microsoft Press\Excel2007SBS\Formulas* folder.

OPEN the *ConveyerBid* workbook.

1. Click cell D20.

2. On the **Formulas** tab, in the **Formula Auditing** group, click **Watch Window**.

The Watch Window opens.

Watch
Window

3. Click **Add Watch**, and then in the **Add Watch** dialog box, click **Add**.

    Cell D20 appears in the Watch Window.

4. Click cell D8.

    =SUM(C3:C7) appears in the formula bar.

5. On the **Formulas** tab, in the **Formula Auditing** group, click the **Trace Precedents** button.

    A blue arrow appears between cell D8 and the cell range C3:C7, indicating that the cells in the range C3:C7 are precedents of the value in cell D8.

6. On the **Formulas** tab, in the **Formula Auditing** group, click the **Remove Arrows** button.

    The arrow disappears.

7. Click cell A1.

Error Checking

8. On the **Formulas** tab, in the **Formula Auditing** group, click the **Error Checking** button.

The Error Checking dialog box opens.

Error Checking	? ⊠
Error in cell D21	Help on this error
=C12/D19	Show Calculation Steps...
Divide by Zero Error	Ignore Error
The formula or function used is dividing by zero or empty cells.	Edit in Formula Bar
Options...	Previous Next

9. Click **Next**.

Excel 2007 displays a message box indicating that there are no more errors in the worksheet.

10. Click **OK**.

The message box and the Error Checking dialog box close.

11. On the **Formulas** tab, in the **Formula Auditing** group, click the **Error Checking** arrow, and then in the list, click **Trace Error**.

Blue arrows appear, pointing to cell D21 from cells C12 and D19. These arrows indicate that using the values (or lack of values, in this case) in the indicated cells generates the error in cell D21.

12. On the **Formulas** tab, in the **Formula Auditing** group, click **Remove Arrows**.

The arrows disappear.

13. In the formula box, delete the existing formula, type =C12/D20, and press [Enter].

The value *14%* appears in cell D21.

14. Click cell D21.

Evaluate Formula

15. On the **Formulas** tab, in the **Formula Auditing** group, click the **Evaluate Formula** button.

The Evaluate Formula dialog box opens, with the formula from cell D21 displayed.

16. Click **Evaluate** three times to step through the formula's elements, and then click **Close**.

    The Evaluate Formula dialog box closes.

17. In the **Watch Window**, click the watch in the list.

18. Click **Delete Watch**.

    The watch disappears.

19. On the **Formulas** tab, in the **Formula Auditing** group, click **Watch Window**.

    The Watch Window closes.

CLOSE the *ConveyerBid* workbook. If you are not continuing directly to the next chapter, exit Excel.

Key Points

- You can add a group of cells to a formula by typing the formula, and then at the spot in the formula in which you want to name the cells, selecting the cells by using the mouse.

- Creating named ranges enables you to refer to entire blocks of cells with a single term, saving you lots of time and effort. You can use a similar technique with table data, referring to an entire table or one or more table columns.

- When you write a formula, be sure you use absolute referencing ($A$1) if you want the formula to remain the same when it's copied from one cell to another or use relative referencing (A1) if you want the formula to change to reflect its new position in the worksheet.

- Instead of typing a formula from scratch, you can use the Insert Function dialog box to help you on your way.

- You can monitor how the value in a cell changes by adding a watch to the Watch Window.

- To see which formulas refer to the values in the selected cell, use Trace Dependents; if you want to see which cells provide values for the formula in the active cell, use Trace Precedents.

- You can step through the calculations of a formula in the Evaluate Formula dialog box or go through a more rigorous error-checking procedure by using the Error Checking tool.

Chapter at a Glance

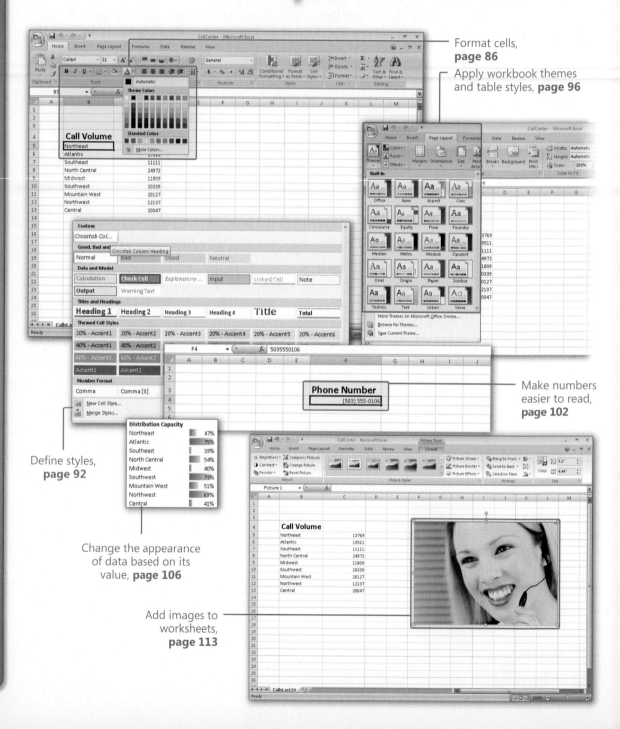

Format cells, **page 86**

Apply workbook themes and table styles, **page 96**

Make numbers easier to read, **page 102**

Define styles, **page 92**

Change the appearance of data based on its value, **page 106**

Add images to worksheets, **page 113**

5 Changing Workbook Appearance

In this chapter, you will learn to:

- ✔ Format cells.
- ✔ Define styles.
- ✔ Apply workbook themes and table styles.
- ✔ Make numbers easier to read.
- ✔ Change the appearance of data based on its value.
- ✔ Add images to worksheets.

Entering data into a workbook efficiently saves you time, but you must also ensure that your data is easy to read. Microsoft Office Excel 2007 gives you a wide variety of ways to make your data easier to understand; for example, you can change the font, character size, or color used to present a cell's contents. Changing how data appears on a worksheet helps set the contents of a cell apart from the contents of surrounding cells. The simplest example of that concept is a data label. If a column on your worksheet has a list of days, you can set a label (for example, Day) apart easily by presenting it in bold type that's noticeably larger than the type used to present the data to which it refers. To save time, you can define a number of custom formats and then apply them quickly to the desired cells.

You might also want to specially format a cell's contents to reflect the value in that cell. For instance, Jenny Lysaker, the chief operating officer of Consolidated Messenger, might want to create a worksheet that displays the percentage of improperly delivered packages from each regional distribution center. If that percentage exceeds a threshold, she could have Excel 2007 display a red traffic light icon, indicating that the center's performance is out of tolerance and requires attention.

In addition to changing how data appears in the cells of your worksheet, you can also use headers and footers to add page numbers, current data, or graphics to the top and bottom of every printed page.

In this chapter, you'll learn how to change the appearance of data, apply existing formats to data, make numbers easier to read, change data's appearance based on its value, make printouts easier to follow, and position your data on the printed page.

See Also Do you need only a quick refresher on the topics in this chapter? See the Quick Reference section at the beginning of this book.

Important Before you can use the practice files in this chapter, you need to install them from the book's companion CD to their default location. See "Using the Companion CD" at the beginning of this book for more information.

Formatting Cells

Excel 2007 spreadsheets can hold and process lots of data, but when you manage numerous spreadsheets it can be hard to remember from a worksheet's title exactly what data is kept in that worksheet. Data labels give you and your colleagues information about data in a worksheet, but it's important to format the labels so that they stand out visually. To make your data labels or any other data stand out, you can change the format of the cells in which the data is stored.

	A	B	C	D	E
1					
2					
3					
4		Call Volume			
5		Northeast	13769		
6		Atlantic	19511		
7		Southeast	11111		
8		North Central	24972		
9		Midwest	11809		
10		Southwest	20339		
11		Mountain West	20127		
12		Northwest	12137		
13		Central	20047		

Most of the tools you need to change a cell's format can be found on the Home tab. You can apply the formatting represented on a button by selecting the cells you want to apply the style to and then clicking the appropriate button. If you want to set your data labels apart by making them appear bold, click the Bold button. If you have already made a cell's contents bold, selecting the cell and clicking the Bold button will remove the formatting.

> **Tip** Deleting a cell's contents doesn't delete the cell's formatting. To delete a selected cell's formatting, on the Home tab, in the Editing group, click the Clear button, and then click Clear Formats.

Buttons in the Home tab's Font group that give you choices, such as the Font Color control, have an arrow at the right edge of the button. Clicking the arrow displays a list of options accessible for that control, such as the fonts available on your system or the colors you can assign to a cell.

Another way you can make a cell stand apart from its neighbors is to add a border around the cell. To place a border around one or more cells, select the cells, and then choose the border type you want by selecting the type of border to apply from the Border list in the Font group. Excel 2007 does provide more options—to display the full range of border types and styles, in the Border list, click More Borders. The Border tab of the Format Cells dialog box contains the full range of tools you can use to define your cells' borders.

Another way you can make a group of cells stand apart from its neighbors is to change its shading, or the color that fills the cells. On a worksheet that tracks total package volume for the past month, Jenny Lysaker could change the fill color of the cells holding her data labels to make the labels stand out even more than by changing the formatting of the text used to display the labels.

> **Tip** You can display the most commonly used formatting controls by right-clicking a selected range. When you do, a Mini toolbar containing a subset of the Home tab formatting tools appears above the shortcut menu.

If you want to change the attributes of every cell in a row or column, you can click the header of the row or column you want to format and then select your desired format.

One task you can't perform using the tools on the Home tab is to change the standard font for a workbook, which is used in the Name box and on the formula bar. The standard font when you install Excel 2007 is Calibri, a simple font that is easy to read on a computer screen and on the printed page. If you want to choose another font, click the Microsoft Office Button, and then click Excel Options. On the Popular page of the Excel Options dialog box, set the values in the Use This Font and Font Size list boxes to pick your new display font.

> **Important** The new standard font doesn't take effect until you exit Excel 2007 and restart the program.

In this exercise, you will emphasize a worksheet's title by changing the format of cell data, adding a border to a cell range, and then changing a cell range's fill color. After those tasks are complete, you will change the default font for the workbook.

> **USE** the *VehicleMileSummary* workbook. This practice file is located in the *Documents\ Microsoft Press\Excel2007SBS\Appearance* folder.
>
> **BE SURE TO** start Excel 2007 before beginning this exercise.
>
> **OPEN** the *VehicleMileSummary* workbook.

1. Click cell D2.

B

Bold

2. On the **Home** tab, in the **Font** group, click the **Bold** button.

Excel 2007 displays the cell's contents in bold type.

11 ▼

Font Size

3. In the **Font** group, click the **Font Size** arrow, and then in the list, click **18**.

Excel 2007 increases the size of the text in cell D2.

4. Select cells B5 and C4.

5. On the **Home** tab, in the **Font** group, click the **Bold** button.

Excel 2007 displays the cells' contents in bold type.

6. Select the cell ranges B6:B15 and C5:H5.

Italic

7. In the **Font** group, click the **Italic** button.

Excel 2007 displays the cells' contents in italic type.

	A	B	C	D	E	F	G	H	I
1									
2			**Vehicle Mile Summary**						
3									
4			Day						
5		**VehicleID**	*Monday*	*Tuesday*	*Wednesday*	*Thursday*	*Friday*	*Saturday*	
6		*V101*	159	144	124	108	125	165	
7		*V102*	113	106	111	116	119	97	
8		*V103*	87	154	124	128	111	100	
9		*V104*	137	100	158	96	127	158	
10		*V105*	86	132	154	97	154	165	
11		*V106*	159	163	155	101	89	160	
12		*V107*	111	165	155	92	91	94	
13		*V108*	101	162	123	87	93	140	
14		*V109*	164	159	116	97	149	120	
15		*V110*	100	107	143	144	152	132	
16									

8. Select the cell range C6:H15.

Border

9. In the **Font** group, click the **Border** arrow, and then in the list, click **Outside Borders**.

Excel 2007 places a border around the outside edge of the selected cells.

10. Select the cell range B4:H15.

11. In the **Border** list, click **Thick Box Border**.

Excel 2007 places a thick border around the outside edge of the selected cells.

12. Select the cell ranges B4:B15 and C4:H5.

Fill Color

13. In the **Font** group, click the **Fill Color** arrow, and then in the **Standard Colors** section of the color palette, click the yellow button.

Excel 2007 changes the selected cells' background color to yellow.

			Vehicle Mile Summary				
	Day						
VehicleID	Monday	Tuesday	Wednesday	Thursday	Friday	Saturday	
V101	159	144	124	108	125	165	
V102	113	106	111	116	119	97	
V103	87	154	124	128	111	100	
V104	137	100	158	96	127	158	
V105	86	132	154	97	154	165	
V106	159	163	155	101	89	160	
V107	111	165	155	92	91	94	
V108	101	162	123	87	93	140	
V109	164	159	116	97	149	120	
V110	100	107	143	144	152	132	

Microsoft Office
Button

14. Click the **Microsoft Office Button**, and then click **Excel Options**.

The Excel Options dialog box opens.

15. If necessary, click **Popular** to display the **Popular** tab.

16. In the **When creating new workbooks** section, in the **Use this font** list, click **Verdana**.

Verdana appears in the Use This Font field.

17. Click **Cancel**.

The Excel Options dialog box closes without saving your change.

CLOSE the *VehicleMileSummary* workbook.

Defining Styles

As you work with Excel 2007, you will probably develop preferred formats for data labels, titles, and other worksheet elements. Instead of adding the format's characteristics one element at a time to the target cells, you can have Excel 2007 store the format and re-call it as needed. You can find the predefined formats available to you by displaying the Home tab, and then in the Styles group, clicking Cell Styles.

Clicking a style from the Cell Styles gallery applies the style to the selected cells, but Excel 2007 goes a step beyond previous versions of the program by displaying a live preview of a format when you point to it. If none of the existing styles is what you want, you can create your own style by displaying the Cell Styles gallery and, at the bottom of the gallery, clicking New Cell Style to display the Style dialog box. In the Style dialog box, type the name of your new style in the Style Name field, and then click Format. The Format Cells dialog box opens.

Format Cells dialog box showing the Font tab selected. Tabs: Number, Alignment, Font, Border, Fill, Protection. Font: Calibri. Font style: Bold. Size: 18. Underline: None. Color. Normal font checkbox. Effects: Strikethrough, Superscript, Subscript. Preview shows AaBbCcYyZz. Text below reads "This is a TrueType font. The same font will be used on both your printer and your screen." OK and Cancel buttons.

After you set the characteristics of your new style, click OK to make your style available in the Cell Styles gallery. If you ever want to delete a style, display the Cell Styles gallery, right-click the style, and then click Delete.

The Style dialog box is quite versatile, but it's overkill if all you want to do is apply formatting changes you made to a cell to the contents of another cell. To do so, use the Format Painter button, found in the Home tab's Clipboard group. Just click the cell that has the format you want to copy, click the Format Painter button, and select the target cells to have Excel 2007 apply the copied format to the target range.

In this exercise, you will create a style, apply the new style to a data label, and then use the Format Painter to apply the style to the contents of another cell.

> **USE** the *HourlyExceptions* workbook. This practice file is located in the *Documents\ Microsoft Press\Excel2007SBS\Appearance* folder.
>
> **OPEN** the *HourlyExceptions* workbook.

1. On the **Home** tab, in the **Styles** group, click **Cell Styles**, and then click **New Cell Style**.

The Style dialog box opens.

2. In the **Style name** field, type Crosstab Column Heading.

3. Click the **Format** button.

   The Format Cells dialog box opens.

4. Click the **Alignment** tab.

5. In the **Horizontal** list, click **Center**.

Center appears in the Horizontal field.

6. Click the **Font** tab.

7. In the **Font style** list, click **Italic**.

The text in the Preview pane appears in italicized text.

8. Click the **Number** tab.

The Number tab of the Format Cells dialog box is displayed.

9. In the **Category** list, click **Time**.

The available time formats appear.

10. In the **Type** pane, click **1:30 PM**.

11. Click **OK** to accept the default time format.

The Format Cells dialog box closes, and your new style's definition appears in the Style dialog box.

12. Click **OK**.

The Style dialog box closes.

13. Select cells C4:N4.

14. On the **Home** tab, in the **Styles** group, click **Cell Styles**.

Your new style appears at the top of the gallery, in the Custom group.

Custom					
Crosstab Col...					
Good, Bad and Crosstab Column Heading					
Normal	Bad	Good	Neutral		
Data and Model					
Calculation	Check Cell	*Explanatory ...*	Input	Linked Cell	Note
Output	Warning Text				
Titles and Headings					
Heading 1	Heading 2	Heading 3	Heading 4	Title	Total
Themed Cell Styles					
20% - Accent1	20% - Accent2	20% - Accent3	20% - Accent4	20% - Accent5	20% - Accent6
40% - Accent1	40% - Accent2	40% - Accent3	40% - Accent4	40% - Accent5	40% - Accent6
60% - Accent1	60% - Accent2	60% - Accent3	60% - Accent4	60% - Accent5	60% - Accent6
Accent1	Accent2	Accent3	Accent4	Accent5	Accent6
Number Format					
Comma	Comma [0]	Currency	Currency [0]	Percent	

New Cell Style...
Merge Styles...

15. Click the **Crosstab Column Heading** style.

Excel 2007 applies your new style to the selected cells.

CLOSE the *HourlyExceptions* workbook.

Applying Workbook Themes and Table Styles

The 2007 Microsoft Office system includes powerful new design tools that enable you to create attractive, professional documents quickly. The Excel 2007 product team implemented the new design capabilities by defining workbook themes and table styles. A *theme* is a way to specify the fonts, colors, and graphic effects that appear in a workbook. Excel 2007 comes with many themes installed.

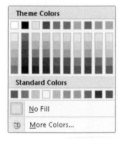

To apply an existing workbook theme, display the Page Layout tab. Then, in the Themes group, click Themes, and click the theme you want to apply to your workbook. By default, Excel 2007 applies the Office theme to your workbooks.

The theme colors appear in the top segment of the color palette—the standard colors and the More Colors link, which displays the Colors dialog box, appear at the bottom of the palette. If you format workbook elements using colors from the theme colors portion of the color palette, applying a different theme changes that object's colors.

You can change a theme's colors, fonts, and graphic effects by displaying the Page Layout tab, and in the Themes group, selecting new values from the Colors, Fonts, and Effects lists. To save your changes as a new theme, display the Page Layout tab, and in the Themes group, click Themes, and then click Save Current Theme. Use the controls in the dialog box that opens to record your theme for later use. Later, when you click the Themes button, your custom theme will appear at the top of the gallery.

> **Tip** When you save a theme, you save it as an Office Theme file. You can apply the theme to Microsoft Office Word 2007 and Microsoft Office PowerPoint 2007 files as well.

Just as you can define and apply themes to entire workbooks, you can apply and define table styles. You select a table's initial style when you create it; to create a new style, display the Home tab, and in the Styles group, click Format As Table. In the Format As Table gallery, click New Table Style to display the New Table Quick Style dialog box.

Type a name for the new style, select the first table element you want to format, and then click Format to display the Format Cells dialog box. Define the element's formatting, and then click OK. When the New Table Quick Style dialog box reopens, its Preview pane displays the overall table style and the Element Formatting section displays the selected element's appearance. Also, in the Table Element list, Excel 2007 displays the element's name in bold to indicate it has been changed. To make the new style the default for new tables created in the current workbook, select the Set As Default Table Quick Style For This Document check box. When you click OK, Excel 2007 saves the new table style.

See Also For more information about creating Excel tables, see "Defining a Table" in Chapter 3, "Working with Data and Data Tables."

In this exercise, you will create a new workbook theme, change a workbook's theme, create a new table style, and apply the new style to a table.

USE the *HourlyTracking* workbook. This practice file is located in the *Documents\ Microsoft Press\Excel2007SBS\Appearance* folder.
OPEN the *HourlyTracking* workbook.

1. If necessary, click any cell in the table.

2. On the **Home** tab, in the **Styles** group, click **Format as Table**, and then click the style at the upper-left corner of the **Table Styles** gallery.

   Excel 2007 applies the style to the table.

3. On the **Home** tab, in the **Styles** group, click **Format as Table**, and then click **New Table Style**.

   The New Table Quick Style dialog box opens.

4. In the **Name** field, type **Exception Default**.

5. In the **Table Element** list, click **Header Row**.

6. Click **Format**.

   The Format Cells dialog box opens.

7. Click the **Fill** tab.

   The Fill tab appears.

8. In the first row of color squares, just below the **No Color** button, click the third square from the left.

   The new background color appears in the Sample pane of the dialog box.

9. Click **OK**.

   The Format Cells dialog box closes. When the New Table Quick Style dialog box reopens, the Header Row table element appears in bold, and the Preview pane's header row is shaded.

10. In the **Table Element** list, click **Second Row Stripe**, and then click **Format**.

    The Format Cells dialog box opens.

11. Click the **No Color** button, and click the third square from the left again.

    The new background color appears in the Sample pane of the dialog box.

12. Click **OK**.

    The Format Cells dialog box closes. When the New Table Quick Style dialog box reopens, the Second Row Stripe table element appears in bold, and every second row is shaded in the Preview pane.

13. Click **OK**.

    The New Table Quick Style dialog box closes.

14. On the **Home** tab, in the **Styles** group, click **Format as Table**. In the gallery that appears, in the **Custom** section, click the new format.

    Excel 2007 applies the new format.

Theme Fonts

15. On the **Page Layout** tab, in the **Themes** group, click the **Theme Fonts** arrow, and then in the list, click **Verdana**.

Excel 2007 changes the theme's font to Verdana.

16. In the **Themes** group, click the **Themes** button, and then click **Save Current Theme**.

The Save Current Theme dialog box opens.

17. In the **File name** field, type Verdana Office, and then click **Save**.

Excel 2007 saves your theme.

18. In the **Themes** group, click the **Themes** button, and then click **Origin**.

Excel 2007 applies the new theme to your workbook.

CLOSE the *HourlyTracking* workbook.

Making Numbers Easier to Read

Changing the format of the cells in your worksheet can make your data much easier to read, both by setting data labels apart from the actual data and by adding borders to define the boundaries between labels and data even more clearly. Of course, using formatting options to change the font and appearance of a cell's contents doesn't help with idiosyncratic data types such as dates, phone numbers, or currency.

For example, consider U.S. phone numbers. These numbers are 10 digits long and have a 3-digit area code, a 3-digit exchange, and a 4-digit line number written in the form (###) ###-####. Although it's certainly possible to type a phone number with the expected formatting in a cell, it's much simpler to type a sequence of 10 digits and have Excel 2007 change the data's appearance.

You can tell Excel 2007 to expect a phone number in a cell by opening the Format Cells dialog box to the Number tab and displaying the formats available for the Special category.

Clicking Phone Number in the Type list tells Excel 2007 to format 10-digit numbers in the standard phone number format. As you can see by comparing the contents of the active cell and the contents of the formula box in the next graphic, the underlying data isn't changed, just its appearance in the cell.

> **Troubleshooting** If you type a 9-digit number in a field that expects a phone number, you won't see an error message; instead, you'll see a 2-digit area code. For example, the number 425555012 would be displayed as (42) 555-5012. An 11-digit number would be displayed with a 4-digit area code.

Just as you can instruct Excel 2007 to expect a phone number in a cell, you can also have it expect a date or a currency amount. You can make those changes from the Format Cells dialog box by choosing either the Date category or the Currency category. The Date category enables you to pick the format for the date (and determine whether the date's appearance changes due to the Locale setting of the operating system on the computer viewing the workbook). In a similar vein, selecting the Currency category displays controls to set the number of places after the decimal point, the currency symbol to use, and the way in which Excel 2007 should display negative numbers.

> **Tip** The new Excel 2007 user interface enables you to set the most common format changes by using the controls in the Home tab's Number group.

You can also create a custom numeric format to add a word or phrase to a number in a cell. For example, you can add the phrase per month to a cell with a formula that calculates average monthly sales for a year to ensure that you and your colleagues will recognize the figure as a monthly average. To create a custom number format, click the Home tab, and then click the Number dialog box launcher to display the Format Cells dialog box. Then, if necessary, click the Number tab.

In the Category list, click Custom to display the available custom number formats in the Type list. You can then click the base format you want and modify it in the Type box. For example, clicking the 0.00 format causes Excel 2007 to format any number in a cell with two digits to the right of the decimal point.

> **Tip** The zeros in the format indicate that the position in the format can accept any number as a valid value.

To customize the format, click in the Type box and add any symbols or text you want to the format. For example, typing a dollar ($) sign to the left of the existing format and then typing *"per month"* to the right of the existing format causes the number 1500 to be displayed as *$1500.00 per month*.

> **Important** You need to enclose any text in quotes so that Excel 2007 recognizes the text as a string to be displayed in the cell.

In this exercise, you will assign date, phone number, and currency formats to ranges of cells. After assigning the formats, you will test them by entering customer data.

> **USE** the *ExecutiveSearch* workbook. This practice file is located in the *Documents\ Microsoft Press\Excel2007SBS\Appearance* folder.
>
> **OPEN** the *ExecutiveSearch* workbook.

1. Click cell A3.

Dialog Box Launcher

2. On the **Home** tab, click the **Font** dialog box launcher.

   The Format Cells dialog box opens.

3. If necessary, click the **Number** tab.

4. In the **Category** list, click **Date**.

   The Type list appears with a list of date formats.

Format Cells

Tabs: Number | Alignment | Font | Border | Fill | Protection

Category:
General
Number
Currency
Accounting
Date
Time
Percentage
Fraction
Scientific
Text
Special
Custom

Sample
1/25/2007

Type:
*3/14/2001
*Wednesday, March 14, 2001
3/14
3/14/01
03/14/01
14-Mar
14-Mar-01

Locale (location):
English (United States)

Date formats display date and time serial numbers as date values. Date formats that begin with an asterisk (*) respond to changes in regional date and time settings that are specified for the operating system. Formats without an asterisk are not affected by operating system settings.

OK | Cancel

5. In the **Type** list, click **3/14/01**.

> **Important** Be sure to click the format without the asterisk (*) in front of the sample date.

6. Click **OK** to assign the chosen format to the cell.

7. Click cell G3.

8. On the **Home** tab, click the **Font** dialog box launcher.

9. If necessary, click the **Number** tab in the **Format Cells** dialog box.

10. In the **Category** list, click **Special**.

    The Type list appears with a list of special formats.

11. In the **Type** list, click **Phone Number**, and then click **OK**.

    The contents of the cell change to (425) 555-0102, matching the format you chose earlier, and the Format Cells dialog box closes.

12. Click cell H3.

13. Click the **Font** dialog box launcher.

14. If necessary, click the **Number** tab in the **Format Cells** dialog box.

15. In the **Category** list, click **Custom**.

    The contents of the Type list are updated to reflect your choice.

16. In the **Type** list, click the **#,##0** item.

#,##0 appears in the Type box.

17. In the **Type** box, click to the left of the existing format, and type $. Then click to the right of the format, and type "before bonuses".

18. Click **OK** to close the dialog box.

CLOSE the *ExecutiveSearch* workbook.

Changing the Appearance of Data Based on Its Value

Recording package volumes, vehicle miles, and other business data in a worksheet enables you to make important decisions about your operations. And as you saw earlier in this chapter, you can change the appearance of data labels and the worksheet itself to make interpreting your data easier.

Another way you can make your data easier to interpret is to have Excel 2007 change the appearance of your data based on its value. These formats are called *conditional formats* because the data must meet certain conditions to have a format applied to it.

For instance, if chief operating officer Jenny Lysaker wanted to highlight any Thursdays with higher-than-average weekday package volumes, she could define a conditional format that tests the value in the cell recording total sales, and that will change the format of the cell's contents when the condition is met.

In previous versions of Excel, you could have a maximum of three conditional formats. There's no such limit in Excel 2007; you may have as many conditional formats as you like. The other major limitation of conditional formats in Excel 2003 and earlier versions was that Excel stopped evaluating conditional formats as soon as it found one that applied to a cell. In other words, you couldn't have multiple conditions be true for the same cell! In Excel 2007, you can control whether Excel 2007 stops or continues after it discovers that a specific condition applies to a cell.

To create a conditional format, you select the cells to which you want to apply the format, display the Home tab, and then in the Styles group, click Conditional Formatting to display a menu of possible conditional formats. Excel 2007 enables you to create all the conditional formats available in previous versions of the program and offers many more conditional formats than were previously available. Prior to Excel 2007, you could create conditional formats to highlight cells that contained values meeting a certain condition. For example, you could highlight all cells that contain a value over 100, contain a date before 1/28/2007, or contain an order amount between $100 and $500. In Excel 2007, you can define conditional formats that change how the program displays data in cells that contain values above or below the average values of the related cells, that contain values near the top or bottom of the value range, or that contain values duplicated elsewhere in the selected range.

When you select which kind of condition to create, Excel 2007 displays a dialog box that contains fields and controls you can use to define your rule. To display all your rules, display the Home tab, and then in the Styles group, click Conditional Formatting. From the menu that appears, click Manage Rules to display the Conditional Formatting Rules Manager.

The Conditional Formatting Rules Manager, which is new in Excel 2007, enables you to control your conditional formats in the following ways:

- Create a new rule by clicking the New Rule button.
- Change a rule by clicking the rule and then clicking the Edit Rule button.
- Remove a rule by clicking the rule and then clicking the Delete Rule button.
- Move a rule up or down in the order by clicking the Move Up or Move Down button.
- Control whether Excel 2007 continues evaluating conditional formats after it finds a rule to apply by selecting or clearing a rule's Stop If True check box.
- Save any new rules and close the Conditional Formatting Rules Manager by clicking OK.
- Save any new rules without closing the Conditional Formatting Rules Manager by clicking Apply.
- Discard any unsaved changes by clicking Cancel.

> **Tip** Clicking the New Rule button in the Conditional Formatting Rules Manager opens the New Formatting Rule dialog box. The commands in the New Formatting Rule dialog box duplicate the options displayed when you click the Conditional Formatting button in the Styles group on the Home tab.

After you create a rule, you can change the format applied if the rule is true by clicking the rule and then clicking the Edit Rule button to display the Edit Formatting Rule dialog box. In that dialog box, click the Format button to display the Format Cells dialog box. After you define your format, click OK.

> **Important** Excel 2007 doesn't check to make sure that your conditions are logically consistent, so you need to be sure that you enter your conditions correctly.

Excel 2007 also enables you to create three new types of conditional formats: data bars, color scales, and icon sets. Data bars summarize the relative magnitude of values in a cell range by extending a band of color across the cell.

Distribution Capacity		
Northeast		47%
Atlantic		75%
Southeast		39%
North Central		54%
Midwest		40%
Southwest		73%
Mountain West		51%
Northwest		69%
Central		41%

Color scales compare the relative magnitude of values in a cell range by applying colors from a two-color or three-color set to your cells. The intensity of a cell's color reflects the value's tendency toward the top or bottom of the values in the range.

Distribution Capacity	
Northeast	47%
Atlantic	75%
Southeast	39%
North Central	54%
Midwest	40%
Southwest	73%
Mountain West	51%
Northwest	69%
Central	41%

Icon sets are collections of three, four, or five images that Excel 2007 displays when certain rules are met.

Distribution Capacity	
Northeast	
Atlantic	
Southeast	
North Central	
Midwest	
Southwest	
Mountain West	
Northwest	
Central	

When you click a color scale or icon set in the Conditional Formatting Rule Manager and then click the Edit Rule button, you can control when Excel 2007 applies a color or icon to your data.

> **Important** Be sure to not include cells that contain summary formulas in your conditionally formatted ranges. The values, which could be much higher or lower than your regular cell data, could throw off your formatting comparisons.

In this exercise, you will create a series of conditional formats to change the appearance of data in worksheet cells displaying the package volume and delivery exception rates of a regional distribution center.

> **USE** the *Dashboard* workbook. This practice file is located in the *Documents\Microsoft Press\Excel2007SBS\Appearance* folder.
>
> **OPEN** the *Dashboard* workbook.

1. Select cells C4:C12.

Conditional Formatting ▾

2. On the **Home** tab, in the **Styles** group, click **Conditional Formatting**. On the menu that appears, point to **Color Scales**, and then in the top row of the palette that appears, click the second pattern from the left.

Excel 2007 formats the selected range.

	Package Exception Rate			Package Volume			Distribution Capacity	
Northeast	0.003%		Northeast	1912447		Northeast	47%	
Atlantic	0.008%		Atlantic	1933574		Atlantic	75%	
Southeast	0.013%		Southeast	1333292		Southeast	39%	
North Central	0.004%		North Central	1811459		North Central	54%	
Midwest	0.018%		Midwest	1140803		Midwest	40%	
Southwest	0.001%		Southwest	1911884		Southwest	73%	
Mountain West	0.045%		Mountain West	1787293		Mountain West	51%	
Northwest	0.002%		Northwest	1631350		Northwest	69%	
Central	0.038%		Central	1660040		Central	41%	
Customer Satisfaction	88%							

3. Select cells F4:F12.

4. On the **Home** tab, in the **Styles** group, click **Conditional Formatting**. From the menu that appears, point to **Data Bars**, and then click the light blue data bar format.

   Excel 2007 formats the selected range.

5. Select cells I4:I12.

6. On the **Home** tab, in the **Styles** group, click **Conditional Formatting**. On the menu that appears, point to **Icon Sets**, and then in the left-hand column of the list of formats that appears, click the three traffic lights.

   Excel 2007 formats the selected cells.

7. With the range I4:I12 still selected, on the **Home** tab, in the **Styles** group, click **Conditional Formatting**, and then click **Manage Rules**.

   The Conditional Formatting Rules Manager opens.

8. Click the icon set rule, and then click **Edit Rule**.

The Edit Formatting Rule dialog box opens.

9. Select the **Reverse Icon Order** check box.

   Excel 2007 reconfigures the rules so the red light icon is at the top and the green light icon is at the bottom.

10. In the red light icon's row, in the **Type** list, click **Percent**.

11. In the red light icon's **Value** field, type 80.

12. In the yellow light icon's row, in the **Type** list, click **Percent**.

13. In the yellow light icon **Value** field, type 67.

14. Click **OK** twice to clear the **Edit Formatting Rule** dialog box and the **Conditional Formatting Rules Manager**.

    Excel 2007 formats the selected cell range.

15. Click cell C15.

16. On the **Home** tab, in the **Styles** group, click **Conditional Formatting**. On the menu that appears, point to **Highlight Cells Rules**, and then click **Less Than**.

    The Less Than dialog box opens.

17. In the left field, type 96%.

18. In the **With** list, click **Red text**.

19. Click **OK**.

The Less Than dialog box closes, and Excel 2007 displays the text in cell C15 in red.

CLOSE the *Dashboard* workbook.

Adding Images to Worksheets

Establishing a strong corporate identity helps customers remember your organization and the products and services you offer. Setting aside the obvious need for sound management, two important physical attributes of a strong retail business are a well-conceived shop space and an eye-catching, easy-to-remember logo. After you or your graphic artist has created a logo, you should add the logo to all your documents, especially any that might be seen by your customers. Not only does the logo mark the documents as coming from your company but it also serves as an advertisement, encouraging anyone who sees your worksheets to call or visit your company.

One way to add a picture to a worksheet is to display the Insert tab, and then in the Illustrations group, click Picture. Clicking Picture displays the Insert Picture dialog box, which enables you to locate the picture you want to add from your hard disk. When you insert a picture, the Picture Tools Format contextual tab appears on the Ribbon. You can use the tools on the Format contextual tab to change the picture's contrast, brightness, and so on. The controls in the Picture Styles group enable you to place a border around the picture, change the picture's shape, or change a picture's effects (such as shadow, reflection, or rotation in three dimensions). Other tools, found in the Arrange and Size groups, enable you to rotate, reposition, and resize the picture.

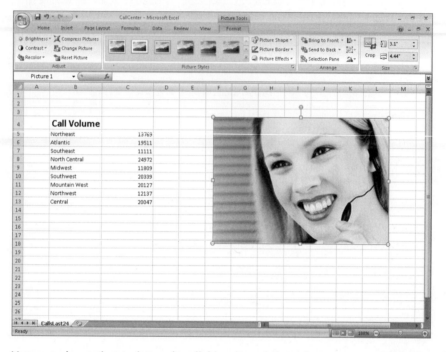

You can also resize a picture by clicking it and then dragging one of the handles that appear on the graphic. If you accidentally resize a graphic by dragging a handle, just click the Undo button to remove your change. If you want to generate a repeating image in the background of a worksheet, forming a tiled pattern behind your worksheet's data, you can display the Page Layout tab, and then in the Page Setup group, click Background. In the Sheet Background dialog box, click the image that you want to serve as the background pattern for your worksheet, and click OK.

> **Tip** To remove a background image from a worksheet, display the Page Layout tab, and then in the Page Setup group, click Delete Background.

To achieve a watermark-type effect with words displayed behind the worksheet data, save the watermark information as an image, and then use the image as the sheet background; or insert the image in the header or footer, and then resize or scale it to position the watermark information where you want it.

In this exercise, you will add an image to an existing worksheet, change the graphic's location on the worksheet, reduce the size of the graphic, change the image's brightness and contrast, rotate and crop the image, delete the image, and then set the image as a repeating background for the worksheet.

> **USE** the *CallCenter* workbook and the *callcenter* and *acbluprt* images. These practice files are located in the *Documents\Microsoft Press\Excel2007SBS\Appearance* folder.
>
> **OPEN** the *CallCenter* workbook.

Picture

1. On the **Insert** tab, in the **Illustrations** group, click **Picture**.

   The Insert Picture dialog box opens.

2. Browse to the *Documents\Microsoft Press\Excel2007SBS\Appearance* folder, and then double-click *callcenter.jpg*.

   The image appears on your worksheet.

3. Move the image to the upper-left corner of the worksheet, grab the handle at the lower-right corner of the image, and drag it up and to the left until it no longer obscures the Call Volume label.

4. On the **Page Layout** tab, in the **Page Setup** group, click **Background**.

The Sheet Background dialog box opens.

5. Browse to the *Documents\Microsoft Press\Excel2007SBS\Appearance* folder, and then double-click *acbluprt.jpg*.

Excel 2007 repeats the image to form a background pattern.

6. On the **Page Layout** tab, in the **Page Setup** group, click **Delete Background**.

Excel 2007 removes the background image.

CLOSE the *CallCenter* workbook. If you are not continuing directly to the next chapter, exit Excel.

Key Points

- If you don't like the default font in which Excel 2007 displays your data, you can change it.

- You can use cell formatting, including borders, alignment, and fill colors, to emphasize certain cells in your worksheets. This emphasis is particularly useful for making column and row labels stand out from the data.

- Excel 2007 comes with a number of existing styles that enable you to change the appearance of individual cells. You can also create new styles to make formatting your workbooks easier.

- If you want to apply the formatting from one cell to another cell, use the Format Painter to copy the format quickly.

- There are quite a few built-in document themes and table formats you can apply to groups of cells. If you see one you like, use it and save yourself lots of formatting time.

- Conditional formats enable you to set rules so that Excel 2007 changes the appearance of a cell's contents based on its value.

- Adding images can make your worksheets more visually appealing and make your data easier to understand.

Chapter at a Glance

Limit data that appears on your screen, **page 120**

Manipulate list data, **page 125**

Define valid sets of values for ranges of cells, **page 130**

6 Focusing on Specific Data by Using Filters

In this chapter, you will learn to:

✔ Limit data that appears on your screen.

✔ Manipulate list data.

✔ Define valid sets of values for ranges of cells.

Microsoft Office Excel 2007 enables you to manage huge data collections, but storing more than 1,000,000 rows of data doesn't help you make business decisions unless you have the ability to zero in on the most important data in a worksheet (whether that data represents the 10 busiest days in a month or low revenue that you might need to reevaluate). Excel 2007 offers a number of powerful and flexible tools with which you can limit the data displayed in your worksheet. After your worksheet displays the subset of the data you need to make a decision, you can perform calculations on that data. You can discover what percentage of monthly sales were made up by the 10 best days in the month, find your total sales for particular days of the week, or locate the slowest business day of the month.

Just as you can limit the data displayed by your worksheets, you can limit the data entered into them as well. Setting rules for data entered into cells enables you to catch many of the most common data entry errors, such as entering values that are too small or too large, or attempting to enter a word in a cell that requires a number. If you add a validation rule to worksheet cells after data has been entered into them, you can circle any invalid data so that you know what to correct.

In this chapter, you'll learn how to limit the data that appears on your screen, manipulate list data, and create validation rules that limit data entry to appropriate values.

See Also Do you need only a quick refresher on the topics in this chapter? See the Quick Reference section at the beginning of this book.

> **Important** Before you can use the practice files in this chapter, you need to install them from the book's companion CD to their default location. See "Using the Companion CD" at the beginning of this book for more information.

Limiting Data That Appears on Your Screen

Excel 2007 spreadsheets can hold as much data as you need them to, but you might not want to work with all the data in a worksheet at the same time. For example, you might want to see the sales figures for your company during the first third, second third, and final third of a month. You can limit the data shown on a worksheet by creating a *filter*, which is a rule that selects rows to be shown in a worksheet.

To create a filter, you click the cell in the group you want to filter and then, on the Home tab, in the Editing group, click Sort & Filter and then click Filter. When you do, Excel 2007 displays a filter arrow at the right edge of the top cell in each column of the selected range. The arrow indicates that the Excel 2007 *AutoFilter* capability is active.

> **Important** When you turn on filtering, Excel 2007 treats the cells in the active cell's column as a range. To ensure that the filtering works properly, you should always add a label to the column you want to filter.

Clicking the filter arrow displays a list of filtering options (greatly expanded over Excel 2003) and a list of the unique values in the column. The first few items in the list are sorting options, followed by the Clear Filter item. The next option that appears on the list depends on the type of data in the column. For example, if the column contains a set of dates, the item will be Date Filters. Clicking the item displays a list of options specific to that data type.

> **Tip** When a column contains several types of data, the filter option becomes Number Filters.

When you click a filtering option, Excel 2007 displays a dialog box that enables you to define the filter's criteria. As an example, you could create a filter that displays only dates after 3/31/2007.

	A	B	C	D	E	F	G
1							
2		ExceptionID ▼	PackageID ▼	Date ▼	Center ▼	Route ▼	
16		EX1000014	PI34920132	4/1/2007	Midwest	RT436	
17		EX1000015	PI34920133	4/1/2007	Midwest	RT758	
18		EX1000016	PI34920134	4/1/2007	Midwest	RT529	
19		EX1000017	PI34920135	4/1/2007	Northeast	RT243	
20		EX1000018	PI34920136	4/1/2007	Northeast	RT189	
21		EX1000019	PI34920137	4/1/2007	Northwest	RT714	
22		EX1000020	PI34920138	4/2/2007	Central	RT151	
23		EX1000021	PI34920139	4/2/2007	Midwest	RT543	
24		EX1000022	PI34920140	4/2/2007	Southwest	RT208	
25		EX1000023	PI34920141	4/2/2007	South	RT145	
26		EX1000024	PI34920142	4/2/2007	Central	RT250	
27		EX1000025	PI34920143	4/2/2007	Midwest	RT852	
28							

If you want to see the highest or lowest values in a data column, you can create a Top 10 filter. Choosing the Top 10 option from the list doesn't just limit the display to the top 10 values. Instead, it opens the Top 10 AutoFilter dialog box. From within this dialog box, you can choose whether to show values from the top or bottom of the list, define the number of items you want to see, and choose whether the number in the middle box indicates the number of items or the percentage of items to be shown when the filter is applied. Using the Top 10 AutoFilter dialog box, you can find your top 10 sales-people or identify the top 5 percent of your customers.

When you choose Custom Filter from the AutoFilter list, you can define a rule that Excel 2007 uses to decide which rows to show after the filter is applied. For instance, you can create a rule that determines only days with package volumes of greater than 100,000 should be shown in your worksheet. With those results in front of you, you might be able to determine whether the weather or another factor resulted in slower business on those days.

Excel 2007 indicates that a column has a filter applied by changing the column's filter arrow to include an icon that looks like a funnel. After you finish examining your data by using a filter, you can remove the filter by clicking the column's filter arrow and then clicking Clear Filter. To turn off filtering, display the Data tab and then, in the Sort & Filter group, click Filter.

In this exercise, you will filter a data list using a series of AutoFilter items, create a filter showing the five days with the highest delivery exception counts in a month, and create a custom filter.

USE the *PackageExceptions* workbook. This practice file is located in the *Documents\ Microsoft Press\Excel2007SBS\Focusing* folder.
BE SURE TO start Excel 2007 before beginning this exercise.
OPEN the *PackageExceptions* workbook.

1. On the **ByRoute** worksheet, click any cell in the cell range B2:F27.

2. On the **Home** tab, in the **Editing** group, click **Sort & Filter**, and then click **Filter**.

   A filter arrow appears in each column's header cell.

   Sort & Filter

3. Click the **Date** column filter arrow and then, from the list of options that appears, clear the **March** check box.

4. Click **OK**.

Excel 2007 hides all rows that contain a date from the month of March.

5. Click the **Center** column filter arrow and then, from the list of options that appears, clear the **Select All** check box.

Excel 2007 clears all the check boxes in the list.

6. Select the **Midwest** check box, and then click **OK**.

Excel 2007 displays only those exceptions that occurred in the Midwest distribution center during the month of April.

7. On the **Home** tab, in the **Editing** group, click **Sort & Filter**, and then click **Clear**.

Excel 2007 clears all active filters but leaves the filter arrows in place.

8. Click the **MarchDailyCount** sheet tab.

   The MarchDailyCount worksheet appears.

9. Click any cell in the data table.

10. Click the **Exceptions** column filter arrow, point to **Number Filters**, and then click **Top 10**.

    The Top 10 AutoFilter dialog box opens.

11. In the middle field, type 5.

12. Click **OK**.

    Excel 2007 displays the table rows that contain the five highest values in the Exceptions column.

	A	B	C	D
2		Date	Exceptions	
18		3/16/2007	144	
21		3/19/2007	128	
22		3/20/2007	144	
23		3/21/2007	138	
24		3/22/2007	137	
34				

13. Click the **Exceptions** column filter arrow, and then click **Clear Filter from "Exceptions"**.

    Excel 2007 removes the filter.

14. Click the **Date** column filter arrow, point to **Date Filters**, and then click **Custom Filter**.

    The Custom AutoFilter dialog box opens.

15. In the upper-left list, click **is after or equal to**.

16. In the upper-right list, click **3/8/2007**.

17. In the lower-left list, click **is before or equal to**.

18. In the lower-right list, click **3/14/2007**.

19. Click **OK**.

    Because you left the And option selected, Excel 2007 displays all table rows that contain a date from 3/8/2007 to 3/14/2007, inclusive.

	A	B	C	D
2		Date ☑	Exceptions ▼	
10		3/8/2007	53	
11		3/9/2007	73	
12		3/10/2007	64	
13		3/11/2007	53	
14		3/12/2007	47	
15		3/13/2007	91	
16		3/14/2007	91	
34				

Undo

20. On the **Quick Access Toolbar**, click the **Undo** button to remove your filter.

Excel 2007 restores the table to its unfiltered state.

✖ **CLOSE** the *PackageExceptions* workbook.

Manipulating List Data

Related tasks you can do in Excel 2007 include choosing rows at random from a list and displaying the unique values in a column in the worksheet (not in the filter list, which you can't normally work with). Generating a list of unique values in a column can give you important information, such as from which states you have customers or which categories of products sold in an hour.

Selecting rows randomly is useful for selecting customers to receive a special offer, deciding which days of the month to audit, or picking prize winners at an employee party. To choose rows, you can use the *RAND* function, which generates a random value between 0 and 1 and compares it with a test value included in the statement. A statement that returns a *TRUE* value 30 percent of the time would be *RAND()<=30%*; that is, whenever the random value was between 0 and .3, the result would be *TRUE*. You could use this statement to select each row in a list with a probability of 30 percent. A formula that displayed *True* when the value was equal to or less than 30 percent, and *False* otherwise, would be *=IF(RAND()<=0.3,"True","False")*.

> **Tip** Because the *RAND* function is a volatile function (it recalculates its results every time you update the worksheet), you should copy the cells that contain the *RAND* function in a formula. Then, on the Home tab, in the Clipboard group, in the Paste list, click Paste Values to replace the formula with its current result.

Excel 2007 has a new function, *RANDBETWEEN*, which enables you to generate a random value within a defined range. For example, the formula *=RANDBETWEEN(1,100)* would generate a random value from 1 to 100, inclusive.

The ability to focus on the data that's most vital to your current needs is important, but there are a few limitations. One limitation is that any formulas you create using the *SUM* and *AVERAGE* functions don't change their calculations if some of the rows used in the formula are hidden by the filter.

Excel 2007 provides two ways to find the total of a group of filtered cells. The first method is to use AutoCalculate. To use AutoCalculate, you select the cells you want to find the total for. When you do, Excel 2007 displays the average of values in the cells, the sum of the values in the cells, and the number of visible cells (count) in the selection. You'll find the display on the status bar at the lower edge of the Excel 2007 window.

When you use AutoCalculate, you aren't limited to finding the sum of the selected cells. To display the other functions you can use, right-click the AutoCalculate pane and select the function you want from the shortcut menu that appears.

AutoCalculate is great for finding a quick total or average for filtered cells, but it doesn't make the result available in the worksheet. Formulas such as *=SUM(C3:C26)* always consider every cell in the range, regardless of whether a cell's row is hidden by a filter, so you need to create a formula using the *SUBTOTAL* function. The *SUBTOTAL* function, which enables you to summarize only the visible cells in a range, has this syntax: *SUBTOTAL(function_num, ref1, ref2, ...)*. The *function_num* argument holds the number of the operation you want to use to summarize your data. The *ref1*, *ref2*, and further arguments represent up to 29 ranges to include in the calculation. For example, the formula *=SUBTOTAL(9, C3:C26, E3:E26, G3:G26)* would find the sum of all values in the ranges C3:C26, E3:E26, and G3:G26.

> **Important** Be sure to place your *SUBTOTAL* formula on a row that is even with or above the headers in the range you're filtering. If you don't, your filter might hide the formula's result!

The following table lists the summary operations available to you in a *SUBTOTAL* formula. The function numbers in the first column include all values in the summary; the function numbers in the second column summarize only those values that are visible within the worksheet.

Number (includes hidden values)	Number (ignores hidden values)	Function	Description
1	101	*AVERAGE*	Returns the average of the values in the range
2	102	*COUNT*	Counts the cells in the selected range that contain a number
3	103	*COUNTA*	Counts the nonblank cells in the selected range
4	104	*MAX*	Returns the largest (maximum) value in the selected range
5	105	*MIN*	Returns the smallest (minimum) value in the selected range
6	106	*PRODUCT*	Returns the result of multiplying all numbers in the selected range
7	107	*STDEV*	Calculates the standard deviation of values in the selected range by examining a sample of the values
8	108	*STDEVP*	Calculates the standard deviation of the values in the range by using all the values
9	109	*SUM*	Returns the result of adding all numbers in the range together
10	110	*VAR*	Calculates the variance of values in the selected range by examining a sample of the values
11	111	*VARP*	Calculates the variance of the values in the range by using all of the values

Tip Excel 2007 displays the available summary operations as part of the Formula AutoComplete functionality, so you don't need to remember the operation codes or look them up in the Help system.

If you want to find a list of the unique values in a data list row, click any cell in the data list, display the Data tab and then, in the Sort & Filter group, click Advanced to display the Advanced Filter dialog box.

In the List Range field, type the reference of the cell range you want to examine for unique values, select the Unique Records Only check box, and then click OK to have Excel 2007 display the first occurrence of each value in the column.

> **Important** Excel 2007 treats the first cell in the data range as a header cell, so it doesn't consider the cell as it builds the list of unique values. Be sure to include the header cell in your data range!

In this exercise, you will select random rows from a list of exceptions to identify package delivery misadventures to investigate, create a *SUBTOTAL* formula to summarize the visible cells in a filtered data list, and find the unique values in one column of a data list.

> **USE** the *ForFollowUp* workbook. This practice file is located in the *Documents\Microsoft Press\Excel2007SBS\Focusing* folder.
>
> **OPEN** the *ForFollowUp* workbook.

1. Select cells G3:G27.

   The average of the values in the selected cells, the number of cells selected, and the total of the values in the selected cells appear in the AutoCalculate section of the status bar.

2. In cell K2, enter the formula =SUBTOTAL(101,G3:G27).

The value *$15.76* appears in cell K2.

Advanced

3. On the **Data** tab, in the **Sort & Filter** group, click **Advanced**.

The Advanced AutoFilter dialog box opens.

4. In the **List range** field, type E2:E27.

5. Select the **Unique records only** check box, and then click **OK**.

Excel 2007 displays the rows that contain the first occurrence of each different value in the selected range.

> **Tip** Remember that you must include cell E2, the header cell, in the List Range field so that the filter doesn't display two occurrences of Northeast in the unique values list. To see what happens when you don't include the header cell, try changing the range in the List Range field to E3:E27, selecting the Unique Records Only check box, and clicking OK.

	A	B	C	D	E	F	G	H	I	J	K
2		ExceptionID	PackageID	Date	Center	Route	Cost	Investigate		Subtotal	$ 15.76
3		EX1000001	PI34920119	3/30/2007	Northeast	RT310	$ 12.08				
4		EX1000002	PI34920120	3/30/2007	Midwest	RT892	$ 14.88				
5		EX1000003	PI34920121	3/30/2007	Northwest	RT424	$ 13.61				
8		EX1000006	PI34920124	3/30/2007	Central	RT341	$ 18.86				
11		EX1000009	PI34920127	3/31/2007	South	RT983	$ 19.87				
12		EX1000010	PI34920128	3/31/2007	Southwest	RT827	$ 18.01				
28											

Clear

6. On the **Data** tab, in the **Sort & Filter** group, click **Clear**.

Excel 2007 removes the filter.

7. In cell H3, type the formula =IF(RAND()<0.15,"Yes","No"), and press [Enter].

A value of *Yes* or *No* appears in cell H3, depending on the *RAND* function result.

8. Select cell H3, and then drag the fill handle down until it covers cell H27.

Excel 2007 copies the formula into every cell in the range H3:H27.

Copy

9. With the range H3:H27 still selected, on the **Home** tab, in the **Clipboard** group, click the **Copy** button.

Excel 2007 copies the cell range's contents to the Clipboard.

10. Click the **Paste** arrow, and then in the list that appears, click **Paste Values**.

Excel 2007 replaces the cells' formulas with the formulas' current results.

CLOSE the *ForFollowUp* workbook.

Defining Valid Sets of Values for Ranges of Cells

Part of creating efficient and easy-to-use worksheets is to do what you can to ensure that the data entered into your worksheets is as accurate as possible. Although it isn't possible to catch every typographical or transcription error, you can set up a *validation rule* to make sure that the data entered into a cell meets certain standards.

To create a validation rule, open the Data Validation dialog box. You can use the Data Validation dialog box to define the type of data that Excel 2007 should allow in the cell and then, depending on the data type you choose, to set the conditions data must meet to be accepted in the cell. In the following graphic, Excel 2007 knows to look for a whole number value between 1000 and 2000.

Setting accurate validation rules can help you and your colleagues avoid entering a customer's name in the cell designated to hold their phone number or setting a credit limit above a certain level. To require a user to enter a numeric value in a cell, display the Settings page of the Data Validation dialog box, and, depending on your needs, choose either Whole Number or Decimal from the Allow list.

If you want to set the same validation rule for a group of cells, you can do so by selecting the cells to which you want to apply the rule (such as a column in which you enter the credit limit of customers of Consolidated Messenger) and setting the rule using the Data Validation dialog box. One important fact you should keep in mind is that Excel 2007 enables you to create validation rules for cells in which you have already entered data. Excel 2007 doesn't tell you whether any cells have data that violate your rule, but you can find out by having Excel 2007 circle any worksheet cells containing data that violates the cell's validation rule. To do so, display the Data tab and then, in the Data Tools group, click the Data Validation arrow. On the menu that appears, click the Circle Invalid Data button to circle cells with invalid data.

When you're ready to hide the circles, in the Data Validation list, click Clear Validation Circles.

Of course, it's frustrating if you want to enter data into a cell and, when a message box appears that tells you the data you tried to enter isn't acceptable, you aren't given the rules you need to follow. Excel 2007 enables you to create messages that tell the user which values are expected before the data is entered and then, if the conditions aren't met, reiterate the conditions in a custom error message.

You can turn off data validation in a cell by displaying the Settings page of the Data Validation dialog box and clicking the Clear All button in the lower-left corner of the dialog box.

In this exercise, you will create a data validation rule limiting the credit line of Consolidated Messenger customers to $25,000, add an input message mentioning the limitation, and then create an error message if someone enters a value greater than $25,000. After you create your rule and messages, you will test them.

USE the *Credit* workbook. This practice file is located in the *Documents\Microsoft Press\ Excel2007SBS\Focusing* folder.
OPEN the *Credit* workbook.

1. Select the cell range J4:J7.

2. On the **Data** tab, in the **Data Tools** group, click **Data Validation**.

Data Validation

The Data Validation dialog box opens and displays the Settings tab.

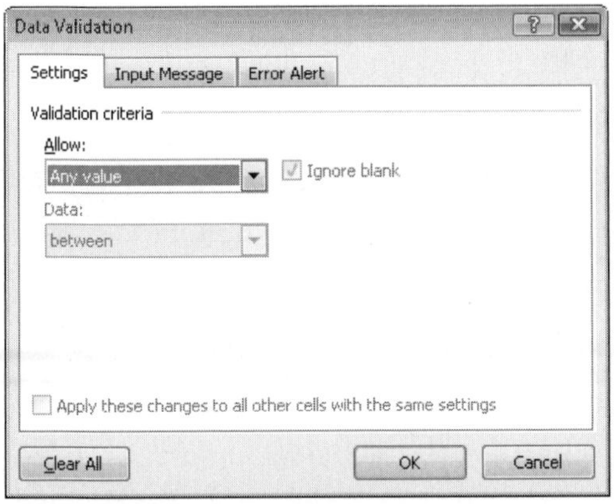

3. In the **Allow** list, click **Whole Number**.

Boxes labeled Minimum and Maximum appear below the Data box.

4. In the **Data** list, click **less than or equal to**.

The Minimum box disappears.

5. In the **Maximum** box, type 25000.

6. Clear the **Ignore blank** check box.

7. Click the **Input Message** tab.

The Input Message tab appears.

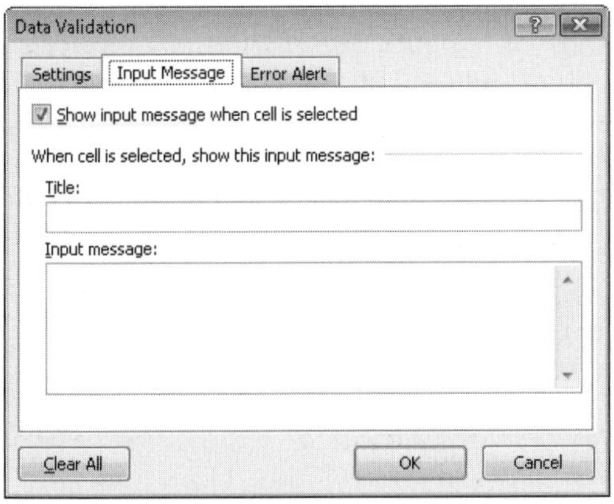

8. In the **Title** box, type Enter Limit.

9. In the **Input Message** box, type Please enter the customer's credit limit, omitting the dollar sign.

10. Click the **Error Alert** tab.

   The Error Alert tab appears.

11. In the **Style** list, click **Stop**.

   The icon that appears on your message box changes to the Stop icon.

12. In the **Title** box, type Error, and then click **OK**.

13. Click cell J7.

   A ScreenTip with the title *Enter Limit* and the text *Please enter the customer's credit limit, omitting the dollar sign* appears near cell J7.

14. Type 25001 and press [Enter].

   A stop box with the title Error appears. Leaving the Error Message box blank in step 12 causes Excel 2007 to use its default message.

15. Click **Cancel**.

   The error box disappears.

> **Important** Clicking Retry enables you to edit the bad value, whereas clicking Cancel deletes the entry.

16. Click cell J7.

Cell J7 becomes the active cell, and the ScreenTip reappears.

17. Type 25000, and press [Enter].

Excel 2007 accepts your input.

18. On the **Data** tab, in the **Data Tools** group, click the **Data Validation** arrow and then, in the list, click **Circle Invalid Data**.

A red circle appears around the value in cell J4.

19. In the **Data Validation** list, click **Clear Validation Circles**.

The red circle around the value in cell K4 disappears.

> **CLOSE** the *Credit* workbook. If you are not continuing directly to the next chapter, exit Excel.

Key Points

- A number of filters are defined in Excel 2007 (you might find the one you want already in place).

- Filtering an Excel 2007 worksheet based on values in a single column is easy to do, but you can create a custom filter to limit your data based on the values in more than one column as well.

- Don't forget that you can get a running total (or an average, or any one of several other summary operations) for the values in a group of cells. Just select the cells and look on the status bar: the result will be there.

- Use data-validation techniques to improve the accuracy of data entered into your worksheets and to identify data that doesn't meet the guidelines you set.

Chapter at a Glance

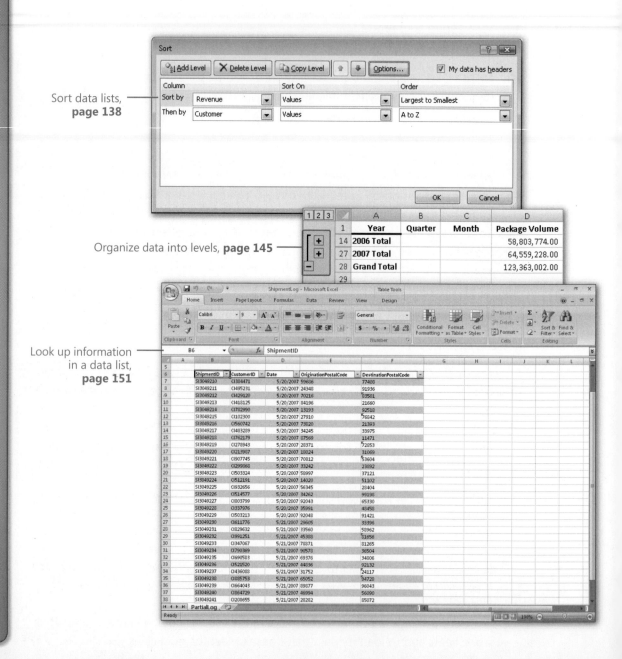

Sort data lists,
page 138

Organize data into levels, **page 145**

Look up information
in a data list,
page 151

7 Reordering and Summarizing Data

In this chapter, you will learn to:

✔ Sort data lists.

✔ Organize data into levels.

✔ Look up information in a data list.

Most of the time, when you enter data in a Microsoft Office Excel 2007 worksheet, you will enter it in chronological order. For instance, you could enter hourly shipment data in a worksheet, starting with the first hour of the day and ending with the last hour. The data would naturally be displayed in the order in which you entered it, but that might not always be the best order to answer your questions. For instance, you might want to sort your data so that the top row in your worksheet shows the day of the month with the highest package volume, with subsequent rows displaying the remaining days in decreasing order of package volumes handled. You can also sort based on the contents of more than one column. A good example is sorting package handling data by week, day, and then hour of the day.

After you have sorted your data into the desired order, Excel 2007 enables you to find partial totals, or *subtotals*, for groups of cells within a given range. Yes, you can create formulas to find the sum, average, or standard deviation of data in a cell range, but you can do the same thing much more quickly by having Excel 2007 calculate the total for cells with the same value in a column. If your worksheet holds sales data for a list of services, you can calculate subtotals for each product category.

When you calculate subtotals in a worksheet, Excel 2007 creates an outline that marks the cell ranges used in each subtotal. For example, if the first 10 rows of a worksheet have overnight shipping data, and the second 10 rows have second-day shipping data, Excel 2007 divides the rows into two units. You can use the markers on the worksheet to hide or display the rows used to calculate a subtotal; in this case, you can hide all the rows that contain overnight shipping data, hide all the rows that contain second-day shipping data, hide both, or show both.

Excel 2007 does have a capability you might expect to find only in a database program—the capability to have a user type a value in a cell and have Excel 2007 look in a named range to find a corresponding value. For instance, you can have a two-column named range with one column displaying the International Standard Book Number (ISBN) of a book and the second column displaying the title of the same book. By using a *VLOOKUP* formula that references the named range, you can let colleagues using your workbook type an ISBN in a cell and have the name of the book with that ISBN appear in the cell with the formula.

In this chapter, you'll learn how to sort your data using one or more criteria, calculate subtotals, organize your data into levels, and look up information in a data list.

See Also Do you need only a quick refresher on the topics in this chapter? See the Quick Reference section at the beginning of this book.

Important Before you can use the practice files in this chapter, you need to install them from the book's companion CD to their default location. See "Using the Companion CD" at the beginning of this book for more information.

Sorting Data Lists

Although Excel 2007 makes it easy to enter your business data and to manage it after you've saved it in a worksheet, your data will rarely answer every question you want to ask it. For example, you might want to discover which of your services generates the most profits, which service costs the most for you to provide, and so on. You can find out that information by sorting your data.

When you *sort* data in a worksheet, you rearrange the worksheet rows based on the contents of cells in a particular column. Sorting a worksheet to find your highest-revenue services might show the results displayed in the following graphic.

	A	B	C	D
1				
2		Service	Revenue	
3		Overnight	$ 1,598,643.00	
4		3Day	$ 1,000,142.00	
5		Ground	$ 994,775.00	
6		2Day	$ 745,600.00	
7		Priority Overnight	$ 502,991.00	
8				

You can sort a group of rows in a worksheet in a number of ways, but the first step is to identify the column that will provide the values by which the rows should be sorted. In the preceding graphic, you could find the highest revenue totals by selecting the cells in the Revenue column and displaying the Home tab. Then, in the Editing group, in the Sort & Filter list, click Sort Descending. Clicking Sort Descending makes Excel 2007 put the row with the highest value in the Revenue column at the top of the worksheet and continue down to the lowest value.

If you want to sort the rows in the opposite order, from the lowest revenue to the highest, select the cells in the Revenue column and then, in the Sort & Filter list, click Sort Ascending.

The Sort Ascending and Sort Descending buttons enable you to sort rows in a worksheet quickly, but you can use them only to sort the worksheet based on the contents of one column, even though you might want to sort by two columns. For example, you might want to order the worksheet rows by service category and then by total so that you can see the customers that use each service category most frequently. You can sort rows in a worksheet by the contents of more than one column through the Sort dialog box, in which you can pick any number of columns to use as sort criteria and choose whether to sort the rows in ascending or descending order.

To display the Sort dialog box, click Custom Sort in the Sort & Filter list.

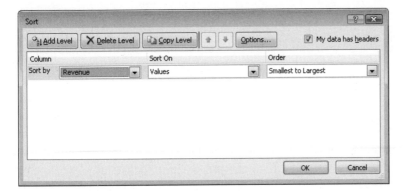

If your data list has a header row, select the My Data Has Headers check box so the column headers will appear in the Sort By list. After you set the column by which you want to sort, the Sort On list enables you to select whether you want to sort by a cell's value (the default), a cell's fill color, a cell's font color, or an icon displayed in the cell.

See Also For more information on creating conditional formats that change a cell's formatting or display icon sets to reflect the cell's value, refer to "Changing the Appearance of Data Based on Its Value" in Chapter 5, "Changing Workbook Appearance."

Finally, from the Order list, you can select how you want Excel 2007 to sort the column values. The exact list changes to reflect the data in your column. If your column contains numerical values, you'll see the options Largest To Smallest, Smallest To Largest, and Custom List. If your column contains text values, the options will be A To Z (ascending order), Z To A (descending order), and Custom List. And if your column contains dates, you'll see Newest To Oldest, Oldest To Newest, and Custom List.

Adding, moving, copying, and deleting sorting levels are a matter of clicking the appropriate button in the Sort dialog box. To manage a data range's sorting levels, click the Add Level button.

> **Tip** In previous versions of Excel, you could create a maximum of three sorting levels. You may create up to 64 sorting levels in Excel 2007.

The Sort dialog box opens, displaying fields to create one sorting level. To create a new level, click Add Level. To delete a level, click the level in the list, and then click Delete Level. Clicking Copy Level enables you to put all the settings from one rule into another, saving you some work if you need to change only one item. The Move Up and Move Down buttons, which display an upward-pointing arrow and a downward-pointing arrow, respectively, enable you to change a sorting level's position in the order. Finally, clicking the Options button displays the Sort Options dialog box, which you can use to make a sorting level case sensitive.

The default setting for Excel 2007 is to sort numbers according to their values and to sort words in alphabetical order, but that pattern doesn't work for some sets of values. One example in which sorting a list of values in alphabetical order would yield incorrect results is with the months of the year. In an "alphabetical" calendar, April is the first month, and September is the last! Fortunately, Excel 2007 recognizes a number of special lists, such as days of the week and months of the year. You can have Excel 2007 sort the contents of a worksheet based on values in a known list; if needed, you can create your own list of values. For example, the default lists of weekdays in Excel 2007 start with Sunday. If you keep your business records based on a Monday–Sunday week, you can create a new list with Monday as the first day and Sunday as the last.

To create a new list, type the list of values you want to use as your list into a contiguous cell range, select the cells, click the Microsoft Office Button, and then click Excel Options. On the Popular page of the dialog box, click the Edit Custom Lists button to display the Custom Lists dialog box.

The following is a screenshot of the Custom Lists dialog box:

Custom Lists

Custom Lists tab

Custom lists:
- NEW LIST
- Sun, Mon, Tue, Wed, Thu, Fri, S
- Sunday, Monday, Tuesday, Wed
- Jan, Feb, Mar, Apr, May, Jun, J
- January, February, March, April

List entries:

Add
Delete

Press Enter to separate list entries.
Import list from cells:
Import

OK   Cancel

The selected cell range's reference appears in the Import list from cells field. To record your list, click the Import button.

To use a custom list as a sorting criterion, display the Sort dialog box, click the rule's Order arrow, click Custom List, and select your list from the dialog box that appears.

> **Important** In previous versions of Excel, your custom list had to be the primary sorting criterion. In Excel 2007, you can use your custom list as any criterion.

In this exercise, you will sort a data list, sort a list by multiple criteria, change the order in which sorting criteria are applied, sort data by using a custom list, and sort data by color.

> **USE** the *ShippingSummary* workbook. This practice file is located in the *Documents\
> Microsoft Press\Excel2007SBS\Sorting* folder.
> **BE SURE TO** start Excel 2007 before beginning this exercise.
> **OPEN** the *ShippingSummary* workbook.

1. Click cell C3.

Sort & Filter

2. On the **Home** tab, in the **Editing** group, click the **Sort & Filter** button and then, in the list, click **Sort A to Z.**

   Excel 2007 sorts the data by season.

3. In the **Sort & Filter** list, click **Custom Sort**.

   The Sort dialog box opens.

4. Select the **My data has headers** check box.

5. In the **Column** list, click **Customer**. If necessary, in the **Sort On** list, click **Values**; then in the **Order** list, click **A to Z**.

6. Click **Add Level**.

   A new Then By sorting level appears.

Sort						? ✕
📋 Add Level	✕ Delete Level	📋 Copy Level	⬆ ⬇	Options...		☑ My data has headers
Column			**Sort On**		**Order**	
Sort by	Customer	▼	Values	▼	A to Z	▼
Then by		▼	Values	▼	A to Z	▼
					OK	Cancel

7. In the new **Column** list, click **Revenue**.

8. In the new **Order** list, click **Largest to Smallest**.

9. Click **OK**.

   Excel 2007 closes the Sort dialog box and sorts the data list.

	A	B	C	D	E
1					
2		Customer	Season	Revenue	
3		Contoso	Spring	$ 201,438.00	
4		Contoso	Winter	$ 183,651.00	
5		Contoso	Fall	$ 118,299.00	
6		Contoso	Summer	$ 114,452.00	
7		Fabrikam	Fall	$ 255,599.00	
8		Fabrikam	Summer	$ 183,632.00	
9		Fabrikam	Spring	$ 139,170.00	
10		Fabrikam	Winter	$ 100,508.00	
11		Northwind Traders	Fall	$ 188,851.00	
12		Northwind Traders	Winter	$ 174,336.00	
13		Northwind Traders	Summer	$ 129,732.00	
14		Northwind Traders	Spring	$ 120,666.00	
15					

10. In the **Sort & Filter** list, click **Custom Sort**.

    The Sort dialog box opens.

11. Click **Then by**.

Excel 2007 highlights the Revenue sorting rule.

12. Click the **Move Up** button.

Excel 2007 moves the Revenue sorting rule above the Customer sorting rule.

13. Click **OK**.

Excel 2007 closes the Sort dialog box and sorts the data list.

14. Select cells G4:G7, click the **Microsoft Office Button**, and then click **Excel Options**.

The Excel Options dialog box opens.

15. On the **Popular** page, click **Edit Custom Lists**.

The Custom Lists dialog box opens.

16. Verify that the cell range $G$4:$G$7 appears in the **Import list from cells** field, and then click **Import**.

The new list appears in the Custom Lists pane.

17. Click **OK** twice to close the **Custom Lists** dialog box and the **Excel Options** dialog box.

18. Click cell C3.

19. On the **Home** tab, in the **Editing** group, click **Sort & Filter**, and then click **Custom Sort**.

The Sort dialog box opens.

20. Click the rule in the **Sort by** row, and then click **Delete Level**.

The sorting rule disappears.

21. In the **Sort by** row, in the **Column** list, click **Season**.

22. In the same row, in the **Order** list, click **Custom List**.

The Custom Lists dialog box opens.

23. In the **Custom lists** pane, click the sequence *Spring, Summer, Fall, Winter.*

24. Click **OK** twice to close the **Custom Lists** dialog box and the **Sort** dialog box.

Excel 2007 sorts the data list.

	A	B	C	D	E
1					
2		Customer	Season	Revenue	
3		Contoso	Spring	$201,438.00	
4		Fabrikam	Spring	$139,170.00	
5		Northwind Traders	Spring	$120,666.00	
6		Fabrikam	Summer	$183,632.00	
7		Northwind Traders	Summer	$129,732.00	
8		Contoso	Summer	$114,452.00	
9		Fabrikam	Fall	$255,599.00	
10		Northwind Traders	Fall	$188,851.00	
11		Contoso	Fall	$118,299.00	
12		Contoso	Winter	$183,651.00	
13		Northwind Traders	Winter	$174,336.00	
14		Fabrikam	Winter	$100,508.00	

25. Click cell C3. Then on the **Home** tab, in the **Editing** group, click **Sort & Filter**, and click **Custom Sort**.

The Sort dialog box opens.

26. In the **Sort by** row, in the **Sort by** list, click **Revenue**.

27. In the **Sort on** ist, click **Cell Color**.

> **Tip** Another benefit of creating a custom list is that dragging the fill handle of a list cell that contains a value causes Excel 2007 to extend the series for you. For example, if you create the list *Spring, Summer, Fall, Winter*, type Summer in a cell, and then drag the cell's fill handle; Excel 2007 extends the series as *Fall, Winter, Spring, Summer, Fall*, and so on.

28. In the final list in the **Sort by** row, click **On Bottom** to have Excel 2007 put the Revenue cells that have no cell color on the bottom.

29. Click **OK**.

Excel 2007 sorts the data list.

> **CLOSE** the *ShippingSummary* workbook.

Organizing Data into Levels

After you have sorted the rows in an Excel 2007 worksheet or entered the data so that it doesn't need to be sorted, you can have Excel 2007 calculate subtotals or totals for a portion of the data. In a worksheet with sales data for three different product categories, for example, you can sort the products by category, select all the cells that contain data, and then open the Subtotal dialog box. To open the Subtotal dialog box, display the Data tab and then, in the Outline group, click Subtotal.

In the Subtotal dialog box, you can choose the column on which to base your subtotals (such as every change of value in the Week column), the summary calculation you want to perform, and the column or columns with values to be summarized. In the worksheet in the preceding graphic, for example, you could also calculate subtotals for the number of units sold in each category. After you define your subtotals, they appear in your worksheet.

As the graphic shows, when you add subtotals to a worksheet, Excel 2007 also defines groups based on the rows used to calculate a subtotal. The groupings form an outline of your worksheet based on the criteria you used to create the subtotals. In the preceding example, all the rows representing months in the year 2006 are in one group, rows representing months in 2007 are in another, and so on. The outline section at the left of your worksheet holds controls you can use to hide or display groups of rows in your worksheet.

There are three types of controls in the outline section: Hide Detail buttons, Show Detail buttons, and level buttons.

The Hide Detail button beside a group can be clicked to hide the rows in that group. In the previous graphic, clicking the Hide Detail button next to row 27 would hide rows 15 through 26 but leave the row holding the subtotal for that group, row 27, visible.

When you hide a group of rows, the button next to the group changes to a Show Detail button. Clicking a group's Show Detail button restores the rows in the group to the worksheet.

The level buttons comprise the other set of buttons in the outline section of a worksheet with subtotals. Each button represents a level of organization in a worksheet; clicking a level button hides all levels of detail below that of the button you clicked. The following table identifies the three levels of organization shown in the preceding graphic.

Level	Description
1	Grand total
2	Subtotals for each group
3	Individual rows in the worksheet

Clicking the Level 2 button in the worksheet shown in the preceding illustration would hide the rows with data on each month's revenue but would leave the row that contains the grand total (Level 1) and all rows that contain the subtotal for each year (Level 2) visible in the worksheet.

	A	B	C	D
1	Year	Quarter	Month	Package Volume
14	2006 Total			58,803,774.00
27	2007 Total			64,559,228.00
28	Grand Total			123,363,002.00
29				

If you like, you can add levels of detail to the outline that Excel 2007 creates. For instance, you might want to be able to hide revenues from January and February, which you know are traditionally strong months. To create a new outline group within an existing group, select the rows you want to group; on the Data tab, in the Outline group, point to Group And Outline, and then click Group.

You can remove a group by selecting the rows in the group and then, in the Outline group, clicking Ungroup.

> **Tip** If you want to remove all subtotals from a worksheet, open the Subtotal dialog box, and click the Remove All button.

In this exercise, you will add subtotals to a worksheet and then use the outline that appears to show and hide different groups of data in your worksheet.

> **USE** the *GroupByQuarter* workbook. This practice file is located in the *Documents\ Microsoft Press\Excel2007SBS\Sorting* folder.
>
> **OPEN** the *GroupByQuarter* workbook.

1. Click any cell in the data list.

2. On the **Data** tab, in the **Outline** group, click **Subtotal**.

   The Subtotal dialog box opens with the default options to add a subtotal at every change in the Year column, to return the sum of the values in the subtotaled rows, and to add a row with the subtotal of values in the Package Volume column below the final selected row.

3. Click **OK**.

The Subtotal dialog box closes. New rows appear with subtotals for package volume during each year represented in the worksheet. The new rows are numbered 14 and 27. A row with the grand total of all rows also appears; that row is row 28. A new section with outline bars and group-level indicators appears to the left of column A.

Row	A Year	B Quarter	C Month	D Package Volume
1	Year	Quarter	Month	Package Volume
2	2006	1	January	5,213,292.00
3	2006	1	February	2,038,516.00
4	2006	1	March	2,489,601.00
5	2006	2	April	9,051,231.00
6	2006	2	May	5,225,156.00
7	2006	2	June	3,266,644.00
8	2006	3	July	2,078,794.00
9	2006	3	August	1,591,434.00
10	2006	3	September	8,518,985.00
11	2006	4	October	1,973,050.00
12	2006	4	November	7,599,195.00
13	2006	4	December	9,757,876.00
14	2006 Total			58,803,774.00
15	2007	1	January	5,304,039.00
16	2007	1	February	5,465,096.00
17	2007	1	March	1,007,799.00
18	2007	2	April	4,010,287.00
19	2007	2	May	4,817,070.00
20	2007	2	June	8,155,717.00
21	2007	3	July	6,552,370.00
22	2007	3	August	2,295,635.00
23	2007	3	September	7,115,883.00
24	2007	4	October	1,362,767.00
25	2007	4	November	8,935,488.00
26	2007	4	December	9,537,077.00
27	2007 Total			64,559,228.00

4. Click the row heading of row 5, and drag to the row heading of row 7.

Rows 5 through 7 are selected.

5. On the **Data** tab, in the **Outline** group, click **Group**.

Rows 5 through 7 are made into a new group. An outline bar appears on a new level in the outline section, and a corresponding Level 4 button appears at the top of the outline section.

Group

6. In the outline section, click the **Hide Detail** button next to row 8.

Rows 5 through 7 are hidden, and the Hide Detail button you clicked changes to a Show Detail button.

Hide Detail

The following table shows the spreadsheet data:

	A	B	C	D
1	Year	Quarter	Month	Package Volume
2	2006	1	January	5,213,292.00
3	2006	1	February	2,038,516.00
4	2006	1	March	2,489,601.00
8	2006	3	July	2,078,794.00
9	2006	3	August	1,591,434.00
10	2006	3	September	8,518,985.00
11	2006	4	October	1,973,050.00
12	2006	4	November	7,599,195.00
13	2006	4	December	9,757,876.00
14	2006 Total			58,803,774.00
15	2007	1	January	5,304,039.00
16	2007	1	February	5,465,096.00
17	2007	1	March	1,007,799.00
18	2007	2	April	4,010,287.00
19	2007	2	May	4,817,070.00
20	2007	2	June	8,155,717.00
21	2007	3	July	6,552,370.00
22	2007	3	August	2,295,635.00
23	2007	3	September	7,115,883.00
24	2007	4	October	1,362,767.00
25	2007	4	November	8,935,488.00
26	2007	4	December	9,537,077.00
27	2007 Total			64,559,228.00
28	Grand Total			123,363,002.00

7. In the outline section, click the **Show Detail** button next to row 8.

   Rows 5 through 7 reappear.

8. In the outline section, click the **Level 1** button.

   All rows except row 1 with the column headings and row 28 with the grand total are hidden.

9. In the outline section, click the **Level 2** button.

   The rows with the subtotal for each week appear.

10. In the outline section, click the **Level 3** button.

    All rows except rows 5 through 7 appear.

11. In the outline section, click the **Level 4** button.

    Rows 5 through 7 reappear.

CLOSE the *GroupByQuarter* workbook.

Looking Up Information in a Data List

Whenever you create a worksheet that holds information about a list of distinct items, such as products offered for sale by a company, you should ensure that at least one column in the list contains a unique value that distinguishes that row (and the item the row represents) from every other row in the list. Assigning each row a column with a unique value means that you can associate data in one worksheet with data in another worksheet. For example, if every customer is assigned a unique identification number, you can store a customer's contact information in one worksheet and all orders for that customer in another worksheet. You can then associate the customer's orders and contact information without writing the contact information in a worksheet every time the customer places an order.

In the case of shipments handled by Consolidated Messenger, the column that contains those unique values, or the *primary key* column, is the ShipmentID column.

If you know a shipment's ShipmentID, it's no trouble to look through a list of 20 or 30 items to find a particular shipment. If, however, you have a list of many thousands of shipments, looking through the list to find one would take quite a bit of time. Instead, you can use the *VLOOKUP* function to let your colleagues type a ShipmentID in a cell and have the corresponding details appear in another cell.

The *VLOOKUP* function finds a value in the leftmost column of a named range, such as a table, and then returns the value from the specified cell to the right of the cell with the found value. A properly formed *VLOOKUP* function has four arguments (data that is passed to the function), as shown in the following definition: *=VLOOKUP(lookup_value, table_array, col_index_num, range_lookup)*.

The following table summarizes the values Excel 2007 expects for each of these arguments.

Argument	Expected value
lookup_value	The value to be found in the first column of the named range specified by the *table_array* argument. The *lookup_value* argument can be a value, a cell reference, or a text string.
table_array	The multicolumn range or name of the range or data table to be searched.
col_index_num	The number of the column in the named range with the value to be returned.
range_lookup	A *TRUE* or *FALSE* value, indicating whether the function should find an approximate match (*TRUE*) or an exact match (*FALSE*) for the *lookup_value*. If left blank, the default value for this argument is *TRUE*.

> **Important** When *range_lookup* is left blank or set to *TRUE*, for *VLOOKUP* to work properly the rows in the named range specified in the *table_array* argument must be sorted in ascending order based on the values in the leftmost column of the named range.

The *VLOOKUP* function works a bit differently depending on whether the *range_lookup* argument is set to *TRUE* or *FALSE*. The following list summarizes how the function works based on the value of *range_lookup*:

- If the *range_lookup* argument is left blank or set to *TRUE*, and *VLOOKUP* doesn't find an exact match for *lookup_value*, the function returns the largest value that is less than *lookup_value*.

- If the *range_lookup* argument is left blank or set to *TRUE*, and *lookup_value* is smaller than the smallest value in the named range, an *#N/A* error is returned.

- If the *range_lookup* argument is left blank or set to *TRUE*, and *lookup_value* is larger than all values in the named range, the largest value in the named range is returned.

- If the *range_lookup* argument is set to *FALSE*, and *VLOOKUP* doesn't find an exact match for *lookup_value*, the function returns an *#N/A* error.

As an example of a *VLOOKUP* function, consider the following worksheet and the accompanying *VLOOKUP* formula.

> **Tip** The related *HLOOKUP* function matches a value in a column of the first row of a table and returns the value in the specified row number of the same column. For more information on using the *HLOOKUP* function, click the Excel Help button, type *HLOOKUP* in the search terms box, and then click Search.

When you type *CI02* in cell E3 and press Enter, the *VLOOKUP* function searches the first column of the table, finds an exact match, and returns the value *Northwind Traders* to cell C3.

> **Important** Be sure to give the cell in which you type the *VLOOKUP* formula the same format as the data you want the formula to display. For example, if you create a *VLOOKUP* formula in cell G14 that finds a date, you must apply a date cell format to cell G14 for the result of the formula to display properly.

In this exercise, you will create a *VLOOKUP* function to return the destination postal code of deliveries with ShipmentIDs typed in a specific cell.

> **USE** the *ShipmentLog* workbook. This practice file is located in the *Documents\ Microsoft Press\Excel2007SBS\Sorting* folder.
>
> **OPEN** the *ShipmentLog* workbook.

1. In cell C3, type the formula =VLOOKUP(B3,Shipments,5,FALSE).

   Cell B3, which the formula uses to look up values in the Shipments table, is blank, so the #*N/A* error code appears in cell C3.

2. In cell B3, type SI3049224, and press Enter.

   The value *51102* appears in cell C3.

3. In cell C3, edit the formula so that it reads =VLOOKUP(B3,Shipments,2,FALSE).

   The formula now finds its target value in table column 2 (the CustomerID column), so the value *CI512191* appears in cell C3.

4. In cell C3, edit the formula so that it reads =VLOOKUP(B3,Shipments,4,TRUE).

   Changing the last argument to *TRUE* enables the *VLOOKUP* formula to find an approximate match for the ShipmentID in cell B3, whereas changing the column to *4* means the formula gets its result from the OriginationPostalCode column. The value *14020* appears in cell C3.

5. In cell B3, type SI3049209.

   The value in cell B3 is smaller than the smallest value in the Shipments table's first column, so the *VLOOKUP* formula displays the *#N/A* error code in cell C3.

6. In cell B3, type SI3049245.

   The ShipmentID typed into cell B3 is greater than the last value in the table's first column, so the *VLOOKUP* formula displays the last value in the target column (in this case, the fourth column). Therefore, the value *44493* appears in cell C3.

> **CLOSE** the *ShipmentLog* workbook. If you are not continuing directly to the next chapter, exit Excel.

Key Points

- You can rearrange the data in a worksheet quickly by clicking either the Sort Ascending or Sort Descending button in the Sort & Filter group on the Data tab.

- Don't forget that you can sort the rows in a worksheet by using orders other than alphabetical or numerical. For example, you can sort a series of days based on their order in the week or by cell color.

- If none of the existing sort orders (days, weekdays, and so on) meets your needs, you can create your own custom sort order.

- You can divide the data in your worksheet into levels and find a subtotal for each level.

- Creating subtotals enables you to show or hide groups of data in your worksheets.

- Use the *VLOOKUP* function to look up a value in one column of a data list and return a value from another column in the same row.

Chapter at a Glance

Use data lists as templates for other lists, **page 158**

Link to data in other worksheets and workbooks, **page 164**

Consolidate multiple sets of data into a single workbook, **page 170**

Group multiple sets of data, **page 173**

8 Combining Data from Multiple Sources

In this chapter, you will learn to:

✔ Use data lists as templates for other lists.

✔ Link to data in other worksheets and workbooks.

✔ Consolidate multiple sets of data into a single workbook.

✔ Group multiple sets of data.

Microsoft Office Excel 2007 gives you a wide range of tools with which to format, summarize, and present your data. After you have created a workbook to hold data about a particular subject, you can create as many worksheets as you need to make that data easier to find within the workbook. For instance, you can create a workbook to store sales data for a year, with each worksheet representing a month in that year. To ensure that the workbook for every year has a similar appearance, you can create a workbook with the desired characteristics (such as more than the standard number of worksheets, custom worksheet formatting, or a particular color for the workbook's sheet tabs) and save it as a pattern for similar workbooks you create in the future. The benefit of ensuring that all your sales data worksheets have the same layout is that you and your colleagues immediately know where to look for specific totals. Also, when you create a summary worksheet, you know in advance which cells to include in your calculations.

If you work with the same workbooks repeatedly, you can group those workbooks in a special file, called a *workspace*. When you open the workspace, Excel 2007 knows to open the files you included in that workspace.

A consequence of organizing your data into different workbooks and worksheets is that you need ways to manage, combine, and summarize data from more than one Excel 2007 document. You can always copy data from one worksheet to another, but if the original value were to change, that change would not be reflected in the cell range to which you copied the data. Rather than remember which cells you need to update when a value changes, you can create a link to the original cell. That way, Excel 2007 will update the value for you whenever you open the workbook. If multiple worksheets hold related values, you can use links to summarize those values in a single worksheet.

In this chapter, you'll learn how to use a data list as a template for other lists, work with more than one set of data, link to data in other workbooks, summarize multiple sets of data, and group multiple data lists.

See Also   Do you need only a quick refresher on the topics in this chapter? See the Quick Reference section at the beginning of this book.

> **Important**   Before you can use the practice files in this chapter, you need to install them from the book's companion CD to their default location. See "Using the Companion CD" at the beginning of this book for more information.

Using Data Lists as Templates for Other Lists

After you decide on the type of data you want to store in a workbook and what that workbook should look like, you probably want to be able to create similar workbooks without adding all the formatting and formulas again. For example, you might have settled on a design for your monthly sales tracking workbook.

When you have settled on a design for your workbooks, you can save one of the workbooks as a *template*, or pattern, for similar workbooks you create in the future. You can leave any labels to aid data entry, but you should remove any existing data from a workbook that you save as a template, both to avoid data entry errors and to remove any confusion as to whether the workbook is a template. You can also remove any worksheets you and your colleagues won't need by right-clicking the tab of an unneeded worksheet and, on the shortcut menu that appears, clicking Delete.

If you want your template workbook to have more than the standard number of worksheets (such as 12 worksheets to track shipments for a year, by month), you can add worksheets by clicking the Insert Worksheet button that appears to the right of the existing worksheet tabs.

To create a template from an existing workbook, save the model workbook as an Excel Template file (a file with an .xltx extension), which you can choose from the Save As Type drop-down list in the Save As dialog box. If you ever want to change the template, you can open it like a standard workbook (that is, an Excel 2007 file with the .xlsx extension) and make your changes. When you have completed your work, resave the file normally—it will still be a template.

See Also You can also save your Excel 2007 workbook either as an Excel 97–2003 template (.xlt) or as a macro-enabled Excel 2007 workbook template (.xltm). For more information on using macros in Excel 2007 workbooks, see "Introducing Macros" in Chapter 13, "Automating Repetitive Tasks by Using Macros."

After you save a workbook as a template, you can use it as a model for new workbooks. To create a workbook from a template in Excel 2007, click the Microsoft Office Button, and then click New to display the New Workbook dialog box.

The leftmost pane of the New Workbook dialog box displays featured templates, which appear by default when you open the New Workbook dialog box, templates that are installed on your computer, and a list of template categories available through the Microsoft Office Online Web site. The middle pane of the dialog box displays the Recently Used Templates section, which contains a list of any previously used templates.

> **Tip** You can also find templates and other tools related to your job functions at the Microsoft Work Essentials Web site, which you can find online by visiting *office.microsoft.com* and clicking Work Essentials in the left pane.

In the Templates dialog box, you can double-click the template you want to use as the model for your workbook. Excel 2007 creates a new workbook (a .xlsx file) with the template's formatting and contents in place.

In addition to creating a workbook template, it's possible to create a template you can add as a worksheet within an existing workbook. To create a worksheet template, design the worksheet you want to use as a template, delete all the other worksheets in that workbook, and save the single-sheet workbook as a template. You can then add a worksheet based on that template to your workbook by right-clicking a sheet tab and then clicking Insert to display the Insert dialog box.

The Insert dialog box splits its contents into two tabs. The General tab contains buttons you can click to insert a blank worksheet, a chart sheet, and any worksheet templates you created. The Spreadsheet Solutions tab contains a set of useful templates for a variety of financial and personal tasks.

To add a spreadsheet from the Insert dialog box to your workbook, click the desired template, and then click OK.

> **Tip** The other two options on the General tab, MS Excel 4.0 Macro and MS Excel 5.0 Dialog, are there to help users integrate older Excel spreadsheet solutions into Excel 2007.

In this exercise, you will create a workbook from an existing template, save a template to track hourly call volumes to each regional center, save another version of the file as a worksheet template, and insert a worksheet based on that template into a new workbook.

> **USE** the *Daily Call Summary* workbook. This practice files is located in the *Documents\Microsoft Press\Excel2007SBS\MultipleFiles* folder.
> **BE SURE TO** start Excel 2007 before starting this exercise.
> **OPEN** the *Daily Call Summary* workbook.

Microsoft Office
Button

1. Click the **Microsoft Office Button**, and then click **Save As**.

   The Save As dialog box opens.

2. In the **Save as type** list, click **Excel Template**.

   Excel 2007 displays the 2007 Microsoft Office system default template folder.

Name	Date modified	Type	Size
Charts	12/10/2007 2:41 PM	File Folder	
Document Themes	11/2/2007 4:51 PM	File Folder	
SmartArt Graphics	10/20/2007 11:37 ...	File Folder	

File name: Daily Call Summary

Save as type: Excel Template

Authors: Curtis Frye   Tags: Add a tag

3. Click **Save**.

Excel 2007 saves the workbook as a template and closes the Save As dialog box.

4. Click the **Microsoft Office Button**, and then click **Close**.

Excel 2007 closes the *Daily Call Summary* workbook.

5. Click the **Microsoft Office Button**, and then click **New**.

The New Workbook dialog box opens.

6. In the **Template Categories** list, click **Installed Templates**.

The Installed Templates list appears.

7. Click **Project To Do List**, and then click **Create**.

Excel 2007 creates a workbook based on the selected template.

8. On the **Quick Access Toolbar**, click the **Save** button.

The Save As dialog box opens.

Save

9. In the **File name** box, type ToDoList. Use the dialog box controls to browse to the *Documents\Microsoft Press\Excel2007SBS\MultipleFiles* folder, and then click **Save**.

Excel 2007 saves your workbook.

10. Click the **Microsoft Office Button** and then, in the **Recent Files** list, click the *Daily Call Summary.xlsx* file.

The *Daily Call Summary* file appears.

11. Right-click the **Sheet2** sheet tab, and then click **Delete**.

    Excel 2007 deletes the worksheet, leaving one worksheet in the workbook.

12. Click the **Microsoft Office Button**, and then click **Save As**.

    The Save As dialog box opens.

13. In the **File name** box, type Daily Call Worksheet.

14. If necessary, in the **Save as type** list, click **Excel Template**.

15. Click **Save**.

    Excel 2007 saves your template.

16. Click the **Microsoft Office Button**, and then click **Close**.

    Excel 2007 closes the workbook.

17. Click the **Microsoft Office Button**, and then click **New**.

    The New Workbook dialog box opens.

18. Click **Blank Workbook**, and then click **Create**.

    A blank workbook appears.

19. Right-click any sheet tab, and then click **Insert**.

    The Insert dialog box opens.

20. On the **General** tab, click **Daily Call Worksheet**, and then click **OK**.

Excel 2007 creates a new worksheet based on the template.

21. On the **Quick Access Toolbar**, click the **Save** button.

The Save As dialog box opens.

22. In the **File name** box, type Current Call Summary. Use the dialog box controls to browse to the *Documents\Microsoft Press\Excel2007SBS\MultipleFiles* folder, and then click **Save**.

Excel 2007 saves your workbook.

CLOSE the *Current Call Summary* workbook.

Linking to Data in Other Worksheets and Workbooks

Cutting and pasting data from one workbook to another is a quick and easy way to gather related data in one place, but there is a substantial limitation: if the data from the original cell changes, the change is not reflected in the cell to which the data was copied. In other words, cutting and pasting a cell's contents doesn't create a relationship between the original cell and the target cell.

You can ensure that the data in the target cell reflects any changes in the original cell by creating a *link* between the two cells. Instead of entering a value into the target cell by typing or pasting, you create a type of formula that identifies the source from which Excel 2007 will derive the target cell's value.

To create a link between cells, open both the workbook with the cell from which you want to pull the value and the workbook with the target cell. Then click the target cell and type an equal sign, signifying that you want to create a formula. After you type the equal sign, activate the workbook with the cell from which you want to derive the value, and then click that cell.

When you switch back to the workbook with the target cell, you see that Excel 2007 has filled in the formula with a reference to the cell you clicked.

The reference from the example =*'[Fleet Operating Costs.xlsx]Truck Fuel'!$C$15* gives three pieces of information: the workbook, the worksheet, and the cell you clicked in the worksheet. The first element of the reference, the name of the workbook, is enclosed in square brackets; the end of the second element is marked with an exclamation point; and the third element, the cell reference, has a dollar sign before both the row and the column identifier. This type of reference is known as a *3-D reference*, reflecting the three dimensions (workbook, worksheet, and cell) that you need to point to a cell in another workbook.

Tip For references to cells in the same workbook, the workbook information is omitted. Likewise, references to cells in the same worksheet don't use a worksheet identifier.

You can also link to cells in an Excel 2007 data table. Such links include the workbook name, worksheet name, name of the table, and row and column references of the cell to which you've linked. Creating a link to the Cost column's cell in a table's Totals row, for example, results in a reference such as ='FleetOperatingCosts.xlsx'!Truck Maintenance[[#Totals],[Cost]].

> **Important** Hiding or displaying a table's Totals row affects a link to a cell in that row. Hiding the Totals row causes any references to that row to display a *#REF!* error message.

Whenever you open a workbook containing a link to another document, Excel 2007 tries to update the information in linked cells. If the program can't find the source, such as when a workbook or worksheet is deleted or renamed, an alert box appears to indicate that there is a broken link. At that point, you can click the Update button and then the Edit Links button to open the Edit Links dialog box and find which link is broken. After you identify the broken link, you can close the Edit Links dialog box, click the cell containing the broken link, and create a new link to the desired data.

If you type a link yourself and you make an error, a *#REF!* error message appears in the cell with the link. To fix the link, click the cell, delete its contents, and then either retype the link or create it with the point-and-click method described earlier in this section.

> **Tip** Excel 2007 is much better at tracking workbook changes, such as new worksheet names, than earlier versions of the program. Unless you delete a worksheet or workbook, or move a workbook to a new folder, odds are good that Excel 2007 can update your link references to reflect the change.

In this exercise, you will create a link to another workbook, make the link's reference invalid, use the Edit Links dialog box to break the link, and then re-create the link correctly.

> **USE** the *Operating Expense Dashboard* and *Fleet Operating Costs* workbooks. These practice files are located in the *Documents\Microsoft Press\Excel2007SBS\MultipleFiles* folder.
>
> **OPEN** the *Operating Expense Dashboard* and *Fleet Operating Costs* workbooks.

1. In the *Operating Expense Dashboard* workbook, in cell I6, type =, but do not press Enter.

Switch Windows ▾

2. On the **View** tab, in the **Window** group, click **Switch Windows** and then, in the list, click *Fleet Operating Costs*.

    The *Fleet Operating Costs* workbook appears.

3. If necessary, click the **Plane Repairs** sheet tab to display the Plane Repairs worksheet, and then click cell C15.

Excel 2007 sets the cell's formula to =*'[Fleet Operating Costs.xlsx]Plane Repairs'!$C$15*.

4. Press Enter .

Excel 2007 displays the *Operating Expense Dashboard* workbook; the value *$2,410,871.00* appears in cell I6.

	Labor			Facilities			Transportation		
Processing	$ 1,400,000.00		Power	$ 1,800,000.00		Truck Fuel		
Driver	$ 2,100,000.00		Water	$ 900,000.00		Truck Maintenance		
Administrative	$ 3,000,000.00		Rent	$ 2,350,000.00		Airplane Fuel	$ 2,410,871.00	
Executive	$ 4,500,000.00		Mortgage	$ 4,590,210.00		Airplane Maintenance		

> **Tip** Yes, cell C15 on the Plane Repairs worksheet contains the wrong total for the Airplane Fuel category; that's why you replace it later in this exercise.

5. In the **Switch Windows** list, click *Fleet Operating Costs*.

The *Fleet Operating Costs* workbook appears.

6. Right-click the **Plane Repairs** sheet tab, and then click **Delete**. In the message box that appears, click **Delete** to confirm that you want to delete the worksheet.

Excel 2007 deletes the Plane Repairs worksheet.

7. In the **Switch Windows** list, click *Operating Expense Dashboard*.

The *Operating Expense Dashboard* workbook appears.

8. On the **Data** tab, in the **Connections** group, click **Edit Links**.

Edit Links

The Edit Links dialog box opens.

9. Click **Break Link**.

Excel 2007 displays a warning box asking if you're sure you want to break the link.

10. Click **Break Links**.

The warning box closes, and Excel 2007 removes the link from the workbook.

11. Click **Close**.

The Edit Links dialog box closes, and the error code *#REF!* appears in cell I6.

12. In cell I6, type =, but do not press Enter .

13. In the **Switch Windows** list, click *Fleet Operating Costs*.

The *Fleet Operating Costs* workbook appears.

14. Click the **Plane Fuel** sheet tab.

The Plane Fuel worksheet appears.

15. Click cell C15, and then press Enter .

Excel 2007 displays the *Operating Expense Dashboard* workbook with the value *$52,466,303.00* in cell I6.

CLOSE the *Operating Expense Dashboard* and *Fleet Operating Costs* workbooks.

Consolidating Multiple Sets of Data into a Single Workbook

When you create a series of worksheets that contain similar data, perhaps by using a template, you build a consistent set of workbooks in which data is stored in a predictable place. For example, the workbook template in the following graphic uses cell C5 to record the number of calls received from 9:00 a.m. to 10:00 a.m. regarding phone calls handled by the Northeast distribution center.

Using links to bring data from one worksheet to another gives you a great deal of power to combine data from several sources in a single spot. For example, you can create a worksheet that lists the total revenue just for certain months of a year, use links to draw the values from the worksheets in which the sales were recorded, and then create a formula to perform calculations on the data. However, for large worksheets with hundreds of cells filled with data, creating links from every cell to cells on another worksheet is time-consuming. Also, to calculate a sum or an average for the data, you would need to include links to cells in every workbook.

Fortunately, there is an easier way to combine data from multiple worksheets in a single worksheet. This process, called *data consolidation*, enables you to define ranges of cells from multiple worksheets and have Excel 2007 summarize the data. You define these ranges in the Consolidate dialog box.

Consolidate dialog box

Function:
Sum

Reference:

Browse...

All references:

Add

Delete

Use labels in
☐ Top row
☐ Left column   ☐ Create links to source data

OK   Close

After you open the dialog box, you move to the worksheet with the cells in the first range you want to include in your summary. When you select the cells, the 3-D reference for the cell range appears in the Consolidate dialog box.

Clicking Add stores the reference, whereas clicking Delete removes the range from the calculation. You can then choose the other cell ranges with data to include in the summary. Cells that are in the same relative position in the ranges have their contents summarized together. So the cell in the upper-left corner of one range is added to the cell in the upper-left corner of another range, even if those ranges are in different areas of the worksheet. After you choose the ranges to be used in your summary, you can choose the calculation to perform on the data (sum, average, and so on). When you're done selecting ranges to use in the calculation, click OK to have Excel 2007 summarize the data on your target worksheet.

> **Important** You can define only one data consolidation summary per workbook.

In this exercise, you will define a series of ranges from two workbooks to be included in a data consolidation calculation. You will then add the contents of the ranges and show the results in a worksheet.

USE the *Consolidate, January Calls,* and *February Calls* workbooks. These practice files are located in the *Documents\Microsoft Press\Excel2007SBS\MultipleFiles* folder.
OPEN the *Consolidate, January Calls,* and *February Calls* workbooks.

Consolidate

1. In the *Consolidate* workbook, on the **Data** tab, in the **Data Tools** group, click **Consolidate**.

The Consolidate dialog box opens.

Collapse Dialog

2. Click the **Collapse Dialog** button at the right edge of the **Reference** field.

   The Consolidate dialog box contracts.

Switch
Windows ▾

3. On the **View** tab, in the **Window** group, click **Switch Windows** and then, in the list, click *January Calls*.

   The *January Calls* workbook appears.

4. Select the cell range C5:O13, and then click the **Expand Dialog** control.

   The Consolidate dialog box reappears.

Expand Dialog

5. Click **Add**.

   The range *'[January Calls.xlsx]January'!$C$5:$O$13* appears in the All References pane.

6. Click the **Contract Dialog** button at the right edge of the **Reference** field.

   The Consolidate dialog box contracts.

7. In the **Switch Windows** list, click *February Calls*.

   The *February Calls* workbook appears.

8. Select the cell range C5:O13, and then click the **Expand Dialog** button.

   The Consolidate dialog box reappears.

9. Click **Add**.

   The range *'[February Calls.xlsx]February'!$C$5:$O$13* appears in the All References pane.

10. Click **OK**.

    Excel 2007 consolidates the *January Calls* and *February Calls* workbook data into the range C5:O13 in the *Consolidate* workbook.

Call Center	Hour												
	9:00 AM	10:00 AM	11:00 AM	12:00 PM	1:00 PM	2:00 PM	3:00 PM	4:00 PM	5:00 PM	6:00 PM	7:00 PM	8:00 PM	9:00 PM
Northeast	15931	15958	13140	25367	19558	20624	18128	26931	25929	22577	10939	27333	20213
Atlantic	28432	22326	15436	20884	30000	19770	29129	16470	9208	23231	23236	15059	15520
Southeast	13132	12568	19732	14762	18885	20882	20917	27571	21751	30970	11432	23216	20173
North Central	17588	26324	24121	24453	20048	21994	29260	30386	21185	17766	24943	11119	23654
Midwest	24875	19965	19386	11374	26007	29378	13125	10730	17250	20811	26705	15531	27786
Southwest	15353	27755	19718	17889	22116	28816	23846	15814	30917	7426	18757	33103	20063
Mountain West	21516	28321	9754	26384	15926	23572	14496	24079	13556	21883	11727	21652	26821
Northwest	19806	24154	12389	10151	24078	11642	22839	24615	19694	21596	27115	17180	16112
Central	21018	24884	18655	31525	13407	19683	17346	8078	16747	17222	17897	32980	9746

CLOSE the *Consolidate*, *January Calls*, and *February Calls* workbooks.

Grouping Multiple Sets of Data

When you work with Excel 2007 for awhile, you'll find that you often work with a number of the same workbooks at a time. For instance, Jenny Lysaker, the chief operating officer of Consolidated Messenger, might always pull up a workbook that tracks labor costs at the same time she opens the package volume summary workbook. She can open the workbooks individually through the Open dialog box, but she can also group the files so that she has the option of opening them all simultaneously.

If you want to open a set of files simultaneously, you can define them as part of a workspace, which uses one file name to reference several workbooks. To define a workspace, you open the files you want to include and then open the Save Workspace dialog box.

Clicking Save in the Save Workspace dialog box saves references to all the Excel 2007 files that are currently open. Whenever you open the workspace you create, all the files that were open when you defined the workspace appear. Including a file in a workspace doesn't remove it from general circulation; you can still open it by itself.

In this exercise, you will save a workspace that consists of two workbooks, close the included files, and then test the workspace by opening it from the Open dialog box.

> **USE** the *Operating Expense Dashboard* and *Fleet Operating Costs* workbooks. These practice files are located in the *Documents\Microsoft Press\Excel2007SBS\MultipleFiles* folder.
>
> **OPEN** the *Operating Expense Dashboard* and *Fleet Operating Costs* workbooks.

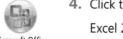

1. In either workbook, on the **View** tab, in the **Window** group, click **Save Workspace**.

The Save Workspace dialog box opens.

2. In the **File name** field, type **Expenses**.

3. Click **Save**.

Excel 2007 saves your workspace and closes the Save Workspace dialog box.

Microsoft Office Button

4. Click the **Microsoft Office Button**, and then click **Close**.

Excel 2007 closes the active workbook.

5. Click the **Microsoft Office Button**, and then click **Close**.

Excel 2007 closes the second workbook.

6. Click the **Microsoft Office Button**, and in the **Recent Documents** list, click **Expenses.xlw**.

Excel 2007 opens the *Operating Expense Dashboard* and *Fleet Operating Costs* workbooks.

	Labor			Facilities			Transportation	
Processing		$ 1,400,000.00		Power	$ 1,800,000.00		Truck Fuel	
Driver		$ 2,100,000.00		Water	$ 900,000.00		Truck Maintenance	
Administrative		$ 3,000,000.00		Rent	$ 2,350,000.00		Airplane Fuel	
Executive		$ 4,500,000.00		Mortgage	$ 4,590,210.00		Airplane Maintenance	

CLOSE the *Operating Expense Dashboard* and *Fleet Operating Costs* workbooks. If you are not continuing directly to the next chapter, exit Excel.

Key Points

- If you create a lot of workbooks with the same layout and design, saving a workbook with the common elements (and no data) takes much less time.

- You can use data in other worksheets or workbooks in your formulas. You make the link by clicking the cell, which creates a 3-D reference to that cell.

- When you create a link to a cell in a table's Totals row, hiding the row doesn't make the link invalid.

- If you always work on a group of workbooks at the same time, create a workspace so that you can open them all at once.

Chapter at a Glance

Define multiple alternative
data sets, **page 181**

Define an alternative
data set, **page 178**

Vary your data to
get a desired result
by using Goal Seek,
page 185

Find optimal solutions by
using Solver, **page 188**

Analyze data by
using descriptive
statistics, **page 194**

9 Analyzing Alternative Data Sets

In this chapter, you will learn to:

- ✔ Define an alternative data set.
- ✔ Define multiple alternative data sets.
- ✔ Vary your data to get a desired result by using Goal Seek.
- ✔ Find optimal solutions by using Solver.
- ✔ Analyze data by using descriptive statistics.

When you store data in a Microsoft Office Excel 2007 workbook, you can use that data, either by itself or as part of a calculation, to discover important information about your business. When you track total sales on a time basis, you can find your best and worst sales periods and correlate them with outside events. For businesses such as Consolidated Messenger, package volume increases dramatically during the holidays as customers ship gifts to friends and family members.

The data in your worksheets is great for asking this question: "What happened?" The data is less useful for asking "what-if" questions such as this: "How much money would we save if we reduced our labor to 20 percent of our total costs?" You can always save an alternative version of a workbook and create formulas that calculate the effects of your changes, but you can do the same thing in your workbook by defining one or more alternative data sets and switching between the original data and the new sets you create.

Excel 2007 also provides the tools to determine the inputs that would be required for a formula to produce a given result. For example, the chief operating officer of Consolidated Messenger, Jenny Lysaker, could find out to what level three-day shipping would need to rise for that category to account for 25 percent of total revenue.

In this chapter, you'll learn how to define alternative data sets and determine the necessary inputs to make a calculation produce a particular result.

See Also Do you need only a quick refresher on the topics in this chapter? See the Quick Reference section at the beginning of this book.

Important Before you can use the practice files in this chapter, you need to install them from the book's companion CD to their default location. See "Using the Companion CD" at the beginning of this book for more information.

Defining an Alternative Data Set

When you save data in an Excel 2007 worksheet, you create a record that reflects the characteristics of an event or object. That data could represent an hour of sales on a particular day, the price of an item you just began offering for sale, or the percentage of total sales accounted for by a category of products. After the data is in place, you can create formulas to generate totals, find averages, and sort the rows in a worksheet based on the contents of one or more columns. However, if you want to perform a *what-if analysis* or explore the impact that changes in your data would have on any of the calculations in your workbooks, you need to change your data.

The problem of working with data that reflects an event or item is that changing any data to affect a calculation runs the risk of destroying the original data if you accidentally save your changes. You can avoid ruining your original data by creating a duplicate workbook and making your changes to it, but you can also create alternative data sets, or *scenarios*, within an existing workbook.

When you create a scenario, you give Excel 2007 alternative values for a list of cells in a worksheet. You can use the Scenario Manager to add, delete, and edit scenarios.

Clicking the Add button displays the Add Scenario dialog box.

From within this dialog box, you can name the scenario and identify the cells that will hold alternative values. After you click OK, a new dialog box opens with spaces for you to enter the new values.

Clicking OK returns you to the Scenario Manager dialog box. From there, clicking the Show button replaces the values in the original worksheet with the alternative values you just defined in a scenario. Any formulas using cells with changed values recalculate their results. You can then remove the scenario by clicking the Undo button on the Quick Access Toolbar.

> **Important** If you save and close a workbook while a scenario is in effect, those values become the default values for the cells changed by the scenario! You should strongly consider creating a scenario that contains the original values of the cells you change or creating a scenario summary worksheet (a topic covered later in this chapter).

In this exercise, you will create a scenario to measure the projected impact on total revenue of a rate increase on two-day shipping.

USE the *2DayScenario* workbook. This practice file is located in the *Documents\Microsoft Press\Excel2007SBS\Alternatives* folder.

BE SURE TO start Excel 2007 before beginning this exercise.

OPEN the *2DayScenario* workbook.

What-If Analysis

1. On the **Data** tab, in the **Data Tools** group, click **What-If Analysis** and then, in the list, click **Scenario Manager**.

The Scenario Manager dialog box opens.

2. Click **Add**.

The Add Scenario dialog box opens.

3. In the **Scenario Name** field, type 2DayIncrease.

Collapse Dialog

4. At the right edge of the **Changing cells** field, click the **Collapse Dialog** button so the worksheet contents are visible.

The Add Scenario dialog box contracts.

Expand Dialog

5. In the worksheet, click cell C5 and then, in the **Add Scenario** dialog box, click the **Expand Dialog** button.

$C$5 appears in the Changing Cells field, and the dialog box title changes to Edit Scenario.

![Edit Scenario dialog box with Scenario name "2DayIncrease", Changing cells "$C$5", Comment "Created by Curt on 11/3/2006", Protection section with "Prevent changes" checked and "Hide" unchecked, OK and Cancel buttons]

6. Click **OK**.

The Scenario Values dialog box opens.

7. In the value field, type 13.2, and then click **OK**.

   The Scenario Values dialog box closes, and the Scenario Manager reappears.

8. If necessary, drag the **Scenario Manager** dialog box to another location on the screen so that you can view the entire table.

9. In the **Scenario Manager** dialog box, click **Show**.

   Excel 2007 applies the scenario, changing the value in cell C5 to *$13.20*, which in turn increases the value in cell E8 to *$747,450,000.00*.

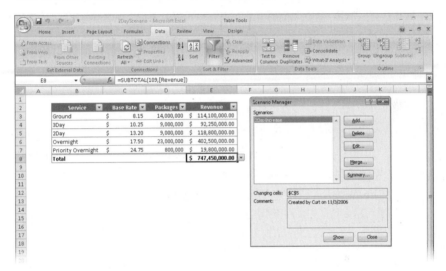

10. Close the **Scenario Manager** dialog box.

11. On the **Quick Access Toolbar**, click the **Undo** button.

    Excel 2007 removes the effect of the scenario.

Undo

CLOSE the *2DayScenario* workbook, saving your changes if you want to.

Defining Multiple Alternative Data Sets

One great feature of Excel 2007 scenarios is that you're not limited to creating one alternative data set—you can create as many as you like and apply them at will by using the Scenario Manager. To apply more than one scenario by using the Scenario Manager, click the name of the first scenario you want to display, click the Show button, and then do the same for the second scenario. The values you defined as part of those scenarios will appear in your worksheet, and Excel 2007 will update any calculations involving the changed cells.

> **Tip** If you apply a scenario to a worksheet and then apply another scenario to the same worksheet, both sets of changes appear. If the second scenario changes a cell changed by the first scenario, the cell reflects the value in the second scenario.

Applying multiple scenarios gives you an overview of how the scenarios affect your calculations, but Excel 2007 also gives you a way to view the results of all your scenarios in a single worksheet. To create a worksheet in your current workbook that summarizes the changes caused by your scenarios, open the Scenario Manager, and then click the Summary button. When you do, the Scenario Summary dialog box opens.

From within the dialog box, you can choose the type of summary worksheet you want to create and the cells you want to appear in the summary worksheet. To choose the cells to appear in the summary, click the button in the box, select the cells you want to appear, and then expand the dialog box. After you verify that the range in the box represents the cells you want included on the summary sheet, click to create the new worksheet.

It's a good idea to create an "undo" scenario named Normal with the original values of every cell before they're changed in other scenarios. For example, if you create a scenario named *High Fuel Costs* that changes the sales figures in three cells, your Normal scenario restores those cells to their original values. That way, even if you accidentally modify your worksheet, you can apply the Normal scenario and not have to reconstruct the worksheet from scratch.

> **Tip** Each scenario can change a maximum of 32 cells, so you might need to create more than one scenario to restore a worksheet.

In this exercise, you will create scenarios to represent projected revenue increases from two rate changes, view the scenarios, and then summarize the scenario results in a new worksheet.

> **USE** the *Multiple Scenarios* workbook. This practice file is located in the *Documents\ Microsoft Press\Excel2007SBS\Alternatives* folder.
> **OPEN** the *Multiple Scenarios* workbook.

What-If Analysis

1. On the **Data** tab, in the **Data Tools** group, click **What-If Analysis** and then, in the list, click **Scenario Manager**.

The Scenario Manager dialog box opens.

2. Click **Add**.

The Add Scenario dialog box opens.

3. In the **Scenario name** field, type 3DayIncrease.

Collapse Dialog

4. At the right edge of the **Changing cells** field, click the **Collapse Dialog** button.

The Add Scenario dialog box collapses.

Expand Dialog

5. In the worksheet, click cell C4 and then, in the dialog box, click the **Expand Dialog** button.

$C$4 appears in the Changing Cells field, and the dialog box title changes to Edit Scenario.

6. Click **OK**.

The Scenario Values dialog box opens.

7. In the value field, type 11.50.

8. Click **OK**.

The Scenario Values dialog box closes, and the Scenario Manager reappears.

9. Click **Add**.

The Add Scenario dialog box opens.

10. In the **Scenario name** field, type Ground and Overnight Increase.

11. At the right edge of the **Changing cells** field, click the **Collapse Dialog** button.

The Add Scenario dialog box collapses.

12. Click cell C3, hold down the Ctrl key, and click cell C6. Then click the **Expand Dialog** button.

$C$3,$C$6 appears in the Changing Cells field, and the dialog box title changes to Edit Scenario.

13. Click **OK**.

    The Scenario Values dialog box opens.

14. In the $C$3 field, type 10.15.

15. In the $C$6 field, type 18.5.

16. Click **OK**.

    The Scenario Values dialog box closes, and the Scenario Manager dialog box reappears.

17. Click the **3DayIncrease** scenario, and then click **Show**.

    Excel 2007 applies the scenario to your worksheet.

18. Click the **Ground and Overnight Increase** scenario, and then click **Show**.

    Excel 2007 applies the scenario to your worksheet.

19. Click **Summary**.

The Scenario Summary dialog box opens.

20. Verify that the **Scenario summary** option is selected and that cell E8 appears in the **Result cells** field.

21. Click **OK**.

Excel 2007 creates a Scenario Summary worksheet.

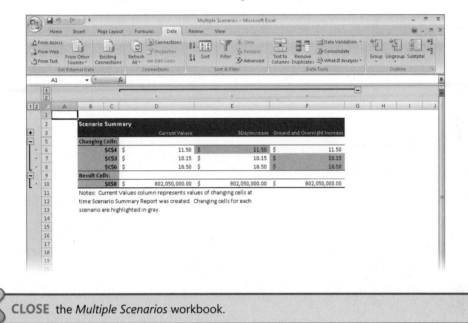

CLOSE the *Multiple Scenarios* workbook.

Varying Your Data to Get a Desired Result by Using Goal Seek

When you run a business, you must know how every department and product is performing, both in absolute terms and in relation to other departments or products in the company. Just as you might want to reward your employees for maintaining a perfect safety record and keeping down your insurance rates, you might also want to stop carrying products you cannot sell.

When you plan how you want to grow your business, you should have specific goals in mind for each department or product category. For example, Jenny Lysaker of Consolidated Messenger might have the goal of reducing the firm's labor cost by

20 percent over the previous year. Finding the labor amount that represents a 20 percent decrease is simple, but expressing goals in other ways can make finding the solution more challenging. Instead of decreasing labor costs 20 percent over the previous year, Jenny might want to decrease labor costs so they represent no more than 20 percent of the company's total outlays.

As an example, consider the following worksheet, which holds cost figures for Consolidated Messenger's operations and uses those figures to calculate both total costs and the share each category has of that total.

	A	B	C	D	E	F	G	H
1								
2			Labor	Transportation	Taxes	Facilities	Total	
3		Cost	$ 18,000,382.00	$35,000,000.00	$ 7,000,000.00	$ 19,000,000.00	$ 79,000,382.00	
4		Share	22.79%	44.30%	8.86%	24.05%		
5								

> **Important** In this worksheet, the values in the Share row are displayed as percentages, but the underlying values are decimals. For example, Excel 2007 represents *0.3064* as *30.64%*.

Although it would certainly be possible to figure the target number that would make labor costs represent 20 percent of the total, there is an easier way to do it in Excel 2007: *Goal Seek*. To use Goal Seek, you display the Data tab and then, in the Data Tools group, click What-If Analysis. From the menu that appears, click Goal Seek to open the Goal Seek dialog box.

In the dialog box, you identify the cell with the target value; in this case, it is cell C4, which has the percentage of costs accounted for by the Labor category. The box has the target value (.2, which is equivalent to *20%*), and the box identifies the cell with the value Excel 2007 should change to generate the target value of *20%* in cell C4. In this example, the cell to be changed is C3.

Clicking OK tells Excel 2007 to find a solution for the goal you set. When Excel 2007 finishes its work, the new values appear in the designated cells, and the Goal Seek Status dialog box opens.

> **Tip** Goal Seek finds the closest solution it can without exceeding the target value. In this case, the closest percentage it could find was 19.97%.

In this exercise, you will use Goal Seek to determine how much you need to decrease transportation costs so those costs comprise no more than 40 percent of Consolidated Messenger's operating costs.

> **USE** the *Target Values* workbook. This practice file is located in the *Documents\Microsoft Press\Excel2007SBS\Alternatives* folder.
>
> **OPEN** the *Target Values* workbook.

What-If Analysis

1. On the **Data** tab, in the **Data Tools** group, click **What-If Analysis** and then, in the list, click **Goal Seek**.

   The Goal Seek dialog box opens.

2. In the **Set cell** field, type D4.

3. In the **To value** field, type .4.

4. In the **By changing cell** field, type D3.

5. Click **OK**.

Excel 2007 displays the solution in both the worksheet and the Goal Seek Status dialog box.

6. Click **Cancel**.

Excel 2007 closes the Goal Seek Status dialog box without saving the new worksheet values.

CLOSE the *Target Values* workbook.

Finding Optimal Solutions by Using Solver

Goal Seek is a great tool for finding out how much you need to change a single input to generate a desired result from a formula, but it's of no help if you want to find the best mix of several inputs. For example, marketing vice president Craig Dewar might want to advertise in four national magazines to drive customers to Consolidated Messenger's Web site, but he might not know the best mix of ads to place among the publications. He asked the publishers for ad pricing and readership numbers, which are reflected in the spreadsheet shown as follows, along with the minimum number of ads per publication (3) and the minimum number of times he wants the ad to be seen (10,000,000). Because one of the magazines has a high percentage of corporate executive readers, Craig does want to take out at least four ads in that publication despite its relatively low readership. The goal of the ad campaign is for the ads to be seen as many times as possible without spending more than the $3,000,000 budget.

> **Tip** It helps to spell out every aspect of your problem so that you can identify the cells you want Solver to use in its calculations.

If you performed a complete installation when you installed Excel 2007 on your system, you see the Solver item on the Data tab in the Analysis group. If not, you need to install the Solver *Add-In*. To do so, click the Microsoft Office Button, and then click Excel Options. In the Excel Options dialog box, click Add-Ins to display the Add-Ins page. At the bottom of the dialog box, in the Manage list, click Excel Add-Ins, and then click Go to display the Add-Ins dialog box. Select the Solver Add-in check box and click OK to install Solver.

> **Tip** You might be prompted for the Microsoft Office system installation CD. If so, put the CD in your CD drive, and click OK.

After the installation is complete, Solver appears on the Data tab, in the Analysis group. Clicking Solver displays the Solver Parameters dialog box.

The first step of setting up your Solver problem is to identify the cell that reflects the results of changing the other cells in the worksheet. To identify that cell, click in the Set Target Cell box, click the target cell, and then select the option representing whether you want to minimize the cell's value, maximize the cell's value, or make the cell take on a specific value. Next you click in the By Changing Cells box and select the cells Solver should vary to change the value in the target cell. Finally, you set the limits for the values Solver can use by clicking Add to display the Add Constraint dialog box.

You add constraints to the Solver problem by selecting the cells to which you want to apply the constraint, selecting the comparison operation (less than or equal to, greater than or equal to, requiring the value to be an integer, and so on), clicking in the Constraint box, and selecting the cell with the value of the constraint. You could also type a value in the Constraint box, but referring to a cell makes it possible for you to change the constraint without opening Solver.

> **Tip** After you run Solver, you can use the controls in the Solver Results, save the results as changes to your worksheet, or create a scenario based on the changed data.

In this exercise, you will use Solver to determine the best mix of ads given the following constraints:

- You want to maximize the number of people who see the ads.
- You must buy at least eight ads in three magazines and at least ten in the fourth.
- You can't buy part of an ad (that is, all numbers must be integers).
- You can buy no more than 20 ads in any one magazine.
- You must reach at least 10,000,000 people.
- Your ad budget is $3,000,000.

> **USE** the *Ad Buy* workbook. This practice file is located in the *Documents\Microsoft Press\ Excel2007SBS\Alternatives* folder.
>
> **OPEN** the *Ad Buy* workbook.

1. If **Solver** doesn't appear in the **Analysis** group on the **Data** tab, follow the instructions on page 190 to install it.

2. In the **Analysis** group on the **Data** tab, click **Solver**.

   The Solver Parameters dialog box opens.

3. Click in the **Set Target Cell** box, and then click cell G9.

   $G$9 appears in the Set Target Cell field.

4. Click **Max**.

5. Click in the **By Changing Cells** field, and select cells E5:E8.

   $E$5:$E$8 appears in the By Changing Cells field.

6. Click **Add**.

   The Add Constraint dialog box opens.

7. Select cells E5:E8.

   $E$5:$E$8 appears in the Cell Reference field.

8. In the operator list, click **int**. Then click **Add**.

   Excel 2007 adds the constraint to the Solver problem, and the Add Constraint dialog box clears to accept the next constraint.

9. Click cell F9.

   $F$9 appears in the Cell Reference field.

10. Click in the **Constraint** field, and then click cell G11.

    $G$11 appears in the Constraint field.

11. Click **Add**.

    Excel 2007 adds the constraint to the Solver problem, and the Add Constraint dialog box clears to accept the next constraint.

12. Click cell G9.

    $G$9 appears in the Cell Reference field.

13. In the operator list, click **=**.

14. Click in the **Constraint** field, and then click cell G12.

    $G$12 appears in the Constraint field.

15. Click **Add**.

Excel 2007 adds the constraint to the Solver problem, and the Add Constraint dialog box clears to accept the next constraint.

16. Select cells E5:E7.

$E$5:$E$7 appears in the Cell Reference field.

17. In the operator list, click =.

18. Click in the **Constraint** field, and then click cell G13.

$G$13 appears in the Constraint field.

19. Click **Add**.

Excel 2007 adds the constraint to the Solver problem, and the Add Constraint dialog box clears to accept the next constraint.

20. Click cell E8.

$E$8 appears in the Cell Reference field.

21. In the operator list, click =.

22. Click in the **Constraint** field, and then click cell G14.

$G$14 appears in the Constraint field.

23. Click **Add**.

Excel 2007 adds the constraint to the Solver problem, and the Add Constraint dialog box clears to accept the next constraint.

24. Select cells E5:E8.

$E$5:$E$8 appears in the Cell Reference field.

25. Click in the **Constraint** field, and then click cell G15.

$G$15 appears in the Constraint field.

26. Click **OK**.

Excel 2007 adds the constraint to the Solver problem, and the Solver Parameters dialog box reappears.

27. Click **Solve**.

The Solver Results dialog box opens, indicating that Solver found a solution. The result is displayed in the body of the worksheet.

28. Click **Cancel**.

The Solver Results dialog box closes.

29. Click **Close**. If you are asked if you want to save your changes, click **No**.

The Solver dialog box closes.

CLOSE the *Ad Buy* workbook.

Analyzing Data by Using Descriptive Statistics

Experienced businesspeople can tell a lot about numbers just by looking at them to see if they "look right" (that is, the sales figures are about where they're supposed to be for a particular hour, day, or month; the average seems about right; and sales have increased from year to year). When you need more than an off-the-cuff assessment, however, you can use the tools in the Analysis ToolPak.

If you don't see the Data Analysis item in the Analysis group on the Data tab, you can install it. To do so, click the Microsoft Office Button, and then click Excel Options. In the Excel Options dialog box, click Add-Ins to display the Add-Ins page. At the bottom of the dialog box, in the Manage list, click Excel Add-Ins, and then click Go to display the Add-Ins dialog box. Select the Analysis ToolPak check box and click OK.

> **Tip** You might be prompted for the Microsoft Office system installation CD. If so, put the CD in your CD drive, and click OK.

After the installation is complete, the Data Analysis item appears in the Analysis group on the Data tab.

You then click the item representing the type of data analysis you want to perform, click OK, and use the controls in the resulting dialog box to analyze your data.

In this exercise, you will use the Analysis ToolPak to generate descriptive statistics of driver sorting time data.

> **USE** the *Driver Sort Times* workbook. This practice file is located in the *Documents\ Microsoft Press\Excel2007SBS\Alternatives* folder.
> **OPEN** the *Driver Sort Times* workbook.

1. On the **Data** tab, in the **Analysis** group, click **Data Analysis**.

The Data Analysis dialog box opens.

2. Click **Descriptive Statistics**, and then click **OK**.

The Descriptive Statistics dialog box opens.

3. Click in the **Input Range** field and point to the top of the **Sorting Minutes** column header. When the pointer changes to a downward-pointing black arrow, click the header.

   $C$3:$C$17 appears in the Input Range field.

4. Select the **Summary Statistics** check box.

5. Click **OK**.

   A new worksheet that contains summary statistics about the selected data appears.

CLOSE the *Driver Sort Times* workbook. If you are not continuing directly to the next chapter, exit Excel.

Key Points

- Scenarios enable you to describe many potential business cases within a single workbook.

- It's usually a good idea to create a "normal" scenario that enables you to reset your worksheet.

- Remember that you can change up to 32 cells in a scenario, but no more.

- You can summarize your scenarios on a new worksheet to compare how each scenario approaches the data.

- Use Goal Seek to determine what value you need in a single cell to generate the desired result from a formula.

- If you want to vary the values in more than one cell to find the optimal mix of inputs for a calculation, use the Solver Add-In.

- Advanced statistical tools are available in the Analysis ToolPak—use them to go over your data thoroughly.

Chapter at a Glance

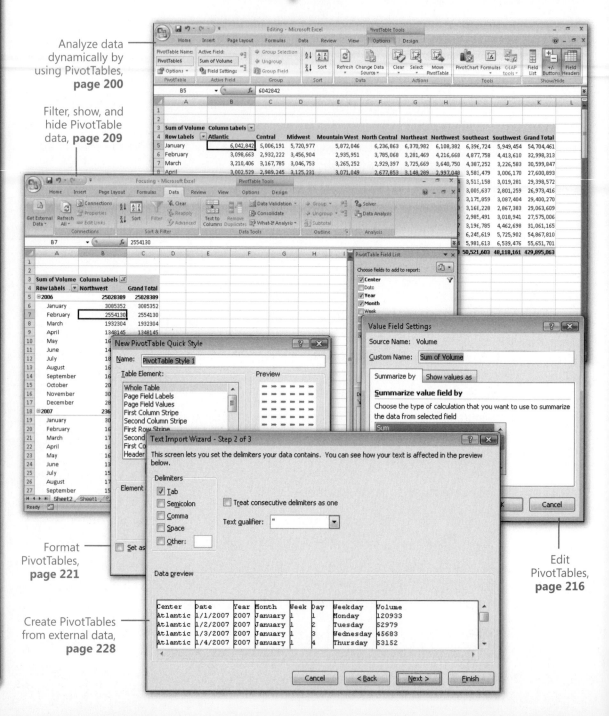

Analyze data dynamically by using PivotTables, **page 200**

Filter, show, and hide PivotTable data, **page 209**

Format PivotTables, **page 221**

Create PivotTables from external data, **page 228**

Edit PivotTables, **page 216**

10 Creating Dynamic Lists by Using PivotTables

In this chapter, you will learn to:

✔ Analyze data dynamically by Using PivotTables.

✔ Filter, show, and hide PivotTable data.

✔ Edit PivotTables.

✔ Format PivotTables.

✔ Create PivotTables from external data.

When you create Microsoft Office Excel 2007 worksheets, you must consider how you want the data to appear when you show it to your colleagues. You can change the formatting of your data to emphasize the contents of specific cells, sort and filter your worksheets based on the contents of specific columns, or hide rows containing data that isn't relevant to the point you're trying to make.

One limitation of the standard Excel worksheet is that you can't change how the data is organized on the page. For example, in a worksheet in which each column represents an hour in the day, each row represents a day in a month, and the body of the worksheet contains the total sales for every hourly period of the month, you can't easily change the worksheet so that it displays only sales on Tuesdays during the afternoon.

An Excel 2007 tool enables you to create worksheets that can be sorted, filtered, and rearranged dynamically to emphasize different aspects of your data. That tool is the *PivotTable*.

In this chapter, you'll learn how to create and edit PivotTables from an existing worksheet and how to create a PivotTable with data imported from a text file.

See Also Do you need only a quick refresher on the topics in this chapter? See the Quick Reference section at the beginning of this book.

> **Important** Before you can use the practice files in this chapter, you need to install them from the book's companion CD to their default location. See "Using the Companion CD" at the beginning of this book for more information.

Analyzing Data Dynamically by Using PivotTables

Excel 2007 worksheets enable you to gather and present important data, but the standard worksheet can't be changed from its original configuration easily. As an example, consider the worksheet in the following graphic.

	January	February	March	April	May	June	July	August	Sept
Atlantic	6,042,842	3,098,663	3,210,406	3,002,529	3,368,888	3,208,696	3,115,294	3,237,645	3,0
Central	6,006,191	2,932,222	3,167,785	2,989,245	3,576,763	2,973,980	3,364,482	3,191,591	2,0
Midwest	5,720,977	3,456,904	3,046,753	3,125,231	3,280,768	3,035,619	2,945,492	3,441,757	3,2
Mountain West	5,872,046	2,935,951	3,265,252	3,071,049	3,159,233	3,063,572	3,456,576	3,371,850	2,9
North Central	6,236,863	3,785,068	2,929,397	2,677,853	3,079,267	3,040,653	3,521,947	3,166,710	2,9
Northeast	6,370,982	3,281,469	3,725,669	3,148,289	3,165,070	2,990,986	3,329,821	3,217,496	3,3
Northwest	6,108,382	4,216,668	3,640,750	2,997,048	3,236,144	2,849,014	3,403,395	3,400,949	3,2
Southeast	6,396,724	4,877,758	4,387,252	3,583,479	3,513,158	3,009,637	3,175,859	3,168,228	2,9
Southwest	5,949,454	4,413,610	3,226,583	3,006,170	3,019,281	2,801,259	3,087,404	2,867,383	3,0
Grand Total	54,704,461	32,998,313	30,599,847	27,600,893	29,398,572	26,973,416	29,400,270	29,063,609	27,9

This worksheet records monthly package volumes for each of nine distribution centers in the United States. The data in the worksheet is organized so that each row represents a distribution center, whereas the columns in the body of the worksheet represent a month of the year. When presented in this arrangement, the monthly totals for all centers and the yearly total for each distribution center are given equal billing: neither set of totals stands out.

Such a neutral presentation of your data is versatile, but it has limitations. First, although you can use sorting and filtering to restrict the rows or columns shown, it's difficult to change the worksheet's organization. For example, in a standard worksheet you can't reorganize the contents of your worksheet so that the hours are assigned to the rows and the distribution centers are assigned to the columns.

The Excel 2007 tool to reorganize and redisplay your data dynamically is the PivotTable. You can create a PivotTable, or dynamic worksheet, that enables you to reorganize and filter your data on the fly. For instance, you can create a PivotTable with the same layout as the worksheet shown previously, which emphasizes totals by month, and then change the PivotTable layout to have the rows represent the months of the year and the columns represent a distribution center. The new layout emphasizes the totals by regional distribution center, as shown in the following graphic.

Row Labels	Atlantic	Central	Midwest	Mountain West	North Central	Northeast	Northwest	Southeast	Southwest	Grand Total
January	6,042,842	6,006,191	5,720,977	5,872,046	6,236,863	6,370,982	6,108,382	6,396,724	5,949,454	54,704,461
February	3,098,663	2,932,222	3,456,904	2,935,951	3,785,068	3,281,469	4,216,668	4,877,758	4,413,610	32,998,313
March	3,210,406	3,167,785	3,046,753	3,265,252	2,929,397	3,725,669	3,640,750	4,387,252	3,226,583	30,599,847
April	3,002,529	2,989,245	3,125,231	3,071,049	2,677,853	3,148,289	2,997,048	3,583,479	3,006,170	27,600,893
May	3,368,888	3,576,763	3,280,768	3,159,233	3,079,267	3,165,070	3,236,144	3,513,158	3,019,281	29,398,572
June	3,208,696	2,973,980	3,035,619	3,063,572	3,040,653	2,990,986	2,849,014	3,009,637	2,801,259	26,973,416
July	3,115,294	3,364,482	2,945,492	3,456,576	3,521,947	3,329,821	3,403,395	3,175,059	3,087,404	29,400,270
August	3,237,645	3,191,591	3,441,757	3,371,850	3,166,710	3,217,496	3,400,949	3,168,228	2,867,383	29,063,609
September	3,072,723	2,807,222	3,166,599	2,942,925	2,996,901	3,364,148	3,220,056	2,985,491	3,018,941	27,575,006
October	3,261,585	3,362,250	3,333,751	3,182,437	3,125,591	3,346,381	3,789,687	3,196,785	4,462,698	31,061,165
November	6,137,174	6,083,306	6,236,356	6,121,929	6,026,826	6,287,815	6,002,883	6,245,619	5,725,902	54,867,810
December	6,279,737	6,546,678	6,099,560	5,880,670	6,093,514	6,462,079	5,768,374	5,981,613	6,539,476	55,651,701
Grand Total	47,036,182	47,001,715	46,889,767	46,323,490	46,680,590	48,690,205	48,633,350	50,521,603	48,118,161	429,895,063

To create a PivotTable, you must have your data collected in a list. The new Excel 2007 data tables mesh perfectly with PivotTable dynamic views; not only do the data tables have a well-defined column and row structure but the ability to refer to a data table by its name also greatly simplifies PivotTable creation and management.

The following graphic shows the first few lines of the data table used to create the PivotTable just shown.

Center	Date	Year	Month	Week	Day	Weekday	Volume
Atlantic	1/1/2007	2007	January	1	1	Monday	120933
Atlantic	1/2/2007	2007	January	1	2	Tuesday	52979
Atlantic	1/3/2007	2007	January	1	3	Wednesday	45683
Atlantic	1/4/2007	2007	January	1	4	Thursday	53152
Atlantic	1/5/2007	2007	January	1	5	Friday	149776
Atlantic	1/6/2007	2007	January	1	6	Saturday	108772
Atlantic	1/7/2007	2007	January	1	7	Sunday	99919
Atlantic	1/8/2007	2007	January	2	8	Monday	138271
Atlantic	1/9/2007	2007	January	2	9	Tuesday	77451
Atlantic	1/10/2007	2007	January	2	10	Wednesday	130536
Atlantic	1/11/2007	2007	January	2	11	Thursday	119809
Atlantic	1/12/2007	2007	January	2	12	Friday	64125
Atlantic	1/13/2007	2007	January	2	13	Saturday	146927
Atlantic	1/14/2007	2007	January	2	14	Sunday	62505
Atlantic	1/15/2007	2007	January	3	15	Monday	56662
Atlantic	1/16/2007	2007	January	3	16	Tuesday	119081
Atlantic	1/17/2007	2007	January	3	17	Wednesday	116136
Atlantic	1/18/2007	2007	January	3	18	Thursday	158629
Atlantic	1/19/2007	2007	January	3	19	Friday	46917
Atlantic	1/20/2007	2007	January	3	20	Saturday	86771
Atlantic	1/21/2007	2007	January	3	21	Sunday	129079
Atlantic	1/22/2007	2007	January	4	22	Monday	82806
Atlantic	1/23/2007	2007	January	4	23	Tuesday	49040
Atlantic	1/24/2007	2007	January	4	24	Wednesday	133663
Atlantic	1/25/2007	2007	January	4	25	Thursday	66235

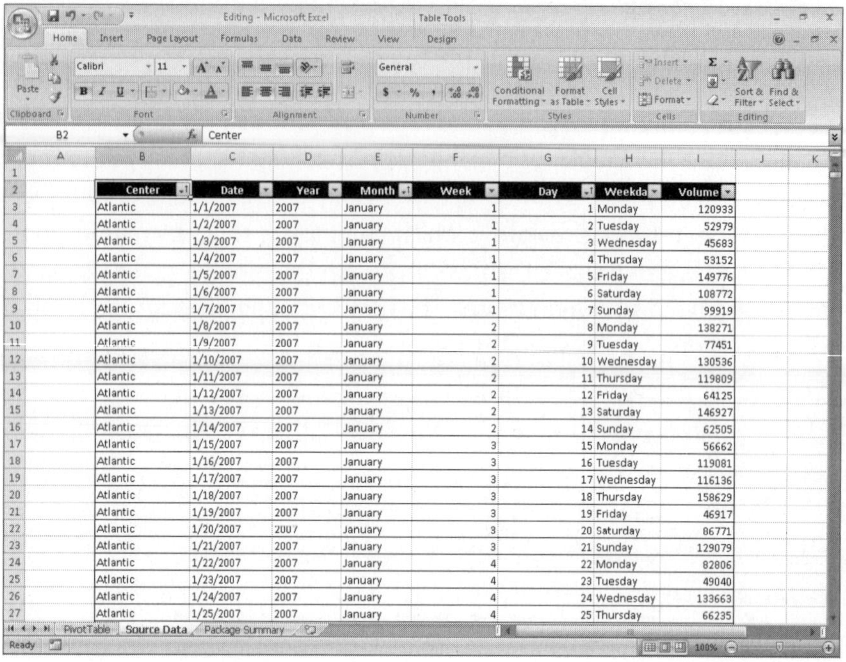

Notice that each line of the table contains a value representing the Distribution Center, Date, Month, Week, Weekday, Day, and Volume for every day of the years 2006 and 2007. Excel 2007 needs that data when it creates the PivotTable so that it can maintain relationships among the data. If you want to filter your PivotTable so that it shows all package volumes on Thursdays in January, for example, Excel 2007 must be able to identify January 11 as a Thursday.

After you create a data table, you can click any cell in that list, display the Insert tab and then, in the Tables group, click PivotTable to display the Create PivotTable dialog box.

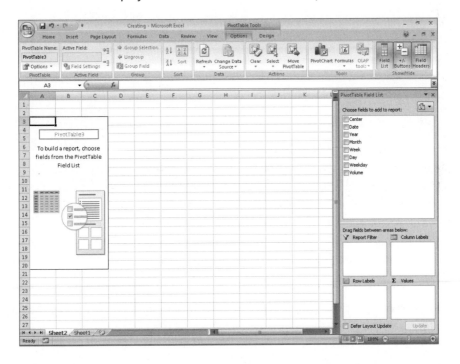

In this dialog box, you verify the data source for your PivotTable and whether you want to create a PivotTable on a new worksheet. After you click OK, Excel 2007 creates a new worksheet and displays the PivotTable Field List task pane.

Tip You should always place your PivotTable on its own worksheet to avoid unwanted edits and reduce the number of cells Excel 2007 must track when you rearrange your data. You might not notice a difference with a small data set, but it's noticeable when your table runs more than a few hundred rows.

To assign a *field*, or column in a data list, to an area of the PivotTable, drag the field head from the Choose Fields To Add To Report area at the top of the PivotTable Field List task pane to the Drag Fields Between Areas Below area at the bottom of the task pane. For example, if you drag the Volume field header to the Values area, the PivotTable displays the total of all entries in the Volume column.

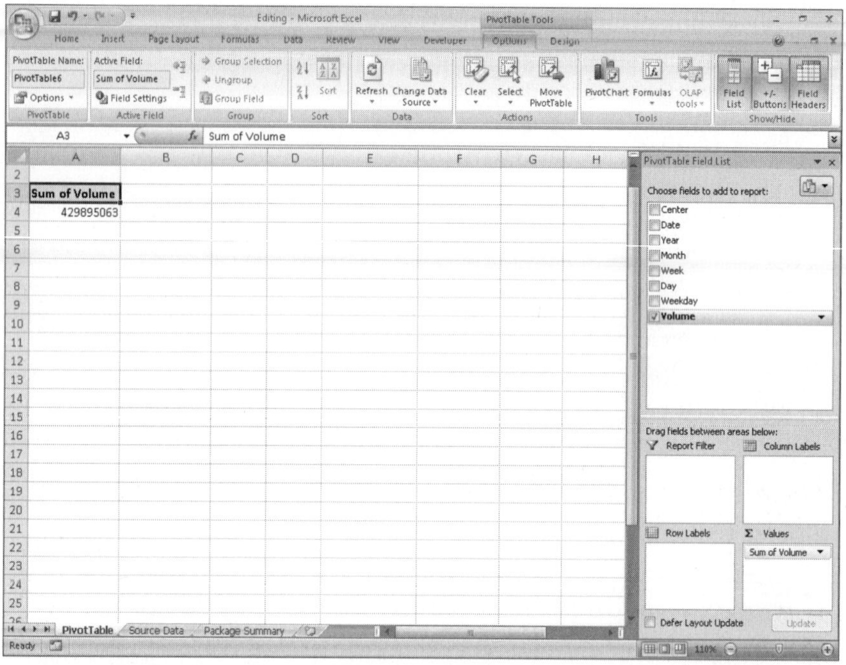

If the PivotTable Field List task pane isn't visible, click any cell in the PivotTable to display it. If you accidentally click the Close button at the upper-right corner of the PivotTable Field List task pane, you can redisplay the task pane by clicking any cell in the PivotTable to display the PivotTable Tools contextual tabs. On the Options contextual tab, in the Show/Hide group, click Field List.

It's important to note that the order in which you enter the fields in the Row Labels and Column Labels areas affects how Excel 2007 organizes the data in your PivotTable. As an example, the following graphic shows a PivotTable that groups the PivotTable rows by distribution center and then by month.

And here is the same PivotTable data, but this time it's organized by month and then by distribution center.

In the preceding examples, all the field headers are in the Row Labels area. If you drag the Center header from the Row Labels area to the Column Labels area, the PivotTable reorganizes (pivots) its data to form this configuration.

To pivot a PivotTable, you drag a field header to a new position in the PivotTable Field List task pane. As you drag the task pane, Excel 2007 displays a blue line in the interior of the target area so you know where the field will appear when you release the left mouse button. If your data set is large or if you based your PivotTable on a data collection on another computer, it might take some time for Excel 2007 to reorganize the PivotTable after a pivot. You can have Excel 2007 delay redrawing the PivotTable by selecting the Defer Layout Update button in the lower-left corner of the PivotTable Field List task pane. When you're ready for Excel 2007 to display the reorganized PivotTable, click Update.

If you expect your PivotTable source data to change, such as when you link to an external database that records shipments or labor hours, ensure that your PivotTable summarizes all the available data. To do that, you can refresh the PivotTable connection to its data source. If Excel 2007 detects new data in the source table, it updates the PivotTable contents accordingly. To refresh your PivotTable, click any cell in the PivotTable and then, on the Options contextual tab, in the Data group, click Refresh.

In this exercise, you will create a PivotTable using data from a table, add fields to the PivotTable, and then pivot the PivotTable.

> **USE** the *Creating* workbook. This practice file is located in the *Documents\Microsoft Press\ Excel2007SBS\PivotTables* folder.
>
> **BE SURE TO** start Excel 2007 before beginning this exercise.
>
> **OPEN** the *Creating* workbook.

1. Click any cell in the data table.

2. On the **Insert** tab, in the **Tables** group, click **PivotTable**.

The Create PivotTable dialog box opens.

3. Verify that the **DailyVolumes** table name appears in the **Table/Range** field and that the **New Worksheet** option is selected.

4. Click **OK**.

Excel 2007 creates a PivotTable on a new worksheet.

5. In the **PivotTable Field List** task pane, drag the **Center** field header to the **Row Labels** area.

Excel 2007 adds the Center field values to the PivotTable row area.

6. In the **PivotTable Field List** task pane, drag the **Year** field header to the **Column Labels** area.

   Excel 2007 adds the Year field values to the PivotTable column area.

7. In the **PivotTable Field List** task pane, drag the **Volume** field header to the **Values** area.

   Excel 2007 fills in the body of the PivotTable with the Volume field values.

8. In the **PivotTable Field List** task pane, in the **Column Labels** area, drag the **Year** field header to the **Row Labels** area, and drop it beneath the **Center** field header.

   Excel 2007 changes the PivotTable to reflect the new organization.

CLOSE the *Creating* workbook.

Filtering, Showing, and Hiding PivotTable Data

PivotTables often summarize huge data sets in a relatively small worksheet. The more details you can capture and write to a table, the more flexibility you have in analyzing the data. As an example, consider all the details captured in the following data table.

Each line of the table contains a value representing the Distribution Center, Date, Month, Week, Weekday, Day, and Volume for every day of the year. Each column, in turn, contains numerous values: there are nine distribution centers, data from two years, twelve months in a year, seven weekdays, and as many as five weeks and 31 days in a month. Just as you can filter the data that appears in a table, you can filter the data displayed in a PivotTable by selecting which values you want the PivotTable to include.

See Also For more information on filtering an Excel 2007 data table, see "Limiting Data That Appears on Your Screen" in Chapter 6, "Focusing on Specific Data by Using Filters."

To filter a PivotTable based on a field's contents, click the field's header in the Choose Fields To Add To Report area of the PivotTable Field List task pane to display a menu of sorting and filtering options.

The PivotTable displays data that's related to the values with a checked box next to them. Clicking the Select All check box clears it, which enables you to select the check boxes of the values you want to display. Selecting only the Northwest check box, for example, leads to the following PivotTable configuration.

If you'd rather display as much PivotTable data as possible, you can hide the PivotTable Field List task pane and filter the PivotTable by using the filter arrows on the Row Labels and Column Labels headers within the body of the PivotTable. Clicking either of those headers enables you to select a field by which you want to filter; you can then define the filter using the same controls you see when you click a field header in the PivotTable Field List task pane.

Excel 2007 indicates that a PivotTable has filters applied by placing a filter indicator next to the Column Labels or Row Labels header, as appropriate, and the filtered field name in the PivotTable Field List task pane.

So far, all the fields by which we've filtered the PivotTable have changed the organization of the data in the PivotTable. Adding some fields to a PivotTable, however, might create unwanted complexity. For example, you might want to filter a PivotTable by weekday, but adding the Weekday field to the body of the PivotTable expands the table unnecessarily.

Instead of adding the Weekday field to the Row Labels or Column Labels area, you can drag the field to the Report Filter area near the bottom of the PivotTable Field List task pane. Doing so leaves the body of the PivotTable in the same position, but adds a new area above the PivotTable in its worksheet.

> **Tip** In Excel 2003 and earlier versions, this area was called the Page Field area.

When you click the filter arrow of a field in the Report Filter area, Excel 2007 displays a list of the values in the field. In previous versions of Excel 2007, you could select only one Report Filter value by which to filter a PivotTable; in Excel 2007, selecting the Select Multiple Items check box enables you to filter by more than one value.

Finally, you can filter values in a PivotTable by hiding and collapsing levels of detail within the report. To do that, you click the Hide Detail control (which looks like a box with a minus sign in it) or the Show Detail control (which looks like a box with a plus sign in it) next to a header. For example, you might have your data divided by year; clicking the Show Detail control next to the 2006 year header would display that year's details. Conversely, clicking the 2007 year header Hide Detail control would hide the individual months' values and display only the year's total.

In this exercise, you will focus the data displayed in a PivotTable by creating a filter, by filtering a PivotTable based on the contents of a field in the Report Filters area, and by showing and hiding levels of detail within the body of the PivotTable.

> **USE** the *Focusing* workbook. This practice file is located in the *Documents\Microsoft Press\ Excel2007SBS\PivotTables* folder.
>
> **OPEN** the *Focusing* workbook.

1. On the PivotTable worksheet, click any cell in the PivotTable.

2. In the **PivotTable Field List** task pane's **Choose fields to add to report** section, click the **Center** field header, click the **Center** field filter arrow, and then clear the **(Select All)** check box.

   Excel 2007 clears all the check boxes in the filter menu.

3. Select the **Northwest** check box, and then click **OK**.

   Excel 2007 filters the PivotTable.

4. On the **Quick Access Toolbar**, click the **Undo** button.

   Excel 2007 removes the filter.

5. In the **PivotTable Field List** task pane, drag the **Weekday** field header from the **Choose fields to add to report** section to the **Report Filter** area in the **Drag fields between areas below** section.

6. In the **PivotTable Field List** task pane, click the **Close** button.

   The PivotTable Field List task pane closes.

7. In the body of the worksheet, click the **Weekday** filter arrow, and then select the **Select Multiple Items** check box.

   Excel 2007 adds check boxes beside the items in the Weekday field filter list.

8. Clear the **All** check box.

   Excel 2007 clears each check box in the list.

9. Select the **Tuesday** and **Thursday** check boxes, and then click **OK**.

Excel 2007 filters the PivotTable, summarizing only those values from Tuesdays and Thursdays.

Hide Detail

10. In cell A5, click the **Hide Detail** button.

Excel 2007 collapses rows that contain data from the year 2006, leaving only the subtotal row that summarizes that year's data.

Row Labels	Atlantic	Central	Midwest	Mountain West	North Central	Northeast	Northwest	Southeast	Southwest	Grand Total
2006	6304269	7050163	6613187	6715681	6830374	6676425	7172546	6868484	7059754	61290883
2007	6408599	6396590	6560131	6770917	6403907	7100828	6958578	7603129	6821849	61024528
January	804732	754373	897073	797919	1046123	1011522	828808	918691	903898	7963139
February	393253	404779	468433	317816	491253	496082	769473	505165	4200859
March	505582	483626	552340	378419	675428	613523	625414	534474	4784265
April	344889	501087	398673	408752	464939	464709	542248	346562	3843676
May	656248	544346	521495	518365	453737	558449	554031	571733	501347	4879751
June	439783	379390	400158	469828	392332	399097	361672	522677	425300	3790237
July	466464	472849	496806	477128	577545	514837	573958	459299	445427	4484313
August	383976	476570	450256	471688	451592	490214	418089	416813	551905	4111103
September	436658	354749	324506	448185	477363	358781	535014	388537	398376	3722169
October	443686	439651	461195	409460	470179	422210	499294	481044	413044	4039763
November	916393	954607	914420	1094284	753727	790101	858666	1088362	977772	8348332
December	718778	776331	704730	664614	676322	923997	754732	818838	818579	6856921
Grand Total	12712868	13446753	13173318	13486598	13234281	13777253	14131124	14471613	13881603	122315411

Sum of Volume
Value: 804732
Row: 2007 - January
Column: Atlantic

CLOSE the *Focusing* workbook.

Editing PivotTables

After you create a PivotTable, you can rename it, edit it to control how it summarizes your data, and use the PivotTable cell data in a formula. As an example, consider the following PivotTable.

Excel 2007 displays the PivotTable name on the Options contextual tab, in the PivotTable Options group. The name PivotTable5 doesn't help you or your colleagues understand the data the PivotTable contains, particularly if you use the PivotTable data in a formula on another worksheet. To give your PivotTable a more descriptive name, click any cell in the PivotTable and then, on the Options contextual tab, in the PivotTable Options group, type the new name in the PivotTable Name field.

When you create a PivotTable with at least one field in the Row Labels area and one field in the Column Labels area of the PivotTable Field List task pane, Excel 2007 adds a grand total row and column to summarize your data. You can control how and where these summary rows and columns appear by clicking any PivotTable cell and then, in the Design contextual tab, in the Layout group, clicking either the Subtotals or Grand Totals button and selecting the desired layout.

After you create a PivotTable, Excel 2007 determines the best way to summarize the data in the column you assign to the Values area. For numeric data, for example, Excel 2007 uses the *Sum* function. If you want to change a PivotTable summary function, right-click any data cell in the PivotTable values area, point to Summarize Data By, and then click the desired operation. If you want to use a function other than those listed, click More Options to display the Value Field Settings dialog box. On the Summarize By tab of the dialog box, you can choose the summary operation you want to use.

You can also change how the PivotTable displays the data in the Values area. On the Show Values As tab of the Value Field Settings dialog box, you can select whether to display each cell's percentage contribution to its column's total, its row's total, or its contribution to the total of all values displayed in the PivotTable.

You can create a link from a cell in another workbook to a cell in your PivotTable. To create a link, you click the cell you want to link to your PivotTable, type an equal sign, and then click the cell in the PivotTable with the data you want linked. A *GETPIVOTDATA* formula appears in the formula box of the worksheet with the PivotTable. When you press Enter, the contents of the PivotTable cell appear in the linked cell.

In this exercise, you will rename a PivotTable, specify whether subtotal and grand total rows will appear, change the PivotTable summary function, display each cell's contribution to its row's total, and create a link to a PivotTable cell.

> **USE** the *Editing* workbook. This practice file is located in the *Documents\Microsoft Press\ Excel2007SBS\PivotTables* folder.
>
> **OPEN** the *Editing* workbook.

1. On the PivotTable worksheet, click any cell in the PivotTable.

2. On the **Options** contextual tab, in the **PivotTable** group, in the **PivotTable Name** field, type VolumeSummary.

   Excel 2007 renames the PivotTable.

3. On the **Design** contextual tab, in the **Layout** group, click **Subtotals**, and then click **Do Not Show Subtotals**.

   Excel 2007 removes the subtotal rows from the PivotTable.

4. On the **Design** contextual tab, in the **Layout** group, click **Grand Totals**, and then click **On for columns only**.

   Excel 2007 removes the cells that calculate each row's grand total.

Undo

5. On the **Quick Access Toolbar**, click the **Undo** button.

   Excel 2007 reverses the last change.

6. Right-click any data cell in the PivotTable, point to **Summarize Data By**, and then click **Average**.

   Excel 2007 changes the Value field summary operation.

3	Average of Volume	Column Labels ▼								
4	Row Labels ▼	Atlantic	Central	Midwest	Mountain West	North Central	Northeast	Northwest	Southeast	Southwest	Grand
5	⊟2006									
6	January	95685.93548	101387.2258	89512.16129	94920.77419	100330.129	99131.3871	99527.48387	111945	97725.48387	9890
7	February	55061.64286	50262.14286	73087.42857	55432.07143	80826.71429	64587.57143	91218.92857	71033.17857	96156.53571	7085
8	March	54452.48387	51433.35484	51642.58065	52936.32258	50108.03226	55006.77419	62332.3871	46512.70968	53127.29032	5306
9	April	48181.2	51606.83333	46526.73333	55127.63333	49206.26667	50513.8	44938.16667	55374.66667	50833.5	5014
10	May	49365.12903	58507.93548	49325.35484	48917.83871	49195.09677	47775.6129	52531.90323	56431.54839	46846	5098
11	June	57525.66667	47717.26667	48600.3	51723.96667	51194.6	51950.53333	49167.93333	47408.83333	47619.36667	5032
12	July	51010.96774	55038.3871	47501.09677	53948.3871	53602.35484	48605.54839	59111.12903	48764.90323	48487.09677	5178
13	August	49017.35484	50891.96774	57972.22581	56295.22581	51214.67742	52330.32258	52696.19355	53911.16129	45637.51613	5221
14	September	49824.5	47335.5	55734.86667	49443.2	41988.36667	58819.2	54600.8	50362.8	46913.4	5055
15	October	56243.25806	55219.67742	51610.54839	53415.03226	54606.80645	55995.3871	65988.35484	46034.3871	93179.51613	5914
16	November	101645.6333	97384.06667	105123.2	49925.06667	107428.1333	100172.0667	100673.9	94954.73333	90964.46667	9925
17	December	96451.09677	111357.129	101385.5484	90766.87097	104208.0323	107328.2581	91452.3871	100385.0645	100006.0323	1003
18	⊟2007									
19	January	99244.45161	92360.87097	95035.48387	94500.06452	100859	106384.1613	97517.09677	94400.93548	94192.3871	9716
20	February	55604.89286	54460.07143	50373.42857	49423.32143	54354.28571	52607.75	59376.35714	103172.4643	61472.39286	6009
21	March	49109	50753.25806	46639.77419	52394.3871	44388.64516	65176.09677	55111.16129	95011.54839	50956.03226	566
22	April	51903.1	48034.66667	57647.63333	47240.66667	40055.5	54429.16667	54963.43333	65074.63333	49372.16667	5208
23	May	59308.67742	56871.51613	56505.87097	52992.90323	50136.09677	54323.41935	51859.83871	56896.12903	50550.16129	5438
24	June	49430.86667	51415.4	52587	50395.1	50160.5	47749	45799.2	52912.4	45755.93333	4957
25	July	49482.3871	53493.29032	47514.77419	57554.06452	60008.83871	58808.03226	50675.80645	53682.16129	51106.58065	5314
26	August	55422.80645	52062.58065	53052.19355	52474.12903	50937.25806	51459.87097	57011.83871	44289.74194	46858.70968	5195
27	September	52599.6	46238.56667	49818.43333	48654.3	57908.33333	53319.06667	52734.4	49153.56667	53717.96667	5157

7. On the **Quick Access Toolbar**, click the **Undo** button.

   Excel 2007 reverses the last change.

8. Right-click any data cell in the PivotTable, and then click **Value Field Settings**.

   The Value Field Settings dialog box opens.

9. Click the **Show values as** tab.

   The Show Values As tab appears.

10. In the **Show values as** list, click **% of row**.

11. Click **OK**.

   Excel 2007 changes how it calculates the values in the PivotTable.

	A	B	C	D	E	F	G	H	I	J	K	L
1												
2												
3	Sum of Volume	Column Labels										
4	Row Labels	Atlantic	Central	Midwest	Mountain West	North Central	Northeast	Northwest	Southeast	Southwest	Grand Total	
5	⊟ 2006											
6	January	10.75%	11.39%	10.06%	10.66%	11.27%	11.14%	11.18%	12.58%	10.98%	100.00%	
7	February	8.63%	7.88%	11.46%	8.69%	12.68%	10.13%	14.31%	11.14%	15.08%	100.00%	
8	March	11.40%	10.77%	10.81%	11.08%	10.49%	11.52%	13.05%	9.74%	11.12%	100.00%	
9	April	10.68%	11.43%	10.31%	12.22%	10.90%	11.19%	9.96%	12.05%	11.26%	100.00%	
10	May	10.76%	12.75%	10.75%	10.66%	10.72%	10.41%	11.45%	12.30%	10.21%	100.00%	
11	June	12.70%	10.54%	10.73%	11.42%	11.30%	11.47%	10.86%	10.47%	10.51%	100.00%	
12	July	10.94%	11.81%	10.19%	11.58%	11.50%	10.43%	12.68%	10.46%	10.40%	100.00%	
13	August	10.43%	10.83%	12.34%	11.98%	10.90%	11.13%	11.21%	11.47%	9.71%	100.00%	
14	September	10.95%	10.40%	12.25%	10.87%	9.23%	12.93%	12.00%	11.07%	10.31%	100.00%	
15	October	10.57%	10.37%	9.70%	10.03%	10.26%	10.52%	12.40%	8.65%	17.51%	100.00%	
16	November	11.38%	10.90%	11.77%	10.63%	12.03%	11.21%	11.27%	10.63%	10.18%	100.00%	
17	December	10.66%	12.33%	11.22%	10.05%	11.54%	11.88%	10.12%	11.11%	11.07%	100.00%	
18	⊟ 2007											
19	January	11.35%	10.56%	10.87%	10.81%	11.53%	12.17%	11.15%	10.79%	10.77%	100.00%	
20	February	10.28%	10.07%	9.31%	9.14%	10.05%	9.73%	10.98%	19.08%	11.37%	100.00%	
21	March	9.64%	9.96%	9.15%	10.28%	8.71%	12.79%	10.82%	18.65%	10.00%	100.00%	
22	April	11.07%	10.25%	12.30%	10.08%	8.55%	11.61%	11.73%	13.88%	10.53%	100.00%	
23	May	12.12%	11.62%	11.54%	10.83%	10.24%	11.10%	10.60%	11.62%	10.33%	100.00%	
24	June	11.08%	11.52%	11.79%	11.29%	11.24%	10.70%	10.26%	11.86%	10.25%	100.00%	
25	July	10.26%	11.09%	9.85%	11.93%	12.44%	12.19%	10.51%	11.13%	10.60%	100.00%	
26	August	11.85%	11.13%	11.35%	11.22%	10.89%	11.01%	12.19%	10.33%	10.02%	100.00%	
27	September	11.33%	9.96%	10.73%	10.48%	12.48%	11.49%	11.36%	10.59%	11.57%	100.00%	

12. On the **Quick Access Toolbar**, click the **Undo** button.

Excel 2007 reverses the last change.

13. On the **Design** tab, in the **Layout** group, click **Subtotals**, and then click **Show All Subtotals at Bottom of Group**.

Excel 2007 displays subtotals in the workbook.

14. Click the **Package Summary** sheet tab.

The Package Summary worksheet appears.

15. In cell C4, type =, but do not press Enter.

16. Click the **PivotTable** sheet tab.

The PivotTable worksheet appears.

17. Click cell K32, and then press Enter.

Excel 2007 creates the formula =GETPIVOTDATA("Volume",PivotTable!$A$3,"Year", 2007) in cell C4.

CLOSE the *Focusing* workbook.

Formatting PivotTables

PivotTables are the ideal tools for summarizing and examining large data tables, even those containing in excess of 10 or even 100,000 rows. Even though PivotTables often end up as compact summaries, you should do everything you can to make your data more comprehensible. One way to improve your data's readability is to apply a number format to the PivotTable Values field. To apply a number format to a field, right-click any cell in the field, and then click Number Format to display the Format Cells dialog box. Select or define the format you want to apply, and then click OK to enact the change.

See Also For more information on selecting and defining cell formats by using the Format Cells dialog box, see "Formatting Cells" in Chapter 5, "Changing Workbook Appearance."

Analysts often use PivotTables to summarize and examine organizational data with an eye to making important decisions about the company. For example, chief operating officer Jenny Lysaker might examine monthly package volumes handled by Consolidated Messenger and notice that there's a surge in package volume during the winter months in the United States.

Sum of Volume	Column Labels									
Row Labels	Atlantic	Central	Midwest	Mountain West	North Central	Northeast	Northwest	Southeast	Southwest	Grand Total
2006	23276049	23727556	23643436	23075900	24118888	24103492	25028389	23785488	24817582	215576788
January	2966264	3143004	2774877	2942544	3110234	3073073	3085352	3470295	3029490	27595133
February	1541726	1407340	2046448	1552098	2263148	1808452	2554130	1988929	2692383	17854654
March	1688027	1594434	1600920	1641026	1553349	1705210	1932304	1441894	1646946	14804110
April	1445436	1548205	1395802	1653829	1476188	1515414	1348145	1631240	1525005	13539264
May	1530319	1813746	1529086	1516453	1525048	1481044	1628489	1749378	1452226	14225789
June	1725770	1431518	1458009	1551719	1535838	1558516	1475038	1422265	1428581	13587254
July	1581340	1706190	1472534	1672400	1661673	1506772	1832445	1511712	1503100	14448166
August	1519538	1577651	1797139	1745152	1587655	1622240	1633582	1671246	1414763	14568966
September	1494735	1420065	1672046	1483296	1259651	1764576	1638024	1510884	1407402	13650679
October	1743541	1711810	1599927	1655866	1692811	1735857	2045639	1427066	2888565	16501082
November	3049369	2921522	3153696	2847752	3222844	3005162	3020217	2848642	2728934	26790138
December	2983904	3452071	3142952	2813773	3230449	3327176	2835024	3111937	3100187	28003553
2007	23760133	23274159	23246331	23247582	22561702	24586713	23604961	26736115	23300579	214318275
January	3076578	2863187	2946100	2929502	3126629	3297909	3023030	2926429	2919964	27109328
February	1556937	1524882	1410456	1383853	1521920	1473017	1662538	2888829	1721227	15143659
March	1522379	1573951	1445833	1624226	1376048	2020459	1708446	2945358	1579637	15795797
April	1557093	1441040	1729429	1417220	1201665	1632075	1648903	1952239	1481165	14061629
May	1838569	1763017	1751682	1642780	1554219	1684026	1607655	1763780	1567055	15172783
June	1482926	1542462	1577610	1511853	1504815	1432470	1373976	1587372	1372678	13386162
July	1533954	1658292	1472958	1784176	1860274	1823049	1570950	1664147	1584304	14952104
August	1718107	1613940	1644618	1626698	1579055	1595256	1767367	1496982	1452620	14494643
September	1577988	1387157	1494553	1459629	1737250	1599572	1582032	1474607	1611539	13924327

Excel 2007 extends the capabilities of your PivotTables by enabling you to apply a conditional format to the PivotTable cells. What's more, you can select whether to apply the conditional format to every cell in the Values area, to every cell at the same level as the selected cell (that is, a regular data cell, a subtotal cell, or a grand total cell) or to every cell that contains or draws its values from the selected cell's field (such as the Volume field in the previous example).

To apply a conditional format to a PivotTable field, click a cell in the Values area. On the Home tab, in the Styles group, click Conditional Formatting, and then create the desired conditional format. After you do, Excel 2007 displays a Formatting Options smart tag, which offers three options on how to apply the conditional format:

- Selected cells, which applies the conditional format to the selected cells only
- All cells showing *Sum of field_name* values, which applies the conditional format to every cell in the data area, regardless of whether the cell is in the data area, a subtotal row or column, or a grand total row or column
- All cells showing *Sum of field_name* values for fields, which applies the conditional format to every cell at the same level (for example, data cell, subtotal, or grand total) as the selected cells

See Also For more information on creating conditional formats, see "Changing the Appearance of Data Based on Its Value" in Chapter 5.

In Excel 2003 and earlier versions of the program, you were limited to a small number of formatting styles, called autoformats, which you could apply to a PivotTable. In Excel 2007, you can take full advantage of the Microsoft Office system enhanced formatting capabilities to apply existing formats to your PivotTables. Just as you can create data table formats, you can also create your own PivotTable formats to match your organization's desired color scheme.

To apply a PivotTable style, click any cell in the PivotTable and then, on the Design contextual tab, in the PivotTable Styles group, click the gallery item representing the style you want to apply. If you want to create your own PivotTable style, click the More button in the PivotTable Styles gallery (in the lower-right corner of the gallery), and then click New PivotTable Style to display the New PivotTable QuickStyle dialog box.

Type a name for the style in the Name field, click the first table element you want to customize, and then click Format. Use the controls in the Format Cells dialog box to change the element's appearance. After you click OK to close the Format Cells dialog box, the New PivotTable Quick Style dialog box Preview pane displays the style's appearance. If you want Excel 2007 to use the style by default, select the Set As Default PivotTable Quick Style For This Document check box. After you finish creating your formats, click OK to close the New PivotTable Quick Style dialog box and save your style.

The Design contextual tab contains many other tools you can use to format your PivotTable, but one of the most useful is the Banded Columns check box, which you can find in the PivotTable Style Options group. If you select a PivotTable style that offers banded rows as an option, selecting the Banded Rows check box turns banding on. If you prefer not to have Excel 2007 band the rows in your PivotTable, clearing the check box turns banding off.

In this exercise, you will apply a number format to a PivotTable values field, apply a PivotTable style, create your own PivotTable style, give your PivotTable banded rows, and apply a conditional format to a PivotTable.

USE the *Formatting* workbook. This practice file is located in the *Documents\Microsoft Press\Excel2007SBS\PivotTables* folder.

OPEN the *Formatting* workbook.

1. On the PivotTable worksheet, right-click any data cell, and then click **Number Format**.

   The Format Cells dialog box opens.

2. In the **Category** list, click **Number**.

   The Number tab page opens.

3. In the **Decimal places** field, type 0.

4. Select the **Use 1000 Separator (,)** check box.

5. Click **OK**.

   Excel 2007 reformats your PivotTable data.

Sum of Volume	Column Labels									
Row Labels	Atlantic	Central	Midwest	Mountain West	North Central	Northeast	Northwest	Southeast	Southwest	Grand Total
2006										
January	2,966,264	3,143,004	2,774,877	2,942,544	3,110,234	3,073,073	3,085,352	3,470,295	3,029,490	27,595,133
February	1,541,726	1,407,340	2,046,448	1,552,098	2,263,148	1,808,452	2,554,130	1,988,929	2,692,383	17,854,654
March	1,688,027	1,594,434	1,600,920	1,641,026	1,553,349	1,705,210	1,932,304	1,441,894	1,646,946	14,804,110
April	1,445,436	1,548,205	1,395,802	1,653,829	1,476,188	1,515,414	1,348,145	1,631,240	1,525,005	13,539,264
May	1,530,319	1,813,746	1,529,086	1,516,453	1,525,048	1,481,044	1,628,489	1,749,378	1,452,226	14,225,789
June	1,725,770	1,431,518	1,458,009	1,551,719	1,535,838	1,558,516	1,475,038	1,422,265	1,428,581	13,587,254
July	1,581,340	1,706,190	1,472,534	1,672,400	1,661,673	1,506,772	1,832,445	1,511,712	1,503,100	14,448,166
August	1,519,538	1,577,651	1,797,139	1,745,152	1,587,655	1,622,240	1,633,582	1,671,246	1,414,763	14,568,966
September	1,494,735	1,420,065	1,672,046	1,483,296	1,259,651	1,764,576	1,638,024	1,510,884	1,407,402	13,650,679
October	1,743,541	1,711,810	1,599,927	1,655,866	1,692,811	1,735,857	2,045,639	1,427,066	2,888,565	16,501,082
November	3,049,369	2,921,522	3,153,696	2,847,752	3,222,844	3,005,162	3,020,217	2,848,642	2,728,934	26,798,138
December	2,989,984	3,452,071	3,142,952	2,813,773	3,230,449	3,327,176	2,835,024	3,111,937	3,100,187	28,003,553
2006 Total	**23,276,049**	**23,727,556**	**23,643,436**	**23,075,908**	**24,118,888**	**24,103,492**	**25,028,389**	**23,785,488**	**24,817,582**	**215,576,788**
2007										
January	3,076,578	2,863,187	2,946,100	2,929,502	3,126,629	3,297,909	3,023,030	2,926,429	2,919,964	27,109,328
February	1,556,937	1,524,882	1,410,456	1,383,853	1,521,920	1,473,017	1,662,538	2,888,829	1,721,227	15,143,659
March	1,522,379	1,573,351	1,445,833	1,624,226	1,376,048	2,020,459	1,708,446	2,945,358	1,579,637	15,795,737

6. If necessary, on the **Design** contextual tab, in the **PivotTable Style Options** group, select the **Banded Rows** check box.

7. On the **Design** contextual tab, in the **PivotTable Styles** group, click the third style from the left (when you point to it, Excel 2007 displays a ScreenTip that reads **Pivot Style Light 2**).

Excel 2007 applies the PivotTable style.

Sum of Volume	Column Labels									
Row Labels	Atlantic	Central	Midwest	Mountain West	North Central	Northeast	Northwest	Southeast	Southwest	Grand Total
2006										
January	2,966,264	3,143,004	2,774,877	2,942,544	3,110,234	3,073,073	3,085,352	3,470,295	3,029,490	27,595,133
February	1,541,726	1,407,340	2,046,448	1,552,098	2,263,148	1,808,452	2,554,130	1,988,929	2,692,383	17,854,654
March	1,688,027	1,594,434	1,600,920	1,641,026	1,553,349	1,705,210	1,932,304	1,441,894	1,646,946	14,804,110
April	1,445,436	1,548,205	1,395,802	1,653,829	1,476,188	1,515,414	1,348,145	1,631,240	1,525,005	13,539,264
May	1,530,319	1,813,746	1,529,086	1,516,453	1,525,048	1,481,044	1,628,489	1,749,378	1,452,226	14,225,789
June	1,725,770	1,431,518	1,458,009	1,551,719	1,535,838	1,558,516	1,475,038	1,422,265	1,428,581	13,587,254
July	1,581,340	1,706,190	1,472,534	1,672,400	1,661,673	1,506,772	1,832,445	1,511,712	1,503,100	14,448,166
August	1,519,538	1,577,651	1,797,139	1,745,152	1,587,655	1,622,240	1,633,582	1,671,246	1,414,763	14,568,966
September	1,494,735	1,420,065	1,672,046	1,483,296	1,259,651	1,764,576	1,638,024	1,510,884	1,407,402	13,650,679
October	1,743,541	1,711,810	1,599,927	1,655,866	1,692,811	1,735,857	2,045,639	1,427,066	2,888,565	16,501,082
November	3,049,369	2,921,522	3,153,696	2,847,752	3,222,844	3,005,162	3,020,217	2,848,642	2,728,934	26,798,138
December	2,989,984	3,452,071	3,142,952	2,813,773	3,230,449	3,327,176	2,835,024	3,111,937	3,100,187	28,003,553
2006 Total	**23,276,049**	**23,727,556**	**23,643,436**	**23,075,908**	**24,118,888**	**24,103,492**	**25,028,389**	**23,785,488**	**24,817,582**	**215,576,788**
2007										
January	3,076,578	2,863,187	2,946,100	2,929,502	3,126,629	3,297,909	3,023,030	2,926,429	2,919,964	27,109,328
February	1,556,937	1,524,882	1,410,456	1,383,853	1,521,920	1,473,017	1,662,538	2,888,829	1,721,227	15,143,659
March	1,522,379	1,573,351	1,445,833	1,624,226	1,376,048	2,020,459	1,708,446	2,945,358	1,579,637	15,795,737

More

8. In the lower-right corner of the **PivotTable Styles** gallery, click the **More** button.

   The gallery expands.

9. Click **New PivotTable Style**.

   The New PivotTable Quick Style dialog box opens.

10. In the **Name** field, type Custom Style 1.

11. In the **Table Element** list, click **Header Row**, and then click **Format**.

    The Format Cells dialog box opens.

12. On the **Font** tab, in the **Color** list, click the white square.

13. On the **Border** tab, in the **Presets** area, click **Outline**.

14. On the **Fill** tab, in the **Background Color** area, click the purple square at the lower-right corner of the color palette.

15. Click **OK**.

    The Format Cells dialog box closes, and the style change appears in the Preview pane of the New PivotTable Quick Style dialog box.

16. In the **Table Element** list, click **Second Row Stripe**, and then click **Format**.

    The Format Cells dialog box opens.

17. On the **Fill** tab, in the middle part of the **Background Color** section, click the eighth square in the second row (it's a light, dusty purple).

18. Click **OK** twice.

    The Format Cells dialog box closes, and your format appears in the PivotTable Styles gallery.

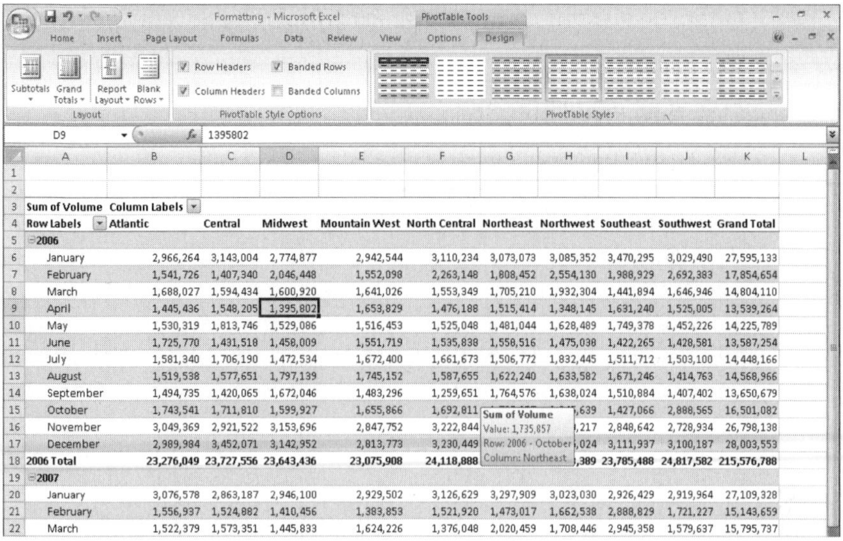

Sum of Volume	Column Labels									
Row Labels	Atlantic	Central	Midwest	Mountain West	North Central	Northeast	Northwest	Southeast	Southwest	Grand Total
2006										
January	2,966,264	3,143,004	2,774,877	2,942,544	3,110,234	3,073,073	3,085,352	3,470,295	3,029,490	27,595,133
February	1,541,726	1,407,340	2,046,448	1,552,098	2,263,148	1,808,452	2,554,130	1,988,929	2,692,383	17,854,654
March	1,688,027	1,594,434	1,600,920	1,641,026	1,553,349	1,705,210	1,932,304	1,441,894	1,646,946	14,804,110
April	1,445,436	1,548,205	1,395,802	1,653,829	1,476,188	1,515,414	1,348,145	1,631,240	1,525,005	13,539,264
May	1,530,319	1,813,746	1,529,086	1,516,453	1,525,048	1,481,044	1,628,489	1,749,378	1,452,226	14,225,789
June	1,725,770	1,431,518	1,458,009	1,551,719	1,535,838	1,558,516	1,475,030	1,422,265	1,428,581	13,587,254
July	1,581,340	1,706,190	1,472,534	1,672,400	1,661,673	1,506,772	1,832,445	1,511,712	1,503,100	14,448,166
August	1,519,538	1,577,651	1,797,139	1,745,152	1,587,655	1,622,240	1,633,582	1,671,246	1,414,763	14,568,966
September	1,494,735	1,420,065	1,672,046	1,483,296	1,259,651	1,764,576	1,638,024	1,510,884	1,407,402	13,650,679
October	1,743,541	1,711,810	1,599,927	1,655,866	1,692,811				2,888,565	16,501,082
November	3,049,369	2,921,522	3,153,696	2,847,752	3,222,844		217	2,848,642	2,728,934	26,798,138
December	2,989,984	3,452,071	3,142,952	2,813,773	3,230,449		024	3,111,937	3,100,187	28,003,553
2006 Total	23,276,049	23,727,556	23,643,436	23,075,908	24,118,888		389	23,785,488	24,817,582	215,576,788
2007										
January	3,076,578	2,863,187	2,946,100	2,929,502	3,126,629	3,297,909	3,023,030	2,926,429	2,919,964	27,109,328
February	1,556,937	1,524,882	1,410,456	1,383,853	1,521,920	1,473,017	1,662,538	2,888,829	1,721,227	15,143,659
March	1,522,379	1,573,351	1,445,833	1,624,226	1,376,048	2,020,459	1,708,446	2,945,358	1,579,637	15,795,737

(Tooltip box over the grid reads: Sum of Volume / Value: 1,735,857 / Row: 2006 - October / Column: Northeast)

19. Click the new style.

Excel 2007 formats your PivotTable using your custom PivotTable style.

20. On the **Design** contextual tab, in the **PivotTable Style Options** group, clear the **Banded Rows** check box.

Excel 2007 removes the banding from your PivotTable.

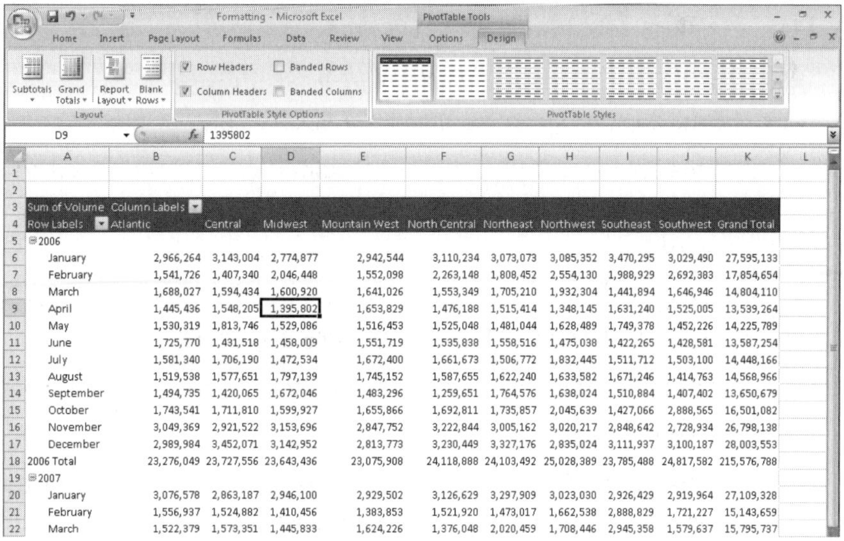

Sum of Volume	Column Labels									
Row Labels	Atlantic	Central	Midwest	Mountain West	North Central	Northeast	Northwest	Southeast	Southwest	Grand Total
2006										
January	2,966,264	3,143,004	2,774,877	2,942,544	3,110,234	3,073,073	3,085,352	3,470,295	3,029,490	27,595,133
February	1,541,726	1,407,340	2,046,448	1,552,098	2,263,148	1,808,452	2,554,130	1,988,929	2,692,383	17,854,654
March	1,688,027	1,594,434	1,600,920	1,641,026	1,553,349	1,705,210	1,932,304	1,441,894	1,646,946	14,804,110
April	1,445,436	1,548,205	1,395,802	1,653,829	1,476,188	1,515,414	1,348,145	1,631,240	1,525,005	13,539,264
May	1,530,319	1,813,746	1,529,086	1,516,453	1,525,048	1,481,044	1,628,489	1,749,378	1,452,226	14,225,789
June	1,725,770	1,431,518	1,458,009	1,551,719	1,535,838	1,558,516	1,475,030	1,422,265	1,428,581	13,587,254
July	1,581,340	1,706,190	1,472,534	1,672,400	1,661,673	1,506,772	1,832,445	1,511,712	1,503,100	14,448,166
August	1,519,538	1,577,651	1,797,139	1,745,152	1,587,655	1,622,240	1,633,582	1,671,246	1,414,763	14,568,966
September	1,494,735	1,420,065	1,672,046	1,483,296	1,259,651	1,764,576	1,638,024	1,510,884	1,407,402	13,650,679
October	1,743,541	1,711,810	1,599,927	1,655,866	1,692,811	1,735,857	2,045,639	1,427,066	2,888,565	16,501,082
November	3,049,369	2,921,522	3,153,696	2,847,752	3,222,844	3,005,162	3,020,217	2,848,642	2,728,934	26,798,138
December	2,989,984	3,452,071	3,142,952	2,813,773	3,230,449	3,327,176	2,835,024	3,111,937	3,100,187	28,003,553
2006 Total	23,276,049	23,727,556	23,643,436	23,075,908	24,118,888	24,103,492	25,028,389	23,785,488	24,817,582	215,576,788
2007										
January	3,076,578	2,863,187	2,946,100	2,929,502	3,126,629	3,297,909	3,023,030	2,926,429	2,919,964	27,109,328
February	1,556,937	1,524,882	1,410,456	1,383,853	1,521,920	1,473,017	1,662,538	2,888,829	1,721,227	15,143,659
March	1,522,379	1,573,351	1,445,833	1,624,226	1,376,048	2,020,459	1,708,446	2,945,358	1,579,637	15,795,737

21. Select the cell ranges K6:K17 and K20:K31.

22. On the **Home** tab, in the **Styles** group, click **Conditional Formatting**, point to **Color Scales**, and in the top row, click the three-color scale with red at the top.

Excel 2007 applies the conditional format to the selected cells.

CLOSE the *Formatting* workbook.

Creating PivotTables from External Data

Although most of the time you will create PivotTables from data stored in Excel 2007 worksheets, you can also bring data from outside sources into Excel 2007. For example, you might need to work with data created in another spreadsheet program with a file format that Excel 2007 can't read directly. Fortunately, you can export the data from the original program into a text file, which Excel 2007 then translates into a worksheet.

Spreadsheet programs store data in cells, so the goal of representing spreadsheet data in a text file is to indicate where the contents of one cell end and those of the next cell begin. The character that marks the end of a cell is a delimiter, in that it marks the end (or "limit") of a cell. The most common cell delimiter is the comma, so the delimited sequence *15, 18, 24, 28* represents data in four cells. The problem with using commas to delimit financial data is that larger values—such as *52,802*—can be written by using commas as thousands markers. To avoid confusion when importing a text file, the most commonly used delimiter for financial data is the Tab character.

To import data from a text file, on the Data tab, in the Get External Data group, click From Text to display the Import Text File dialog box.

From within the Import Text File dialog box, you browse to the directory that contains the text file you want to import. Double-clicking the file launches the Text Import Wizard.

The first page of the Text Import Wizard enables you to indicate whether the data file you are importing is Delimited or Fixed Width; Fixed Width means that each cell value will fall within a specific position in the file. Clicking Next to accept the default choice, Delimited (which Excel 2007 assigns after examining the data source you selected), advances you to the next wizard screen.

This screen enables you to choose the delimiter for the file (in this case, Excel 2007 detected tabs in the file and selected the Tab check box for you) and gives you a preview of what the text file will look like when imported. Clicking Next advances you to the final wizard screen.

This screen enables you to change the data type and formatting of the columns in your data list. Because you'll assign number styles and PivotTable Quick Styles after you create the PivotTable, you can click Finish to import the data into your worksheet. After the data is in Excel 2007, you can work with it normally.

In this exercise, you will import a data list into Excel 2007 from a text file and then create a PivotTable based on that list.

USE the *Creating* text file.

1. On the **Data** tab, in the **Get External Data** group, click **From Text**.

   The Import Text File dialog box opens.

2. Navigate to the *Documents\Microsoft Press\Excel2007SBS\PivotTables* folder, and then double-click **Creating.txt**.

   The Text Import Wizard starts.

3. Verify that the **Delimited** option is selected, and then click **Next**.

   The next Text Import Wizard page appears.

4. In the **Delimiters** section, verify that the **Tab** check box is selected and also verify that the data displayed in the **Data preview** area reflects the structure you expect.

5. Click **Finish**.

   The Import Data dialog box opens.

6. Verify that the **Existing worksheet** option is selected, and then click **OK**.

   Excel 2007 imports the data into your workbook.

7. On the **Insert** tab, in the **Tables** group, click **PivotTable**.

   The Create PivotTable dialog box opens.

8. Verify that the **Select a table or range** option is selected, that the range Sheet1$A$1:$H$6571 appears in the **Table/Range** field, and that the **New Worksheet** option is selected.

9. Click **OK**.

   Excel 2007 creates a new worksheet.

10. In the **PivotTable Field List** task pane, drag the **Volume** field header to the **Values** area.

11. Drag the **Weekday** field header to the **Column Labels** area.

12. Drag the **Center** field header to the **Row Labels** data area.

Sum of Volume	Column Labels							
Row Labels	Sunday	Monday	Tuesday	Wednesday	Thursday	Friday	Saturday	Grand Total
Atlantic	6681849	6718491	6065016	6999145	6647852	6592351	7331478	47036182
Central	6930783	6787961	6530917	6543992	6915836	6523218	6769008	47001715
Midwest	6923875	6358123	6705800	6629517	6467518	7011908	6793026	46889767
Mountain West	6673339	6661710	6698354	6563217	6788244	6457215	6481411	46323490
North Central	6937060	6295847	6767203	7093316	6467078	6443849	6676237	46680590
Northeast	7166215	6941642	7068465	6808329	6708788	7049366	6947400	48690205
Northwest	6974586	6750727	7213121	7087334	6918003	6639912	7049667	48633350
Southeast	7229898	7272423	7600639	7193113	6870974	7236536	7118020	50521603
Southwest	7148300	6736137	7145226	7010575	6736377	6863256	6478290	48118161
Grand Total	62665905	60523061	61794741	61928530	60520670	60817611	61644537	429895063

Save

13. On the **Quick Access Toolbar**, click the **Save** button.

The Save As dialog box opens.

14. Browse to the *Documents\Microsoft Press\Excel2007SBS\PivotTables* folder.

15. In the **File name** field, type *Imported Data*.

16. Click **OK**.

Excel 2007 saves your file.

CLOSE the *Imported Data* workbook. If you are not continuing directly to the next chapter, exit Excel.

Key Points

- A PivotTable is a versatile tool you can use to rearrange your data dynamically, enabling you to emphasize different aspects of your data without creating new worksheets.

- PivotTable data must be formatted as a list. Using a data table as the PivotTable data source enables you to streamline the creation process by referring to the table name instead of being required to select the entire range that contains the data you want to summarize.

- Excel 2007 comes with many attractive styles for PivotTables; you'll probably find one you like.

- The PivotTable Field List task pane enables you to create your PivotTable by using a straightforward, compact tool.

- Just as you can limit the data shown in a static worksheet, you can use filters to limit the data shown in a PivotTable.

- If you have data in a compatible format, such as a text file, you can import that data into Excel 2007 and create a PivotTable from it.

Chapter at a Glance

Customize the appearance of charts, **page 242**

Create dynamic charts by using PivotCharts, **page 251**

Find trends in your data, **page 248**

Create diagrams by using SmartArt, **page 256**

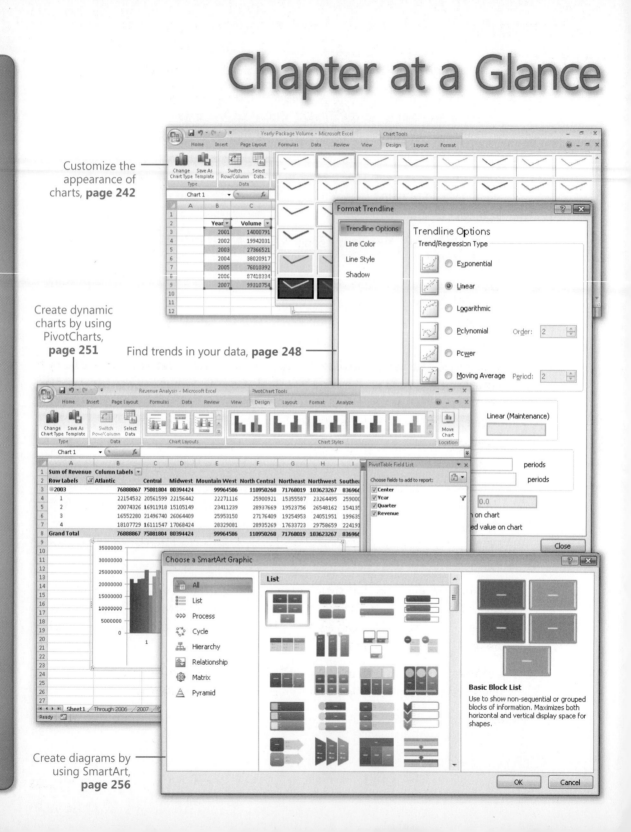

11 Creating Charts and Graphics

In this chapter, you will learn to:

✔ Create charts.

✔ Customize the appearance of charts.

✔ Find trends in your data.

✔ Create dynamic charts by using PivotCharts.

✔ Create diagrams by using SmartArt.

When you enter data into a Microsoft Office Excel 2007 worksheet, you create a record of important events, whether they are individual sales, sales for an hour of a day, or the price of a product. What a list of values in cells can't communicate easily, however, is the overall trends in the data. The best way to communicate trends in a large collection of data is by creating a *chart*, which summarizes data visually.

You have a great deal of control over your charts' appearance—you can change the color of any chart element, choose a different chart type to better summarize the underlying data, and change the display properties of text and numbers in a chart. If the data in the worksheet used to create a chart represents a progression through time, such as sales over a number of months, you can have Excel 2007 extrapolate future sales and add a *trendlline* to the graph representing that prediction.

Just as you can create PivotTable dynamic views to reorganize a data list dynamically, you can create a *PivotChart* dynamic view that reflects the contents and organization of the associated PivotTable. You can also create diagrams, such as organizational charts, that are useful in many organizations.

In this chapter, you'll learn how to create a chart and customize its elements, find trends in your overall data, create dynamic charts, and create and format diagrams.

See Also Do you need only a quick refresher on the topics in this chapter? See the Quick Reference section at the beginning of this book.

Important Before you can use the practice files in this chapter, you need to install them from the book's companion CD to their default location. See "Using the Companion CD" at the beginning of this book for more information.

Creating Charts

To create a chart, select the data you want to summarize visually and then, on the Insert tab, in the Charts group, click the type of chart you want to create to have Excel 2007 display the available chart subtypes.

When you click your desired chart subtype, Excel 2007 creates the chart using the default layout and color scheme defined in your workbook's theme. The following graphic shows a column chart and the data used to create it.

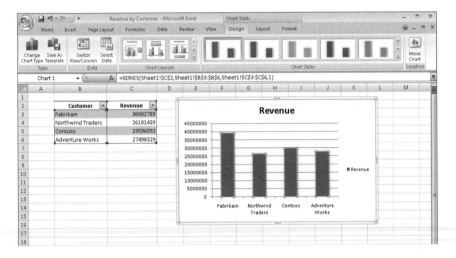

If Excel 2007 doesn't plot your data the way you want, you can change the axis on which Excel 2007 plots a data column. The most common situation in which Excel 2007 plots data incorrectly is when the column you want to provide values for the horizontal axis contains numerical data. For example, if your data list contains a Year column and a Volume column, Excel 2007 plots both of those columns in the body of the chart and creates a sequential series to provide values for the horizontal axis. If your data set contains one column of text values and another column of numerical values, the Excel 2007 chart engine plots the data correctly.

You can change which data it applies to the vertical axis (also known as the y-axis) and the horizontal axis (also known as the x-axis). To make that change, select the chart and then, on the Design tab, in the Data group, click Select Data to display the Select Data Source dialog box.

The Year column doesn't belong in the Legend Entries (Series) pane, which corresponds to a column chart's vertical axis. To remove a column from an axis, select the column's name, and then click Remove. To add the column to the Horizontal (Category) Axis Labels pane, click that pane's Edit button to display the Axis Labels dialog box.

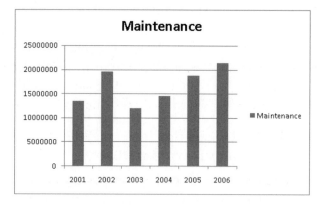

In the Axis Labels dialog box, click the Contract Dialog button at the right edge of the Axis Label Range field, select the cells to provide the values for the horizontal axis (not including the column header, if any), click the Expand Dialog button, and then click OK. Click OK again to close the Select Data Source dialog box and revise your chart.

After you create your chart, you can change its size to reflect whether you want the chart to dominate its worksheet or take on a role as another informative element on the worksheet. For example, Gary Schare, the chief executive officer of Consolidated Messenger, could create a dashboard to summarize the performance of each of his company's business units. In that case, he would display multiple measures on the same worksheet, so he would want to make his charts as small as possible without sacrificing comprehensibility.

To resize a chart, select the chart, and then drag one of the handles on the chart's edges. Handles in the middle of the edges enable you to resize the chart in one direction. Dragging a handle on the left or right edge enables you to make the chart narrower or wider, whereas dragging the handles on the chart's upper and lower edges enable you to make the chart shorter or taller. Dragging a corner handle enables you to change the chart's height and width at the same time; holding down the Shift key as you drag the corner handle changes the chart's size proportionally.

Just as you can control a chart's size, you can also control its location. To move a chart within a worksheet, drag the chart to the desired location. If you want to move the chart to a new worksheet, click the chart and then, on the Design contextual tab, in the Location group, click Move Chart to display the Move Chart dialog box.

To move the chart to a new chart sheet, select the New Sheet option and type the new sheet's name in the accompanying field. Selecting the New Sheet option creates a chart sheet, which contains only your chart. You can still resize the chart on that sheet, but when Excel 2007 creates the new chart sheet, the chart takes up the full sheet.

To move the chart to an existing worksheet, select the Object In option and then, in the Object In list, click the worksheet to which you want to move the chart.

In this exercise, you will create a chart, change how the chart plots your data, resize your chart, move your chart within a worksheet, and move your chart to its own chart sheet.

> **USE** the *Yearly Package Volume* workbook. This practice file is located in the *Documents\ Microsoft Press\Excel2007SBS\Charting* folder.
> **BE SURE TO** start Excel 2007 before beginning this exercise.
> **OPEN** the *Yearly Package Volume* workbook.

1. On the **Data** worksheet, click any cell in the data table.

2. On the **Insert** tab, in the **Charts** group, click **Bar** and then, in the **2D Bar** group, click the first chart subtype (the chart subtype is named *Clustered Bar*).

   Excel 2007 creates the chart, with both the Year and Volume data series plotted in the body of the chart.

3. On the **Design** tab, in the **Data** group, click **Select Data**.

   The Select Data Source dialog box opens.

4. In the **Legend Entries (Series)** area, click **Year**.

5. Click **Remove**.

   The Year series disappears.

6. In the **Horizontal (Category) Axis Labels** area, click **Edit**.

   The Axis Labels dialog box opens.

7. Select cells B3:B9, and then click **OK**.

   The Axis Labels dialog box closes, and the Select Data Source dialog box reappears with the years in the Horizontal (Category) Axis Labels area.

8. Click **OK**.

   Excel 2007 redraws your chart, using the years as the values for the horizontal axis.

9. Point to an edge of the chart.

   The mouse pointer changes to a four-headed arrow.

10. Drag the chart up and to the left so that it covers the data table.

11. On the **Design** tab, in the **Location** group, click **Move Chart**.

    The Move Chart dialog box opens.

12. Click **New sheet**, and then click **OK**.

    Your chart appears on its own chart sheet.

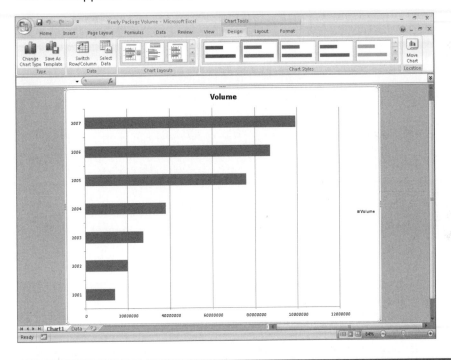

CLOSE the *Yearly Package Volume* workbook.

Customizing the Appearance of Charts

If you want to change a chart's appearance, select the chart and then, on the Design tab, click a style in the Chart Styles gallery. The gallery contains far more chart styles than are shown on the Ribbon—to select a new look for your chart, click the More button at the gallery's lower-right corner, and then click the design you want.

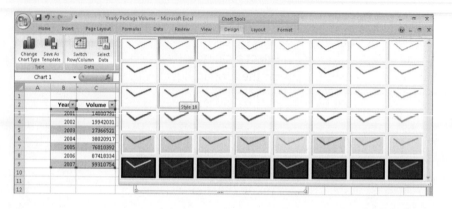

> **Important** The styles in the Chart Styles gallery are tied to your workbook's theme. If you change your workbook's theme, Excel 2007 changes your chart's appearance to reflect the new theme's colors.

When you create a chart by using the tools in the Insert tab's Charts group, Excel 2007 creates an attractive chart that focuses on the data. In most cases, the chart has a title, legend (list of data series displayed in the chart), horizontal lines in the body of the chart to make it easier to discern individual values, and axis labels. If you want to create a chart that has more or different elements, such as by adding data labels to each data point plotted on your chart, you can do so by selecting the chart and then, on the Design tab, in the Chart Layouts group, clicking the layout you want.

If you don't find the exact chart layout you like, you can use the tools on the Layout contextual tab to control each element's appearance and placement.

In the Axes group, clicking Gridlines enables you to determine whether the chart displays horizontal and vertical gridlines and, if it does, at what value intervals they should appear.

In addition to changing your chart's layout, you can control the appearance of each element within the chart. To select a chart element to format, click that element. For example, if you want to change the formatting of the data series named Volume in the column chart shown in the previous graphic, clicking any column in the series selects the entire series. Any formatting changes you make now apply to every point in the entire series. If you want to change a single data point, select the entire series, and then click the chart element (for example, a column) that represents the data point you want to change. For example, you can highlight the column representing the year 2005 in the chart shown in the previous graphic.

You can display a list of the selectable chart elements by selecting the chart and then, on the Format tab, in the Current Selection group, clicking the Chart Elements control arrow. Just click the desired chart element to select it.

After you select the chart element, you can drag one of the elements' handles to resize the chart or drag the element to another location within the chart. To change the chart element's format, use the tools and dialog box launchers in the Shape Styles, Word Art Styles, Arrange, and Size groups to change the element's appearance. You can also select the chart element and then, on the Format tab, in the Current Selection group, click Format Selection to display a Format dialog box that enables you to change the chart element's fill, line, line style, shadow, 3-D format, and alignment.

If you think you want to apply the same set of changes to charts you'll create in the future, you can save your chart as a chart template. When you select the data you want to summarize visually and apply the chart template, you'll create consistently formatted charts in a minimum of steps. To save a chart as a chart template, select the chart you want to use as a template and then, on the Design tab, in the Type group, click Save Template. Use the controls in the dialog box that appears to name and save your template. Then, to create a chart based on that template, select the data you want to summarize and then, on the Insert tab, in the Charts group, click any chart type, and then click All Chart Types to display the Create Charts dialog box. Under Choose A Chart Type, click Templates, and then click the template you want to use.

> **Tip** You can apply a template to an existing chart by selecting the chart and then, on the Design tab, in the Type group, clicking Change Chart Type to display the Change Chart Type dialog box. Click Templates, and then click the template you want to use.

In this exercise, you will change a chart's layout, apply a new Chart Style, reposition the chart's legend, change the number format of the values on the vertical axis, and save the chart as a chart template.

> **USE** the *Volume by Center* workbook. This practice file is located in the *Documents\Microsoft Press\Excel2007SBS\Charting* folder.
>
> **OPEN** the *Volume by Center* workbook.

1. On the **Presentation** worksheet, select the chart.

2. On the **Design** tab, in the **Chart Layouts** group, click the first chart layout (its screen tip says the layout name is *Layout 1*).

   Excel 2007 changes the chart's layout.

3. On the **Design** contextual tab, in the **Chart Styles** group, click the **More** button.

   The Chart Styles gallery expands.

4. Click **Style 7** (it's the next-to-last style on the top row of the gallery).

   Excel 2007 changes the chart's style.

5. Right-click the values on the vertical axis, and then click **Format Axis**.

   The Format Axis dialog box opens.

6. In the left pane, click **Number**.

   The Format Axis dialog box displays the Number tab.

7. In the **Category** list, click **Number**.

   The Format Axis dialog box displays the Number style's controls.

8. In the **Decimal places** field, type 0.

9. Select the **Use 1000 Separator (,)** check box.

10. Click **Close**.

   Excel 2007 changes the format of the values on the vertical axis.

11. On the **Design** contextual tab, in the **Type** group, click **Save As Template**.

The Save Chart Template dialog box opens.

12. In the **File name** field, type Cool Blue.

13. Click **Save**.

Excel 2007 saves your template.

14. On the tab bar, click the **Yearly Summary** sheet tab.

The Yearly Summary worksheet appears.

15. Select the chart and then, on the **Design** tab, in the **Type** group, click **Change Chart Type**.

The Change Chart Type dialog box opens.

16. Click **Templates**.

The My Templates list appears.

17. Click the **Cool Blue** custom template, and then click **OK**.

Excel 2007 applies the template to your chart.

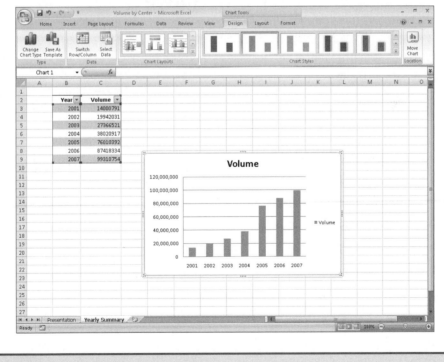

CLOSE the *Volume by Center* workbook.

Finding Trends in Your Data

You can use the data in Excel 2007 workbooks to discover how your business has performed in the past, but you can also have Excel 2007 make its best guess as to future shipping revenues if the current trend continues. As an example, consider the following graph for Consolidated Messenger.

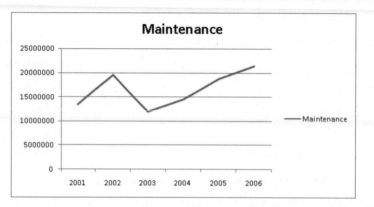

This graph shows the fleet maintenance costs for the years 2001 through 2006. The total has increased from 2001 to 2006, but the growth hasn't been uniform, so guessing how much maintenance costs would increase if the overall trend continued would require difficult mathematical computations. Fortunately, Excel 2007 knows that math. To have Excel 2007 project future values in the maintenance costs data series, click the chart and then, on the Layout tab, in the Analysis group, click Trendline. Click More Trendline Options to display the Format Trendline dialog box.

The Trendline Options tab of the Format Trendline dialog box enables you to choose the data distribution that Excel 2007 should expect when it makes its projection. The right choice for most business data is Linear—the other distributions (such as Exponential, Logarithmic, and Polynomial) are used for scientific and operations research applications.

Tip If you don't know which distribution to choose, try Linear first.

After you pick the distribution type, you need to tell Excel 2007 how far ahead to project the data trend. The horizontal axis of the chart used in this example shows revenues by year from 2001 to 2006. To tell Excel 2007 how far in the future to look, type a number in the Forecast section's Forward box. In this case, to look ahead one year, type 1 in the Forward box, and then click OK to add the trendline to the chart.

Tip When you click the Trendline button in the Analysis group, one of the options Excel 2007 displays is Linear Forecast Trendline, which adds a trendline with a two-period forecast.

As with other chart elements, you can double-click the trendline to open a formatting dialog box and change the line's appearance.

In this exercise, you will add a trendline to a chart.

USE the *Future Volumes* workbook. This practice file is located in the *Documents\Microsoft Press\Excel2007SBS\Charting* folder.

OPEN the *Future Volumes* workbook.

1. Select the chart.

2. On the **Layout** contextual tab, in the **Analysis** group, click **Trendline**, and then click **More Trendline Options**.

   The Format Trendline dialog box opens.

3. In the **Trend/Regression Type** area, click **Linear**.

4. In the **Forecast** area, in the **Forward** field, type 3.

5. Click **Close**.

   Excel 2007 adds the trendline to the chart.

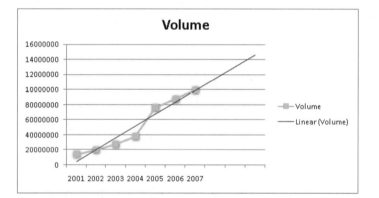

CLOSE the *Future Volumes* workbook.

Creating Dynamic Charts by Using PivotCharts

Just as you can create tables that you can reorganize on the fly to emphasize different aspects of the data in a list, you can also create dynamic charts, or PivotCharts, to reflect the contents and organization of a PivotTable.

Creating a PivotChart is fairly straightforward. Just click any cell in a list or data table you would use to create a PivotTable, and then click the Insert tab. In the Tables group, in the PivotTable list, click PivotChart. In a worksheet with an existing PivotTable, click a cell in the PivotTable, display the Insert tab and then, in the Charts group, click the type of chart you want to create.

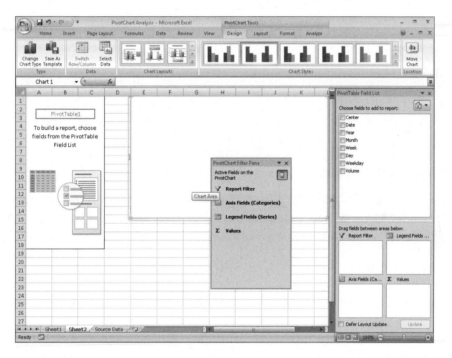

Any changes to the PivotTable on which the PivotChart is based are reflected in the PivotChart. For example, if the data in an underlying data list changes, clicking the Refresh Data button in the Data group on the Options contextual tab will change the PivotChart to reflect the new data. Also, you can filter the contents of the PivotTable shown here by clicking 2003 in the Year list and then clicking OK. The PivotTable then shows revenues from 2003. The PivotChart also reflects the filter.

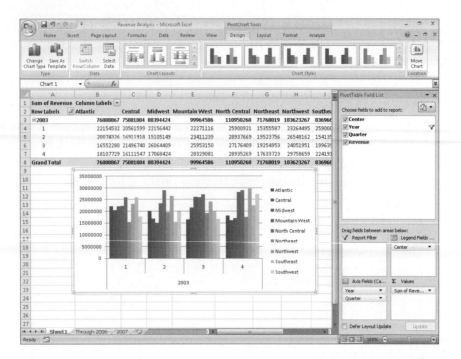

See Also For more information on manipulating PivotTables, see "Filtering, Showing, and Hiding PivotTable Data" in Chapter 10, "Creating Dynamic Lists by Using PivotTables."

The PivotChart has controls with which you can filter the data in the PivotChart and PivotTable. Clicking the Weekday arrow, clicking (All) in the list that appears, and then clicking OK will restore the PivotChart to its original configuration.

If you ever want to change the chart type of an existing chart, you can do so by selecting the chart and then, on the Design tab, in the Type group, clicking Change Chart Type to display the Change Chart Type dialog box. When you select the desired type and click OK, Excel 2007 re-creates your chart.

> **Important** If your data is the wrong type to be represented by the chart type you select, Excel 2007 displays an error message.

In this exercise, you will create a PivotTable and associated PivotChart, change the underlying data and update the PivotChart to reflect that change, and then change the PivotChart's type.

> **USE** the *Revenue Analysis* workbook. This practice file is located in the *Documents\Microsoft Press\Excel2007SBS\Charting* folder.
>
> **OPEN** the *Revenue Analysis* workbook.

1. On the **Through 2006** worksheet, click any cell in the data table.

PivotTable

Insert PivotTable

2. On the **Insert** tab, in the **Tables** group, click the **PivotTable** arrow and then, in the list that appears, click **PivotChart**.

   The Create PivotTable With PivotChart dialog box opens.

   Create PivotTable with PivotChart

   Choose the data that you want to analyze
   - ⦿ Select a table or range
     - Table/Range: QuarterlyRevenue
   - ⦾ Use an external data source
     - Choose Connection...
     - Connection name:

   Choose where you want the PivotTable and PivotChart to be placed
   - ⦿ New Worksheet
   - ⦾ Existing Worksheet
     - Location:

   OK   Cancel

3. Verify that the QuarterlyRevenue table appears in the **Table/Range** field and that the **New Worksheet** option is selected.

4. Click **OK**.

   Excel 2007 creates the PivotTable and associated PivotChart.

5. In the **PivotTable Field List** task pane, drag the **Center** field header from the **Choose fields to add to report** area to the **Legend Fields** area.

6. Drag the **Year** field header from the **Choose fields to add to report** pane to the **Axis Fields** area.

7. Drag the **Quarter** field header from the **Choose fields to add to report** area to the **Axis Fields** area, positioning it below the **Year** field header.

8. Drag the **Revenue** field header from the **Choose fields to add to report** area to the **Values** area.

Excel 2007 updates the PivotChart to reflect the field placements.

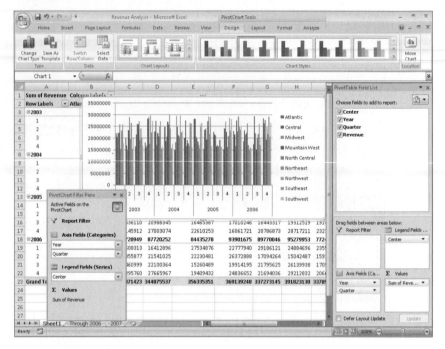

9. Click the **2007** sheet tab.

The 2007 worksheet appears.

10. Select the data in cells B2:E10, and then press ⌃Ctrl+C.

Excel 2007 copies the data to the Clipboard.

11. On the tab bar, click the **Through 2006** sheet tab.

The Through 2006 worksheet appears.

12. Select cell B147, and then press ⌃Ctrl+V.

Excel 2007 pastes the data into the worksheet and includes it in the table.

13. Click the tab of the worksheet that contains the PivotChart.

The PivotChart appears.

14. Select the PivotChart and then, on the **Analyze** contextual tab, in the **Data** group, click **Refresh**.

Excel 2007 adds the new table data to your PivotChart.

15. On the **Design** contextual tab, in the **Type** group, click **Change Chart Type**.

The Change Chart Type dialog box opens.

16. Click **Line**, and then click the second Line chart subtype.

17. Click **OK**.

Excel 2007 changes your PivotChart to a line chart.

18. In the **PivotTable Field List** task pane, in the **Choose fields to add to report** area, click the **Center** field header.

19. Click the filter arrow that appears and then, in the filter menu, clear the **Select All** check box.

Excel 2007 removes the check boxes from the filter list items.

20. Select the **Northeast** check box, and then click **OK**.

Excel 2007 filters the PivotChart.

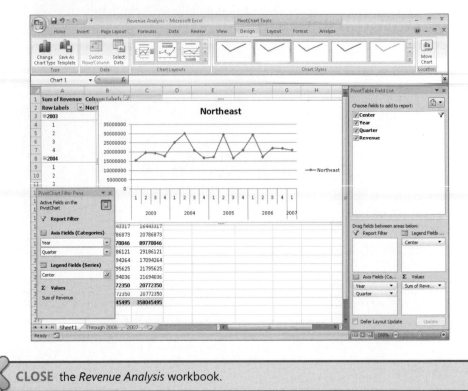

CLOSE the *Revenue Analysis* workbook.

Creating Diagrams by Using SmartArt

As an international delivery company, Consolidated Messenger's business processes are quite complex. Many times, chief operating officer Jenny Lysaker summarizes the company's processes for the board of directors by creating diagrams. Excel 2007 has just the tool she needs to create those diagrams: SmartArt. To create a SmartArt graphic, on the Insert tab, in the Illustrations group, click SmartArt to display the Choose A SmartArt Graphic dialog box.

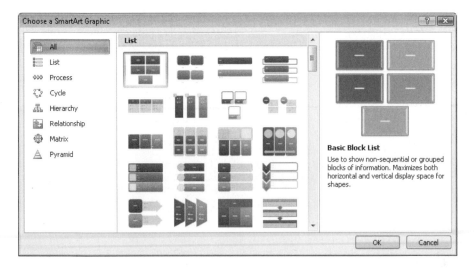

See Also For more information on adding pictures from existing files to your worksheets, see "Adding Images to Worksheets" in Chapter 5, "Changing Workbook Appearance."

Clicking one of the buttons in the Choose A SmartArt Graphic dialog box selects the type of diagram the button represents and causes a description of the diagram type to appear in the rightmost pane of the dialog box. Clicking All displays every available SmartArt graphic type. The following table lists the seven types of diagrams you can create by using the Choose A SmartArt Graphic dialog box.

Diagram	Description
List	Shows a series of items that typically require a large amount of text to explain.
Process	Shows a progression of sequential steps through a task, process, or workflow.
Hierarchy	Shows hierarchical relationships, such as those within a company.
Cycle	Shows a process with a continuous cycle or to show relationships of a core element.
Relationship	Shows the relationships between two or more items.
Pyramid diagram	Shows proportional, foundation-based, or hierarchical relationships such as a series of skills.
Matrix diagram	Shows the relationship of components to a whole by using quadrants.

> **Tip** Some of the diagram types can be used to illustrate several types of relationships. Be sure to examine all your options when you decide on the type of diagram to use to illustrate your point.

After you click the button representing the type of diagram you want to create, clicking OK adds the diagram to your worksheet.

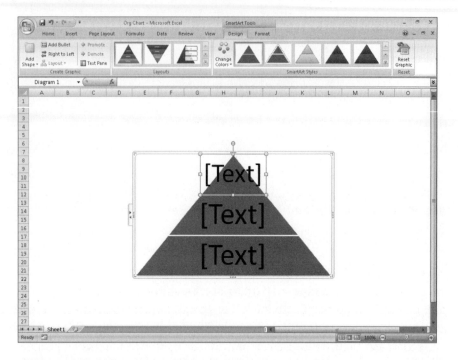

While the diagram is selected, Excel 2007 displays the SmartArt Tools contextual tabs named Design and Format. You can use the tools on the Design contextual tab to change the graphic's layout, style, or color scheme. The Design contextual tab also contains the Create Graphic group, which is home to tools you can use to add a shape to the SmartArt graphic, add text to the graphic, and promote or demote shapes within the graphic.

As an example, consider a process diagram that describes how Consolidated Messenger handles a package within one of the company's regional distribution centers.

The Text Pane, located to the left of the SmartArt graphic, enables you to add text to a shape without having to click and type within the shape. If you enter the process steps in the wrong order, you can move a shape by right-clicking the shape you want to move and then clicking Cut on the shortcut menu that appears. To paste the shape back into the graphic, right-click the shape to the left of where you want the pasted shape to appear, and then click Paste. For example, if you have a five-step process and accidentally switch the second and third steps, you can move the third step to the second position by right-clicking the third step, clicking Cut, right-clicking the first shape, and then clicking Paste.

If you want to add a shape to a SmartArt graphic, such as add a step to a process, click a shape next to the position you want the new shape to occupy and then, on the Design contextual tab, in the Create Graphic group, click Add Shape, and then click the option that represents where you want the new shape to appear in relation to the selected shape.

> **Tip** The options that appear when you click Add Shape depend on the type of SmartArt graphic you created and which graphic element is selected. For an organizational chart, the options are Add Shape After, Add Shape Before, Add Shape Above, Add Shape Below, and Add Assistant.

You can edit the graphic's elements by using the controls on the Formatting contextual tab as well as by right-clicking the shape and then clicking Format Shape to display the Format Shape dialog box. If you have selected the text in a shape, you can use the tools in the Font group on the Home tab to change the text's appearance.

> **Tip**   The controls in the Format Shape dialog box enable you to change the shape's fill color, borders, shadow, 3-D appearance, and text box properties.

In this exercise, you will create an organization chart, fill in the shapes, delete a shape, add a shape, change the layout of the diagram without changing the information it embodies, and change the formatting of one of the diagram elements.

> **USE** the *Org Chart* workbook. This practice file is located in the *Documents\Microsoft Press\Excel2007SBS\Charting* folder.
>
> **OPEN** the *Org Chart* workbook.

1. On the **Insert** tab, in the **Illustrations** group, click **SmartArt**.

The Choose A SmartArt Graphic dialog box opens.

2. Click **Hierarchy**.

The Hierarchy graphic subtypes appear.

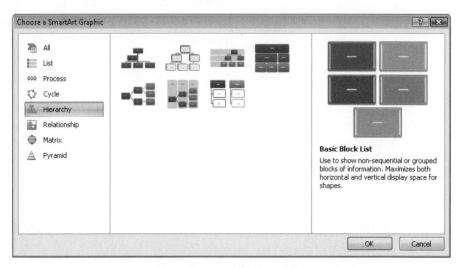

3. Click the first subtype (**Organization Chart**), and then click **OK**.

Excel 2007 creates the organization chart graphic.

4. In the **Type your text here** pane, in the first text box, type CEO, and then press the ⬇ key.

The value CEO appears in the shape at the top level of the organization chart.

5. In the SmartArt diagram, right-click the assistant box, located below the CEO shape, and then click **Cut**.

Excel 2007 removes the shape and moves the shapes on the third level of the organization chart to the second level.

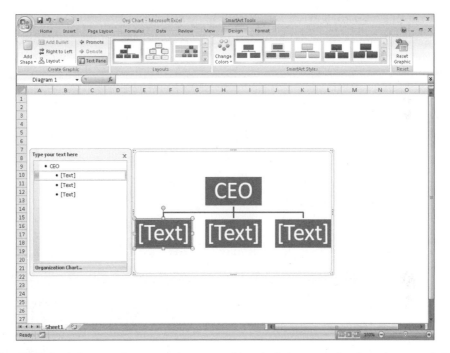

6. Click the leftmost shape on the second level of the organization chart, and then type COO.

7. Click the middle shape on the second level of the organization chart, and then type CIO.

8. Click the rightmost shape on the second level of the organization chart, and then type CFO.

9. Click the CFO shape. On the **Design** contextual tab, in the **Create Graphic** group, in the **Add Shape** list, click **Add Shape Below**.

A new shape appears below the CFO shape.

10. In the new shape, type Comptroller.

11. On the **Design** contextual tab, in the **Layouts** group, click the second layout.

    Excel 2007 applies the new layout to your organization chart.

12. Right-click the Comptroller shape, and then click **Format Shape**.

    The Format Shape dialog box opens.

13. If necessary, click the **Fill** category.

    Excel 2007 displays the fill controls.

14. Verify that the **Solid fill** option is selected, click the **Color** control and then, in the **Standard** color area of the color picker, click the red square.

15. Click **Close**.

    Excel 2007 changes the shape's fill to red.

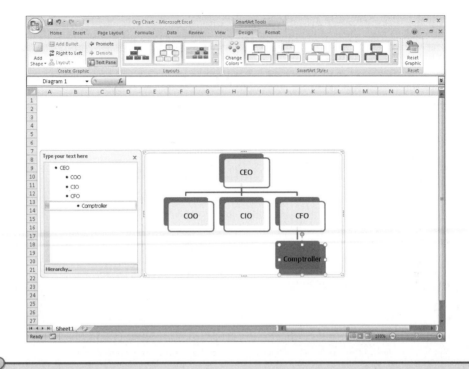

CLOSE the *Org Chart* workbook. If you are not continuing directly to the next chapter, exit Excel.

Key Points

- You can use charts to summarize large sets of data in an easy-to-follow visual format.
- You're not stuck with the chart you create; if you want to change it, you can.
- If you format a lot of your charts the same way, creating a chart template can save you a lot of work in the future.
- Adding chart labels and a legend makes your chart much easier to follow.
- If your chart data represents a series of events over time (such as monthly or yearly sales), you can use trendline analysis to extrapolate future events based on the past data.
- A PivotChart enables you to rearrange your chart on the fly, emphasizing different aspects of the same data without having to create a new chart for each view.
- Excel 2007 enables you to quickly create and modify common business and organizational diagrams, such as organization charts and process diagrams.

Chapter at a Glance

Add headers and footers to printed pages, **page 266**

Prepare worksheets for printing, **page 271**

Print data lists, **page 279**

Print parts of data lists, **page 281**

Print charts, **page 286**

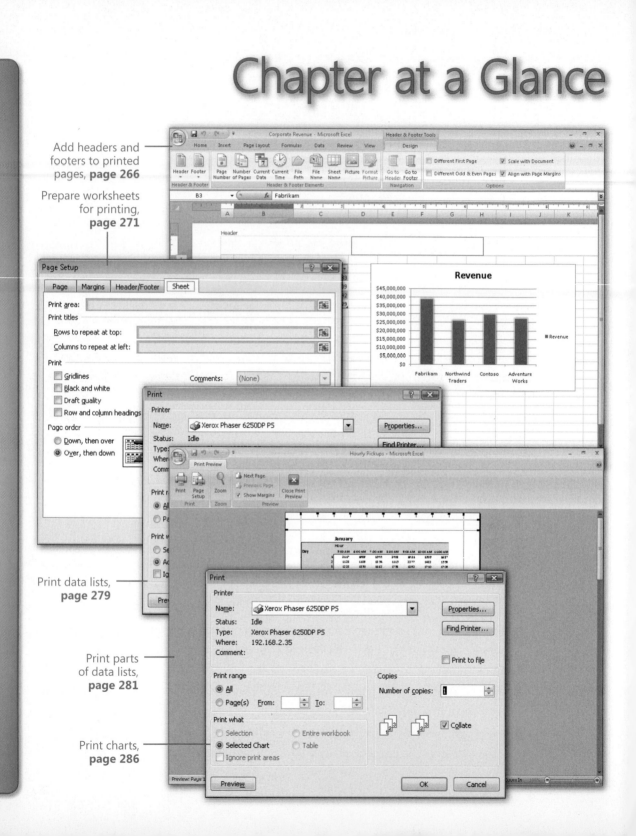

12 Printing

In this chapter, you will learn to:

✔ Add headers and footers to printed pages.

✔ Prepare worksheets for printing.

✔ Print data lists.

✔ Print parts of data lists.

✔ Print charts.

Microsoft Office Excel 2007 gives you a wide range of tools to create and manipulate your data lists. By using filters, by sorting, and by creating PivotTables and charts, you can change your worksheets so that they convey the greatest possible amount of information. After you configure your worksheet so that it shows your data to best advantage, you can print your Excel 2007 documents to use in a presentation or include in a report. You can choose to print all or part of any of your worksheets, change how your data and charts appear on the printed page, and even suppress any error messages that might appear in your worksheets.

In this chapter, you'll learn how to print all or part of a data list, how to print charts, and how to add headers and footers to your worksheets.

See Also Do you need only a quick refresher on the topics in this chapter? See the Quick Reference section at the beginning of this book.

Important Before you can use the practice files in this chapter, you need to install them from the book's companion CD to their default location. See "Using the Companion CD" at the beginning of this book for more information.

Adding Headers and Footers to Printed Pages

Changing how your data appears in the body of your worksheets can make your information much easier to understand, but it doesn't communicate when the worksheet was last opened or to whom it belongs. You could always add that information to the top of every printed page, but you would need to change the current date every time you opened the document. And if you wanted the same information to appear at the top of every printed page, any changes to the body of your worksheets could mean that you would need to edit your workbook so that the information appeared in the proper place.

If you want to ensure that the same information appears at the top or bottom of every printed page, you can do so by using headers or footers. (A header is a section that appears at the top of every printed page; a footer is a section that appears at the bottom of every printed page.) To create a header or footer in Excel 2007, you display the Insert tab and then, in the Text group, click Header & Footer to display the Header & Footer Tools Design contextual tab.

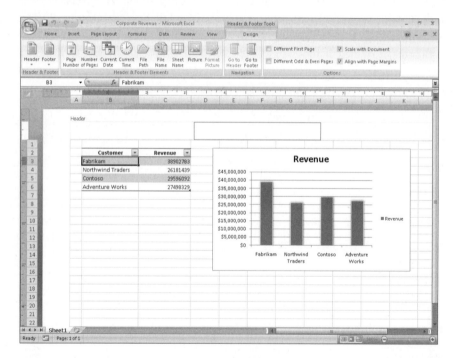

When you display your workbook's headers and footers, Excel 2007 displays the workbook in Page Layout view, which is new in Excel 2007. The Excel 2007 product team's goal in creating Page Layout view was to show you exactly how your workbook will look when printed while still enabling you to edit your file, a capability not provided by Print Preview. You can also switch to Page Layout view quickly by displaying the View tab and then, in the Workbook Views group, clicking Page Layout.

See Also For more information on editing your workbook in Print Preview mode, see the section titled "Previewing Worksheets Before Printing" later in this chapter.

Excel 2007 divides its headers and footers into left, middle, and right sections. When you point to an editable header or footer section, Excel 2007 highlights the section to indicate that clicking the left mouse button will open that header or footer section for editing.

> **Important** If you have a chart selected when you click the Header & Footer button on the Insert tab, Excel 2007 displays the Header/Footer page of the Page Setup dialog box instead of opening a header or footer section for editing.

When you click a header or footer section, Excel 2007 displays the Design contextual tab on the Ribbon. The Design contextual tab holds a number of standard headers and footers, such as page numbers by themselves or followed by the name of the workbook. To add an Auto Header to your workbook, display the Design contextual tab and then, in the Auto Header & Footer group, click Auto Header. Then click the Auto Header you want to apply.

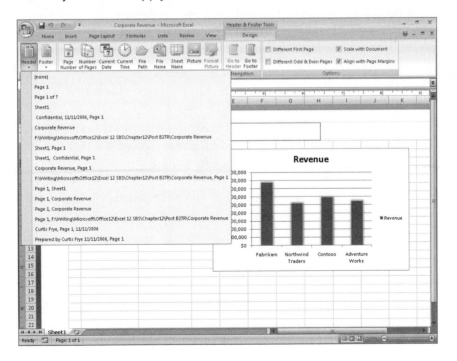

You can also create custom headers by typing your own text or by using the controls in the Header & Footer Elements group to insert a date, time, worksheet name, or page number. Beginning with Excel 2002, you have had the option of adding a graphic to a header or footer. Adding a graphic such as a company logo to a worksheet enables you to identify the worksheet as referring to your company and helps reinforce your company's identity if you include the worksheet in a printed report distributed outside your company. After you insert a graphic into a header or footer, the Format Picture button in the Header & Footer Elements group will become available. Clicking that button opens a dialog box with tools to edit your graphic.

In this exercise, you will create a custom header for a workbook. You will add a graphic to the footer and then edit the graphic using the Format Picture dialog box.

> **USE** the *Revenue by Customer* workbook. This practice file is located in the *Documents\ Microsoft Press\Excel2007SBS\Printing* folder.
>
> **BE SURE TO** start Excel 2007 before starting this exercise.
>
> **OPEN** the *Revenue by Customer* workbook.

1. On the **View** tab, in the **Workbook Views** group, click **Page Layout**.

   Excel 2007 displays your workbook in Page Layout view.

2. At the top of the worksheet, click **Click to add header**.

   Excel 2007 opens the middle header section for editing.

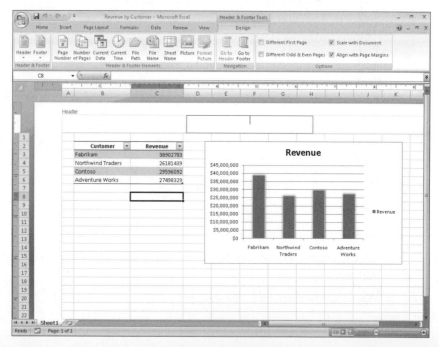

3. In the middle header section, type Q1 2006, and then press Enter.

4. On the **Design** contextual tab, in the **Header & Footer Elements** group, click **File Name**.

   Excel 2007 adds the *&[File]* code to the header.

5. To the right of the *&[File]* code, type a comma, and then press Space.

6. On the **Design** contextual tab, in the **Header & Footer Elements** group, click **Current Date**.

   Excel 2007 changes the contents of the middle header section to *&[File], &[Date]*.

7. Press Tab.

   Excel 2007 highlights the right header section; the workbook name and current date appear in the middle header section.

8. On the **Design** contextual tab, in the **Navigation** group, click **Go to Footer**.

   Excel 2007 highlights the right footer section.

9. Click the middle footer section.

10. On the **Design** contextual tab, in the **Header & Footer Elements** group, click **Picture**.

    The Insert Picture dialog box opens.

11. Browse to the *Documents\Microsoft Press\Excel2007SBS\Printing* folder, and then double-click *ConsolidatedMessenger.png*.

    The code *&[Picture]* appears in the middle footer section.

12. Click any worksheet cell above the footer.

    Excel 2007 displays the worksheet as it will be printed.

13. Click the image in the footer and then, on the **Design** contextual tab, click **Format Picture**.

    The Format Picture dialog box opens.

14. Click the **Size** tab if it is not already displayed.

15. In the **Height** field, type 80%, and then press Enter .

    The Format Picture dialog box closes.

16. Click any worksheet cell above the footer.

    Excel 2007 displays the newly formatted picture.

CLOSE the *Revenue by Customer* workbook.

Preparing Worksheets for Printing

After you have your data and any headers or footers in your workbook, you can change your workbook properties to ensure that your worksheets display all your information and that printing is centered on the page.

One of the workbook properties you can change is its margins, or the boundaries between different sections of the printed page. You can view a document's margins and where the contents of the header, footer, and body appear in relation to those margins in the Print Preview window.

You can drag each margin line to change the corresponding margin's position, increasing or decreasing the amount of space allocated to each worksheet section. Do bear in mind that increasing the size of the header or footer reduces the size of the worksheet body, meaning that fewer rows can be printed on a page.

Excel 2007 comes with three margin settings: Normal, Wide, and Narrow. Excel 2007 applies the Normal setting by default, but you can select any of the three options by displaying the Page Layout tab and then, in the Page Setup group, by clicking Margins. If you want finer control over your margins, click Custom Margins to display the Margins tab of the Page Setup dialog box.

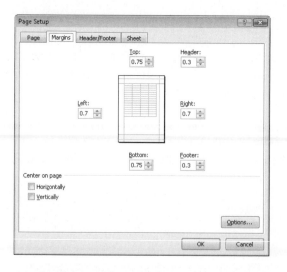

Another issue with printing worksheets is that the data in worksheets tends to be wider horizontally than a standard sheet of paper. For example, the data in the worksheet in the previous graphic is several columns wider than a standard piece of paper. You can use the controls on the Page Layout tab to change the alignment of the rows and columns on the page. When the columns follow the long edge of a piece of paper, the page is laid out in *portrait mode*; when the columns follow the short edge of a piece of paper, it is in *landscape mode*. The following graphic displays the contents of the previous worksheet laid out in landscape mode.

This arrangement is a better fit, but not all the data fits on the printed page. This is where the tools in the Scale To Fit group on the Page Layout tab come to the rescue. You can use the tools in that group to have Excel 2007 reduce the size of the worksheet's contents until the entire worksheet can be printed on a single page. You can make the same changes (and more) by using the controls in the Page Setup dialog box. To display the Page Setup dialog box, click the Page Layout tab, and then click the Page Setup dialog box launcher.

Previewing Worksheets Before Printing

You can view your Excel 2007 worksheet as it will be printed by clicking the Microsoft Office Button, pointing to Print, and then clicking Print Preview. When you do, Excel 2007 displays the active worksheet in the Print Preview window.

When the Print Preview window opens, it shows the active worksheet as it will be printed with its current settings. In the lower-left corner of the Print Preview window, Excel 2007 indicates how many pages the worksheet will require when printed and the number of the page you are viewing.

> **Tip** You can view the next printed page by pressing the Page Down key; to move to the previous page, press the Page Up key.

Changing Page Breaks in a Worksheet

Another way to change how your worksheet will appear on the printed page is to change where Excel 2007 assigns its page breaks or the point where Excel 2007 prints all subsequent data on a new sheet of paper. You can do that indirectly by changing a worksheet's margins, but you can do it directly by displaying your document in Page Break Preview mode. To display your worksheet in Page Break Preview mode, on the View tab, in the Workbook Views group, click Page Break Preview.

> **Tip** If you prefer not to display your workbook in Page Break Preview mode, you can insert a page break by clicking a cell, row header, or column header. Then, on the Page Layout tab, in the Page Setup group, click Breaks, and click Insert Page Break.

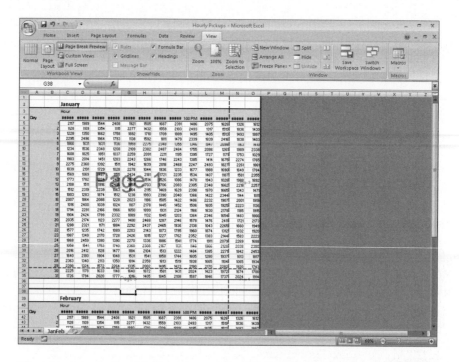

The blue lines in the window represent the page breaks. If you want to set a page break manually, you can do so by displaying your worksheet in Page Break Preview mode and then right-clicking the row header of the row below where you want the new page to start. In other words, if you right-click the row header of row 15 and click Insert Page Break, row 14 will be the last row on the first printed page, and row 15 will be the first row on the second printed page. The same technique applies to columns: if you right-click the column H column header and click Insert Page Break, column G will be the last column on the first printed page, and column H will be the first column on the second printed page.

You can also add page breaks without displaying your workbook in Page Break Preview mode. To add a page break while your workbook is open in Normal view, click a row or column header and then, on the Page Layout tab, in the Page Setup area, click Break. Then click Insert Page Break. Items in the Breaks list also enable you to delete a page break or to reset all of the page breaks in your worksheets.

Important Be sure to right-click a row header or column header when you want to insert a single page break. If you view a workbook in Page Break Preview mode, right-click a cell within the body of a worksheet, and then click Insert Page Break, Excel 2007 creates both a vertical page break above the selected cell and a horizontal page break below the selected cell.

To move a page break, drag the line representing the break to its new position. Excel 2007 will change the worksheet's properties so that the area you defined will be printed on a single page.

Changing the Page Printing Order for Worksheets

When you view a document in Page Break Preview mode, Excel 2007 indicates the order in which the pages will be printed with light gray words on the worksheet pages. (These indicators appear only in Page Break Preview mode; they don't show up when the document is printed.) You can change the order in which the pages are printed by displaying the Page Layout tab, clicking the Page Setup dialog box launcher, and displaying the Sheet tab of the Page Setup dialog box.

On the Sheet tab, selecting the Over, Then Down option changes the order in which the worksheets will be printed from the default Down, Then Over. You might want to change the printing order to keep certain information together on consecutive printed pages. For example, suppose you have a worksheet that holds hourly package pickup information; the columns represent hours of the day, and the rows represent days of the month. If you want to print out consecutive days for each hour, you use Down, Then Over, as shown in the following graphic. Pages 1 and 2 enable you to see the 5:00 a.m. to 11:00 a.m. pickups for the months of January and February, pages 3 and 4 enable you to see the 12:00 p.m. to 5:00 p.m. pickups for the months, and so on.

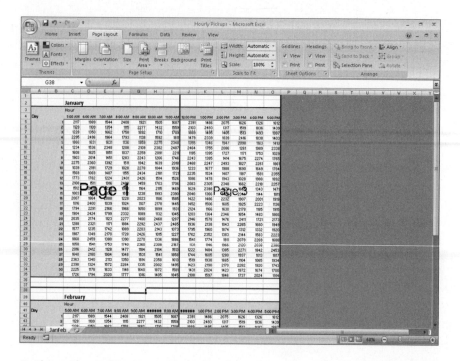

As the next graphic shows, changing the print order to Over, Then Down prints consecutive hours for each day. Pages 1 and 2 enable you to see the 5:00 a.m. to 5:00 p.m. pickups for January, and pages 3 and 4 enable you to see the same pickups for February.

In this exercise, you will preview a worksheet before printing, change a worksheet's margins, change a worksheet's orientation, reduce a worksheet's size, add a page break, and change the page printing order.

> **USE** the *Pickups by Hour* workbook. This practice file is located in the *Documents\Microsoft Press\Excel2007SBS\Printing* folder.
>
> **OPEN** the *Pickups by Hour* workbook.

Microsoft Office
Button

1. While displaying the **JanFeb** worksheet, click the **Microsoft Office Button**, point to **Print**, and then click **Print Preview**.

The workbook appears in Print Preview mode.

2. On the **Print Preview** tab, in the **Preview** group, click **Close Print Preview**.

The workbook appears in Normal view.

3. On the **Page Layout** tab, in the **Page Setup** group, click **Orientation**, and then click **Landscape**.

Excel 2007 reorients the worksheet.

4. On the **Page Layout** tab, in the **Scale to Fit** group, in the **Scale** field, type 80%, and then press Enter.

Excel 2007 resizes your worksheet.

5. Click the row header for row 38.

Excel 2007 highlights row 38.

6. On the **Page Layout** tab, in the **Page Setup** group, click **Breaks**, and then click **Insert Page Break**.

Excel 2007 sets a horizontal page break above row 38.

Pickups by Hour - Microsoft Excel

	A	B	C	D	E	F	G	H	I	J	K	L	M	N	O
24			20	2035	2174	1123	2277	1400	2468	1287	2146	1578	1476	2411	1721
25			21	1288	2321	1171	1884	2292	2437	2465	1936	2138	1043	2265	1660
26			22	1577	1235	1742	1089	2203	2143	1073	1795	1960	1874	1312	1332
27			23	1997	1249	2170	1778	2476	1015	1777	1762	2352	1383	2144	1583
28			24	1868	2459	1380	1390	2270	1336	1886	1541	1774	1911	2079	2269
29			25	1058	1541	1753	1740	2360	2308	2167	1131	1146	1966	2120	2038
30			26	2016	2412	1128	1477	1184	2104	1513	1222	1484	1385	2271	1842
31			27	1640	2180	1904	1048	1531	1541	1858	1744	1605	1280	1937	1013
32			28	2363	1340	2113	1350	1814	2358	1613	1519	1938	1665	1104	1065
33			29	2398	1324	1572	2264	1335	2002	1495	1423	2190	2170	2282	1920
34			30	2225	1178	1633	1148	1640	1872	1581	1431	2024	1423	1972	1674
35			31	1726	1794	2020	1777	1016	1405	1845	2108	1597	1846	1737	2024
38	February														
40				Hour											
41	Day			5:00 AM	6:00 AM	7:00 AM	8:00 AM	9:00 AM	10:00 AM	11:00 AM	12:00 PM	1:00 PM	2:00 PM	3:00 PM	4:00 PM
42			1	2117	1989	1544	2408	1921	1505	1687	2391	1486	2075	1626	1326
43			2	1128	1109	1354	1115	2277	1432	1559	2103	2493	1317	1519	1836
44			3	1228	1350	1662	1758	1892	1710	1709	1889	1495	1405	1513	1493
45			4	2295	2496	1964	1793	1138	1592	1811	1479	2339	1839	2416	1838
46			5	1866	1631	1631	1136	1959	2275	2348	1355	1346	1947	2098	1163
47			6	1234	1536	2348	1208	2109	2382	2487	2464	1755	2086	1261	1989
48			7	1608	1825	1851	1037	2259	2091	2211	1195	1395	1727	1171	1753
49			8	1903	2014	1451	1283	2243	1266	1746	2243	1385	1414	1675	2274

JanFeb / MarJun

7. On the tab bar, click the **MarJun** sheet tab.

The MarJun worksheet appears.

8. On the **Page Layout** tab, in the **Page Setup** group, click **Margins**, and then click **Wide**.

Excel 2007 applies wide margins to the worksheet.

9. On the **Page Layout** tab, click the **Page Setup** dialog box launcher.

The Page Setup dialog box opens.

10. If necessary, click the **Sheet** tab.

The Sheet tab appears.

11. In the **Page order** section, click **Over, then down**.

12. Click **OK**.

13. If desired, click the **Microsoft Office Button**, point to **Print**, and then click **Quick Print**.

Excel 2007 prints your worksheet.

CLOSE the *Pickups by Hour* workbook.

Printing Data Lists

When you're ready to print a worksheet, all you have to do is click the Microsoft Office Button, point to Print, and then click Quick Print. If you want a little more say in how Excel 2007 prints your worksheet, you can use the controls in the Print dialog box to determine how Excel 2007 prints your worksheet. For example, you can choose the printer to which you want to send this job, print multiple copies of the worksheet, and select whether the copies are collated (all pages of a document together) or not (multiple copies of the same page are printed together).

Important The exact version of the Print dialog box that Excel 2007 presents depends on the printer you select, so your Print dialog box might differ from the one shown in the preceding graphic.

If you want to print more than one worksheet from the active workbook, but not every worksheet in the workbook, you can select the worksheets to print from the tab bar. To select the worksheets to print, hold down the Ctrl key while you click the sheet tabs of the worksheets you want to print. Then click the Microsoft Office Button, point to Print, and click Quick Print.

Tip The worksheets you select for printing do not need to be next to one another in the workbook.

A helpful option on the Sheet tab of the Page Setup dialog box is the Cell Errors As box, which enables you to select how Excel 2007 will print any errors in your worksheet. You can print an error as it normally appears in the worksheet, print a blank cell in place of the error, or choose one of two other indicators that are not standard error messages.

After you prepare your worksheet for printing, you can print it by opening the Print dialog box. To print every page in the worksheet, select the All option in the Print Range section, and then click OK. To print every worksheet in the active workbook, select the Entire Workbook option in the Print What section.

In this exercise, you will print nonadjacent worksheets in your workbook and suppress errors in the printed worksheet.

> **USE** the *Summary by Customer* workbook. This practice file is located in the *Documents\Microsoft Press\Excel2007SBS\Printing* folder.
>
> **OPEN** the *Summary by Customer* workbook.

1. If necessary, display the **Summary** worksheet.

2. On the **Page Layout** tab, click the **Page Setup** dialog box launcher.

   The Page Setup dialog box opens.

3. Click the **Sheet** tab.

   The Sheet tab appears.

4. In the **Cell errors as** list, click **<blank>**.

5. Click **OK**.

6. Hold down the Ctrl key and then, on the tab bar, click the **Northwind** sheet tab.

   Excel 2007 selects the Summary and Northwind worksheets.

Microsoft Office
Button

7. Click the **Microsoft Office Button**, and then click **Print**.

The Print dialog box opens.

8. In the **Print what** area, verify that the **Active sheet(s)** option is selected.

Print		? ✕
Printer		
Na<u>m</u>e:	🖨 Xerox Phaser 6250DP PS ▼	<u>P</u>roperties...
Status:	Idle	Fin<u>d</u> Printer...
Type:	Xerox Phaser 6250DP PS	
Where:	192.168.2.35	
Comment:		☐ Print to fi<u>l</u>e
Print range		**Copies**
⦿ <u>A</u>ll		Number of <u>c</u>opies: 1 ▲▼
◯ Pa<u>g</u>e(s) <u>F</u>rom: ▲▼ <u>T</u>o: ▲▼		
Print what		☑ C<u>o</u>llate
◯ Selection ◯ Entire workbook		
⦿ Acti<u>v</u>e sheet(s) ◯ Table		
☐ Ignore print areas		
Pre<u>v</u>iew		OK Cancel

9. Click **Cancel** (or click **OK** if you want to print the worksheets).

✖ **CLOSE** the *Summary by Customer* workbook.

Printing Parts of Data Lists

Excel 2007 gives you a great deal of control over what your worksheets look like when you print them, but you also have a lot of control over which parts of your worksheets will be printed. For example, you can use the Print dialog box to choose which pages of a multipage worksheet you want to print.

Selecting the Page(s) option in the Print Range section of the dialog box enables you to fill in the page numbers you want to print in the From and To boxes.

> **Tip** You can use the Page Break Preview window to determine which pages you want to print, and if the pages aren't in an order you like, you can use the controls on the Sheet tab of the Page Setup dialog box to change the order in which they will be printed.

Another way you can modify how a worksheet will be printed is to have Excel 2007 fit the entire worksheet on a specified number of pages. For example, you can have Excel 2007 resize a worksheet so that it will fit on a single printed page. Fitting a worksheet onto a single page is a handy tool when you need to add a sales or other summary to a report and don't want to spread important information across more than one page.

To have Excel 2007 fit a worksheet on a set number of pages, display the Page Layout tab and use the controls in the Scale To Fit group. In the Width and Height lists, you can select how many pages wide or tall you want your printout to be.

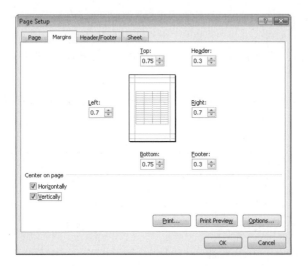

If you want to print a portion of a worksheet instead of the entire worksheet, you can define the area or areas you want to have printed. To identify the area of the worksheet you want to print, select the cells with the data you want to print and, on the Page Layout tab, in the Page Setup group, click Print Area. Then click Set Print Area. Excel 2007 marks the area with a dotted line around the border of the selected cells and prints only the cells you selected. To remove the selection, click Print Area, and then click Clear Print Area.

> **Tip** You can include noncontiguous groups of cells in the area to be printed by holding down the Ctrl key as you select the cells.

After you define a print area, you can use the Page Setup dialog box to position the print area on the page. Specifically, you can have Excel 2007 center the print area on the page by selecting the Horizontally and Vertically check boxes on the Margins tab.

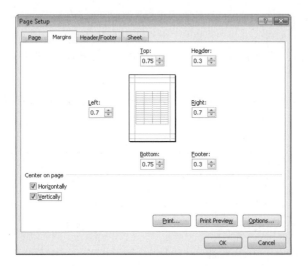

If the contents of a worksheet will take up more than one printed page, you can have Excel 2007 repeat one or more rows at the top of the page or columns at the left of the page. For example, if you want to print a lengthy data list containing the mailing addresses of customers signed up to receive your company's monthly newsletter, you could repeat the column headings Name, Address, City, and so forth at the top of the page. To repeat rows at the top of each printed page, on the Page Layout tab, in the Page Setup group, click Print Titles. Excel 2007 will display the Sheet tab of the Page Setup dialog box.

On the Sheet tab of the Page Setup dialog box, you can use the controls in the Print Titles section of the dialog box to select the rows or columns to repeat. To choose rows to repeat at the top of the page, click the Collapse Dialog button next to the Rows To Repeat At Top box, select the rows, and then click the Expand Dialog button. The rows you selected appear in the Rows To Repeat At Top box.

Similarly, to have a set of columns appear at the left of every printed page, click the Collapse Dialog button next to the Columns To Repeat At Left box, select the columns, and then click the Expand Dialog button. When you're done, click OK to accept the settings.

A final feature that comes in handy when you print Excel 2007 worksheets is Intelliprint, which was introduced in Excel 2003. Intelliprint prevents Excel 2007 from printing any blank pages at the end of a document. The end result is that you don't need to set a print area manually unless you want to print a subset of the data in your worksheet or if you do want to print blank pages after the rest of your data.

In this exercise, you will select certain pages of a worksheet to print, have Excel 2007 fit your printed worksheet on a set number of pages, define a multiregion print area, center the printed material on the page, and repeat columns at the left edge of each printed page.

> **USE** the *Hourly Pickups* workbook. This practice file is located in the *Documents\Microsoft Press\Excel2007SBS\Printing* folder.
> **OPEN** the *Hourly Pickups* workbook.

1. On the **Page Layout** tab, in the **Page Setup** group, click **Print Titles**.

   The Page Setup dialog box opens, displaying the Sheet tab.

Collapse Dialog

2. At the right edge of the **Columns to repeat at left** field, click the **Collapse Dialog** button.

   The dialog box collapses.

3. Select the column header of column A, and drag to select the column header of column B, too.

   The reference *$A:$B* appears in the **Columns to repeat at left** field.

Expand Dialog

4. At the right edge of the **Columns to repeat at left** field, click the **Expand Dialog** button.

   The dialog box expands.

5. Click **Print Preview**.

   Excel 2007 displays your worksheet as it will appear when printed.

6. Click **Close Print Preview**.

   Excel 2007 displays your worksheet in Normal view.

7. Click the **Microsoft Office Button**, and then click **Print**.

   The Print dialog box opens.

Microsoft Office
Button

8. Click **Page(s)**.

9. In the **From** field, type 1; in the **To** field, type 2.

10. Click **Cancel** (or click **OK** to print the selected pages).

    The Print dialog box closes.

11. On the **Page Layout** tab, in the **Scale to Fit** group, click the **Width** arrow and then, in the list that appears, click **1 page**.

12. Click the **Height** arrow and then, in the list that appears, click **2 pages**.

Excel 2007 resizes your worksheet so that it will fit on two printed pages. The new scaling and size values appear in the Scale To Fit group on the Page Layout tab.

13. Select the cell range A1:E8, hold down the ⌷ key, and then select the cell range A38:E45.

14. On the **Page Layout** tab, in the **Page Setup** group, click **Print Area**, and then click **Set Print Area**.

15. Click the **Page Setup** dialog box launcher.

The Page Setup dialog box opens.

16. On the **Margins** tab of the dialog box, select the **Horizontally** and **Vertically** check boxes.

17. Click **Print Preview**.

Excel 2007 displays your worksheet as it will appear when printed.

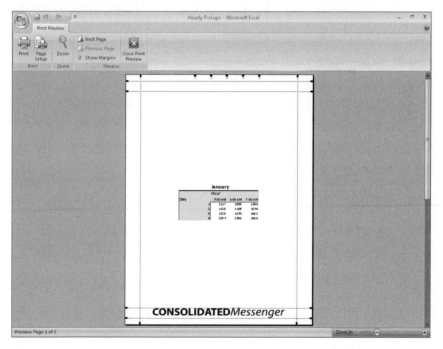

18. Click **Close Print Preview**.

Excel 2007 displays your worksheet in Normal view.

19. On the **Page Layout** tab, in the **Page Setup** group, click **Print Area**, and then click **Clear Print Area**.

   Excel 2007 removes the print areas defined for the JanFeb worksheet.

> **CLOSE** the *Hourly Pickups* workbook.

Printing Charts

Charts, which are graphic representations of your Excel 2007 data, enable you to communicate lots of information with a picture. Depending on your data and the type of chart you make, you can show trends across time, indicate the revenue share for various departments in a company for a month, or project future sales using trendline analysis. After you create a chart, you can print it to include in a report or use in a presentation.

If you embed a chart in a worksheet, however, the chart will probably obscure some of your data unless you move the chart to a second page in the worksheet. That's one way to handle printing a chart or the underlying worksheet, but there are other ways that don't involve changing the layout of your worksheets.

To print a chart, click the chart, click the Microsoft Office Button, point to Print, and then click Print to display the Print dialog box. In the Print What section, Selected Chart is the only option available. If you click anywhere on the worksheet outside the chart, the Print What section appears with the Active Sheet(s) option selected, meaning that the chart and underlying worksheet are printed as they appear on the screen.

In this exercise, you will print a chart.

> **USE** the *Corporate Revenue* workbook. This practice file is located in the *Documents\Microsoft Press\Excel2007SBS\Printing* folder.
> **OPEN** the *Corporate Revenue* workbook.

1. Select the chart.

Microsoft Office
Button

2. Click the **Microsoft Office Button**, and then click **Print**.

   The Print dialog box opens.

3. Verify that the **Selected Chart** option is selected, and then click **OK** (or click **Cancel** if you don't want to print the chart).

CLOSE the *Corporate Revenue* workbook. If you are not continuing directly to the next chapter, exit Excel.

Key Points

● Excel 2007 gives you complete control over how your worksheets appear on the printed page. Don't be afraid to experiment until you find a look you like.

● Use Print Preview to see what your worksheet will look like on paper before you print, especially if you're using an expensive color printer.

● You can preview where the page breaks will fall when you print a worksheet and change them if you so desire.

● Don't forget that you can have Excel 2007 avoid printing error codes! Be sure to use your power wisely.

● You can repeat rows or columns in a printed worksheet.

● If you want to print a chart without printing the rest of the accompanying worksheet, be sure to select the chart before you open the Print dialog box.

Chapter at a Glance

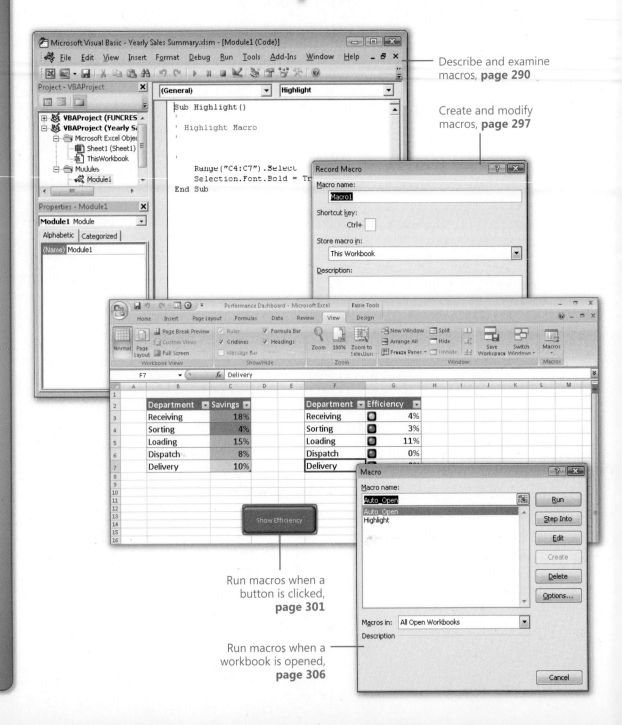

Describe and examine macros, **page 290**

Create and modify macros, **page 297**

Run macros when a button is clicked, **page 301**

Run macros when a workbook is opened, **page 306**

13 Automating Repetitive Tasks by Using Macros

In this chapter, you will learn to:

✔ Describe and examine macros.

✔ Create and modify macros.

✔ Run macros when a button is clicked.

✔ Run macros when a workbook is opened.

Many tasks you perform in Microsoft Office Excel 2007 (for example, entering sales data for a particular day or adding formulas to a worksheet) are done once or (for example, changing the format of a cell range) can be repeated quickly using available tools in Excel 2007. However, you will often perform one or two tasks frequently that require a lot of steps to accomplish. For example, you might have a number of cells in a worksheet that contain important data you use quite often in presentations to your colleagues. Instead of going through a lengthy series of steps to highlight the cells with the important information, you can create a macro, or a recorded series of actions, to perform the steps for you. After you have created a macro, you can run, edit, or delete it as needed.

In Excel 2007, you run and edit macros using the items available in the Macros group on the View tab. You can make your macros easier to access by creating new buttons on the Quick Access Toolbar, to which you can assign your macros. If you run a macro to highlight specific cells in a worksheet every time you show that worksheet to a colleague, you can save time by adding a Quick Access Toolbar button that runs a macro to highlight the cells for you.

Another handy feature of Excel 2007 macros is that you can create macros that run when a workbook is opened. For example, you might want to ensure that no cells in a worksheet are highlighted when the worksheet opens. You can create a macro that removes any special formatting from your worksheet cells when its workbook opens, enabling you to emphasize the data you want as you present the information to your colleagues.

In this chapter, you'll learn how to open, run, create, and modify macros; create Quick Access Toolbar buttons and shapes that enable you to run macros with a single mouse click; define macro security settings; and run a macro when a workbook is opened.

See Also Do you need only a quick refresher on the topics in this chapter? See the Quick Reference section at the beginning of this book.

> **Important** Before you can use the practice files in this chapter, you need to install them from the book's companion CD to their default location. See "Using the Companion CD" at the beginning of this book for more information.

Introducing Macros

After you have worked with your Excel 2007 documents for awhile, you will probably discover some series of actions you perform repeatedly. Although many of these actions (such as saving your changes and printing) can be accomplished quickly, some sequences involve many steps and take time to accomplish by hand. For example, you might want to highlight a number of cells in a worksheet to emphasize an aspect of your data. Instead of highlighting the cells by hand every time you present your findings, you can create a *macro*, or series of automated actions, to do the highlighting for you.

Macro Security in Excel 2007

It's possible for unscrupulous programmers to write viruses and other harmful programs using the Microsoft Visual Basic for Applications (VBA) programming language, so you need to be sure that you don't run macros from unknown sources. In versions of Office Excel prior to Excel 2007, you could define macro security levels to determine which macros, if any, your workbooks would be allowed to run, but there was no workbook type in which all macros were disallowed. Excel 2007 has several file types you can use to control whether the workbook will allow macros to be run. The following table summarizes the macro-related file types.

Extension	Description
.xlsx	Regular Excel 2007 workbook; macros are *disabled*
.xlsm	Regular Excel 2007 workbook; macros are *enabled*
.xltx	Excel 2007 template workbook; macros are *disabled*
.xltxm	Excel 2007 template workbook; macros are *enabled*

When you open a macro-enabled workbook, the Excel 2007 program-level security settings might prevent the workbook from running the macro code. When that happens, Excel 2007 displays a security warning on the Message Bar.

Clicking the Options button displays the Microsoft Office Security Options dialog box.

If you are expecting a workbook that contains macros and recognize the source of the workbook, you can select the Enable This Content option and then click OK to enable the workbook macros. Please take the time to verify the workbook's source and whether you expected the workbook to contain macros before enabling the content.

You can change your program-level security settings to make them more or less restrictive; to do so, click the Microsoft Office Button, click the Excel Options button and then, in the Excel Options dialog box, click the Trust Center category. On the page that appears, click the Trust Center Settings button to display a dialog box of the same name.

The Excel 2007 default macro security level is Disable All Macros With Notification, which means that Excel 2007 displays a warning on the Message Bar, but you can enable the macros by clicking the Options button and selecting the Enable This Content option. Selecting the Disable All Macros Without Notification option does exactly what the label says. If Consolidated Messenger's company policy is to disallow all macros in all Excel 2007 workbooks, you would select the Disable All Macros Without Notification option.

> **Important** Because it is possible to write macros that act as viruses, potentially causing harm to your computer and spreading copies of themselves to other computers, you should never choose the Enable All Macros security setting, even if you have virus-checking software installed on your computer.

Examining Macros

The best way to get an idea of how macros work is to examine an existing macro. To do that, display the View tab. In the Macros group, click the Macros button, and then click View Macros.

> **Tip** In the Macro dialog box, you can display the macros available in other workbooks by clicking the Macros In box and selecting a workbook by name or by selecting All Open Workbooks to display every macro in any open workbook. If you select either of those choices, the macro names displayed include the name of the workbook in which the macro is stored. Clicking This Workbook displays the macros in the active workbook.

The Macro dialog box has a list of macros in your workbook. To view the code behind a macro, you click the macro's name and then click Edit to open the Microsoft Visual Basic Editor.

Excel 2007 macros are recorded using VBA. The preceding graphic shows the code for a macro that highlights the cell range C4:C7 and changes the cells' formatting to bold. After introductory information about the macro (its name and when it was created), the first line of the macro identifies the cell range to be selected (in this case, cells C4:C7). After the macros selects the cells, the next line of the macro changes the formatting of the selected cells to bold, which has the same result as clicking a cell and then clicking the Bold button in the Font group on the Home tab.

To see how the macro works, you can open the Macro dialog box, click the name of the macro you want to examine, and then click Step Into. The Microsoft Visual Basic Editor appears, with a highlight around the instruction that will be executed next.

To execute an instruction, press F8. The highlight moves to the next instruction, and your worksheet then changes to reflect the action that resulted from executing the preceding instruction.

You can run a macro without stopping after each instruction by opening the Macro dialog box, clicking the macro to run, and then clicking Run. You'll usually run the macro this way; after all, the point of using macros is to save time.

In this exercise, you will examine a macro in the Visual Basic Editor, move through the first part of the macro one step at a time, and then run the entire macro without stopping.

USE the *VolumeHighlights* workbook. This practice file is located in the *Documents\Microsoft Press\Excel2007SBS\Macros* folder.

BE SURE TO start Excel 2007 before beginning this exercise.

OPEN the *VolumeHighlights* workbook.

1. On the **Message Bar**, click **Options**.

   The Microsoft Office Security Options dialog box opens.

2. Select the **Enable this content** option.

3. Click **OK**.

   The security warning disappears, and macros are enabled.

Macros

4. On the **View** tab, in the **Macros** group, click the **Macros** arrow and then, in the list that appears, click **View Macros**.

   The Macro dialog box opens.

Macro   [?] [×]

Macro name:

HighlightSouthern			**Run**

HighlightSouthern

Step Into

Edit

Create

Delete

Options...

Macros in: All Open Workbooks

Description

Cancel

5. Click the **HighlightSouthern** macro, and then click **Edit**.

   The Visual Basic Editor opens, with the code for the HighlightSouthern macro displayed in the Module1 (Code) window.

Close

6. In the Visual Basic Editor window, click the **Close** button.

   The Visual Basic Editor closes, and Excel displays the *VolumeHighlights* workbook.

7. In the **Macros** list, **View Macros**.

   The Macro dialog box opens.

8. Click the **HighlightSouthern** macro, and then click **Step Into**.

   The macro appears in the Visual Basic Editor, with the first macro instruction highlighted.

9. Press the **F8** key.

   Excel 2007 highlights the next instruction.

10. Press the **F8** key.

    The macro selects the Atlantic row in the table.

11. Press the **F8** key twice.

The macro changes the Atlantic row's text color to red.

12. Click the Visual Basic Editor **Close** button.

    A warning dialog box appears, indicating that closing the Visual Basic Editor will stop the debugger.

13. Click **OK**.

    The Visual Basic Editor closes.

14. In the **Macros** list, click **View Macros**.

    The Macro dialog box opens.

15. Click the **HighlightSouthern** macro.

16. Click **Run**.

    The Macro dialog box closes, and Excel 2007 runs the entire macro.

17. On the **Quick Access Toolbar**, click the **Save** button.

Save

Excel 2007 saves your work.

CLOSE the *VolumeHighlights* workbook.

Creating and Modifying Macros

The first step of creating a macro is to plan the process you want to automate. Computers today are quite fast, so adding an extra step that doesn't affect the outcome of a process doesn't slow you down noticeably, but leaving out a step means you will need to rerecord your macro. After you plan your process, you can create a macro by clicking the View tab and then, in the Macros group, clicking the Macros arrow. In the list that appears, click Record Macro. When you do, the Record Macro dialog box opens.

After you type the name of your macro in the Macro Name box, click OK. You can now perform the actions you want Excel 2007 to repeat later; when you're done, in the Macros list, click Stop Recording to add your macro to the list of macros available in your workbook.

To modify an existing macro, you can simply delete the macro and rerecord it. Or if you just need to make a quick change, you can open it in the Visual Basic Editor and add to or change the macro's instructions. To delete a macro, open the Macro dialog box, click the macro you want to delete, and then click Delete.

In this exercise, you will record, save, and run a macro that removes the bold formatting from selected cells.

USE the *Yearly Sales Summary* workbook. This practice file is located in the *Documents\ Microsoft Press\Excel2007SBS\Macros* folder.

OPEN the *Yearly Sales Summary* workbook.

1. On the **View** tab, in the **Macros** group, click the **Macros** arrow and then, in the list that appears, click **Record Macro**.

   The Record Macro dialog box opens.

2. In the **Macro name** box, delete the existing name, and then type RemoveHighlight.

3. Click **OK**.

   The Record Macro dialog box closes.

4. Select the cell range C4:C7.

   The text in these cells is currently bold.

5. On the **Home** tab, in the **Font** group, click the **Bold** button.

6. On the **View** tab, in the **Macros** list, click **Stop Recording**.

   Excel 2007 stops recording the macro.

7. In the **Macros** list, click **View Macros**.

   The Macro dialog box opens.

8. In the **Macro name** section, click **RemoveHighlight**, and then click **Edit**.

   The Visual Basic Editor starts.

```
Microsoft Visual Basic - Yearly Sales Summary.xlsm - [Module3 (Code)]
File  Edit  View  Insert  Format  Debug  Run  Tools  Add-Ins  Window  Help

Project - VBAProject                    (General)              RemoveHighlight

  Microsoft Excel Objec                 Sub RemoveHighlight()
    Sheet1 (Sheet1)                     '
    ThisWorkbook                        ' RemoveHighlight Macro
  Modules                               '
    Module1                             '
    Module2                                 Range("C4:C7").Select
    Module3                                 Selection.Font.Bold = False
                                        End Sub

Properties - Module3

Module3 Module

Alphabetic | Categorized

(Name) Module3
```

9. Click at the end of the line just above End Sub, press [Enter], type Range("C9"). Select, and press [Enter].

   This macro statement selects cell C9.

10. Type Selection.Font.Bold = False, and then press [Enter].

    This macro statement removes bold formatting from the selected cell (C9).

11. On the **Standard** toolbar of the Visual Basic Editor, click the **Save** button to save your change.

    A dialog box opens, informing you that you can't save macros in a simple workbook.

12. In the dialog box, click **No**.

    The Save As dialog box opens.

13. In the **Save as type** list, click **Excel Macro-Enabled Workbook (*.xlsm)**, and then click **Save**.

    Excel saves a marco-enabled version of the workbook.

Close

14. On the title bar of the **Microsoft Visual Basic** window, click the **Close** button.

   The Visual Basic Editor closes.

15. Select cells C3:C9, and format them as bold.

16. In the **Macros** list, click **View Macros**.

   The Macro dialog box opens.

17. Click **Remove Highlight**, and then click **Run**.

   The bold formatting is removed from cells C4, C5, C6, C7, and C9.

18. On the **Quick Access Toolbar**, click the **Save** button.

   Excel 2007 saves your workbook.

CLOSE the *Yearly Sales Summary* workbook.

Running Macros When a Button Is Clicked

The Ribbon, which is the most visible indicator of the new Microsoft Office Fluent user interface, enables you to discover the commands built into Excel 2007 quickly. However, it can take a few seconds to display the View tab, open the Macro dialog box, select the macro you want to run, and click the Run button. When you're in the middle of a presentation, taking even those few seconds can reduce your momentum and force you to regain your audience's attention. Excel 2007 offers several ways for you to make your macros more accessible.

If you want to display the Macro dialog box quickly, you can add the View Macros button to the Quick Access Toolbar. To do so, click the Customize Quick Access Toolbar button at the right edge of the Quick Access Toolbar, and then click More Commands to display the Customize tab of the Excel Options dialog box.

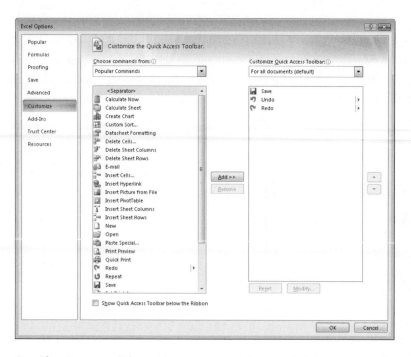

See Also For more information on customizing the Quick Access Toolbar, see Chapter 2, "Setting Up a Workbook."

When you display the Popular Commands command group, you'll see that the last item in the command pane is View Macros. When you click the View Macros item, click the Add button, and then click OK, Excel 2007 adds the command to the Quick Access Toolbar and closes the Excel Options dialog box. Clicking the View Macros button on the Quick Access Toolbar displays the Macro dialog box, which saves a significant amount of time compared to displaying the View tab and moving the mouse to the far right edge of the Ribbon.

If you prefer to run a macro without having to display the Macro dialog box, you can do so by adding a button representing the macro to the Quick Access Toolbar. Clicking that button runs the macro immediately, which is very handy when you create a macro for a task you perform frequently. To add a button representing a macro to the Quick Access Toolbar, click the Customize Quick Access Toolbar button at the right edge of the Quick Access Toolbar, and then click More Commands to display the Customize tab of the Excel Options dialog box. From there, in the Choose Commands From list, click Macros. Click the macro you want represented on the Quick Access Toolbar, click Add, and then click OK.

If you add more than one macro button to the Quick Access Toolbar or if you want to change the button that represents your macro on the Quick Access Toolbar, you can select a new button from more than 160 options. To assign a new button to your macro, click the macro item in the Customize Quick Access Toolbar pane and click the Modify button to display your choices. Click the button you want, type a new text value to appear when a user points to the button, and then click OK twice (the first time to close the Modify Button dialog box and the second to close the Excel Options dialog box).

Finally, you can have Excel 2007 run a macro when you click a shape in your workbook. Assigning macros to shapes enables you to create "buttons" that are graphically richer than those available on the Quick Access Toolbar. If you're so inclined, you can even create custom button layouts that represent other objects, such as a remote control. To run a macro when you click a shape, right-click the shape, and then click Assign Macro on the shortcut menu that appears. In the Assign Macro dialog box, click the macro you want to run when you click the shape, and then click OK.

> **Important** When you assign a macro to run when you click a shape, don't change the name of the macro that appears in the Assign Macro dialog box. The name that appears refers to the object and what the object should do when it is clicked; changing the macro name breaks that connection and prevents Excel 2007 from running the macro.

In this exercise, you will add the View Macros button to the Quick Access Toolbar, add a macro button to the Quick Access Toolbar, assign a macro to a workbook shape, and then run the macros.

> **USE** the *Performance Dashboard* workbook. This practice file is located in the *Documents\Microsoft Press\Excel2007SBS\Macros* folder.
>
> **OPEN** the *Performance Dashboard* workbook.

1. If necessary, click the **Options** button that appears on the Message Bar. Then in the **Microsoft Office Security Options** dialog box, click **Enable this content option**, and click **OK**.

2. On the **Quick Access Toolbar**, click the **Customize Quick Access Toolbar** button, and then click **More Commands**.

   The Customize page of the Excel Options dialog box appears, displaying the Popular Commands category in the Choose Commands From panel.

Customize Quick
Access Toolbar

3. In the **Choose commands from** panel, click **View Macros**.

4. Click **Add**.

   The View Macros command appears in the Customize Quick Access Toolbar panel.

5. In the **Choose commands from** list, click **Macros**.

   The available macros appear in the panel below.

6. In the **Choose commands from** panel, click **SavingsHighlight**.

> **Troubleshooting** If macros in the workbook are not enabled, the SavingsHighlight macro will not appear in the list.

7. Click **Add**.

   The SavingsHighlight macro appears in the Customize Quick Access Toolbar panel.

8. In the **Customize Quick Access Toolbar** panel, click the **SavingsHighlight** command.

9. Click **Modify**.

   The Modify Button dialog box opens.

10. Click the blue button with the white circle inside it (the fourth button from the left on the top row).

11. Click **OK** twice to close the **Modify Button** dialog box and the **Excel Options** dialog box.

    The Excel Options dialog box closes, and the View Macros and SavingsHighlight buttons appear on the Quick Access Toolbar.

12. Right-click the **Show Efficiency** shape, and then click **Assign Macro**.

    The Assign Macro dialog box opens.

13. Click **EfficiencyHighlight**, and then click **OK**.

    The Assign Macro dialog box closes.

SavingsHighlight

14. On the **Quick Access Toolbar**, click the **SavingsHighlight** button.

Excel 2007 runs the macro, which applies a conditional format to the values in the Savings column of the table on the left.

15. Click the **Show Efficiency** shape.

Excel 2007 runs the macro, which applies a conditional format to the values in the Efficiency column of the table on the right.

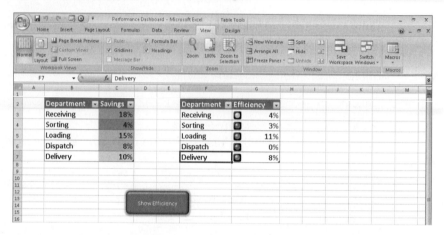

16. On the **Quick Access Toolbar**, click the **Save** button to save your work.

Save

CLOSE the *Performance Dashboard* workbook.

Running Macros When a Workbook Is Opened

One advantage of writing Excel 2007 macros in VBA is that you can have Excel 2007 run a macro whenever a workbook is opened. For example, if you use a worksheet for presentations, you can create macros that render the contents of selected cells in bold type, italic, or different typefaces to set the data apart from data in neighboring cells. If you close a workbook without removing that formatting, however, the contents of your workbook will have highlights when you open it. Although this is not a catastrophe, returning the workbook to its original formatting might take a few seconds to accomplish.

Instead of running a macro by hand, or even from a toolbar button or a menu, you can have Excel 2007 run a macro whenever a workbook is opened. The trick of making that happen is in the name you give the macro. Whenever Excel 2007 finds a macro with the name Auto_Open, it runs the macro when the workbook to which it is attached is opened.

> **Tip** If you have your macro security set to the Disable With Notification level, clicking the Options button that appears on the Message Bar, selecting the Enable This Content option, and then clicking OK allows the Auto_Open macro to run.

In this exercise, you will create a macro to run whenever someone opens the workbook to which it is attached.

> **USE** the *RunOnOpen* workbook. This practice file is located in the *Documents\Microsoft Press\Excel2007SBS\Macros* folder.
> **OPEN** the *RunOnOpen* workbook.

1. If necessary, click the **Options** button that appears on the **Message Bar**.

   The Microsoft Office Security Options dialog box opens.

2. Click **Enable this content**, and then click **OK**.

   The Microsoft Office Security Options dialog box closes.

3. On the **View** tab, in the **Macros** group, click the **Macros** arrow and then, in the list that appears, click **Record Macro**.

   The Record Macro dialog box opens.

4. In the **Macro name** box, delete the existing name, and then type Auto_Open.

5. Click **OK**.

   The Record Macro dialog box closes.

6. Select the cell range B3:C11.

Bold

7. On the **Home** tab, in the **Font** group, click the **Bold** button twice.

   The first click of the Bold button formats all the selected cells in bold; the second click removes the bold formatting from all the selected cells.

8. In the **Macros** list, click **Stop Recording**.

   Excel 2007 stops recording your macro.

9. In the **Macros** list, click **View Macros**.

   The Macro dialog box opens.

Macro	? ✕
Macro name:	
Auto_Open	Run
Auto_Open	
Highlight	Step Into
	Edit
	Create
	Delete
	Options...
Macros in: All Open Workbooks	
Description	
	Cancel

10. Click **Highlight**, and then click **Run**.

    The contents of cells C4, C6, and C10 appear in bold type.

Save

11. On the **Quick Access Toolbar**, click the **Save** button to save your work.

Close

12. Click the **Close** button to close the *RunOnOpen* workbook.

13. Click the **Microsoft Office Button** and then, in the **Recent Documents** list, click **RunOnOpen.xlsm**. If a warning appears, click **Options**, click **Enable this content**, and then click **OK** to enable macros.

    RunOnOpen opens, and the contents of cells C4, C6, and C10 change immediately to regular type.

14. On the **Quick Access Toolbar**, click the **Save** button to save your work.

> **CLOSE** the *RunOnOpen* workbook. If you are not continuing directly to the next chapter, exit Excel.

Key Points

- Macros are handy tools you can use to perform repetitive tasks quickly, such as inserting blocks of text.

- You don't have to be a programmer to use macros; you can record your actions and have Excel 2007 save them as a macro.

- Excel 2007 uses macro-enabled workbook types, which have the file extensions .xlsx (a macro-enabled workbook) and .xlstx (a macro-enabled template workbook).

- If you're curious about what a macro looks like, you can display it in the Visual Basic Editor. If you know a little VBA, or if you just want to experiment, feel free to modify the macro code and see what happens.

- You can create Quick Access Toolbar buttons and shapes that, when clicked, run a macro.

Chapter at a Glance

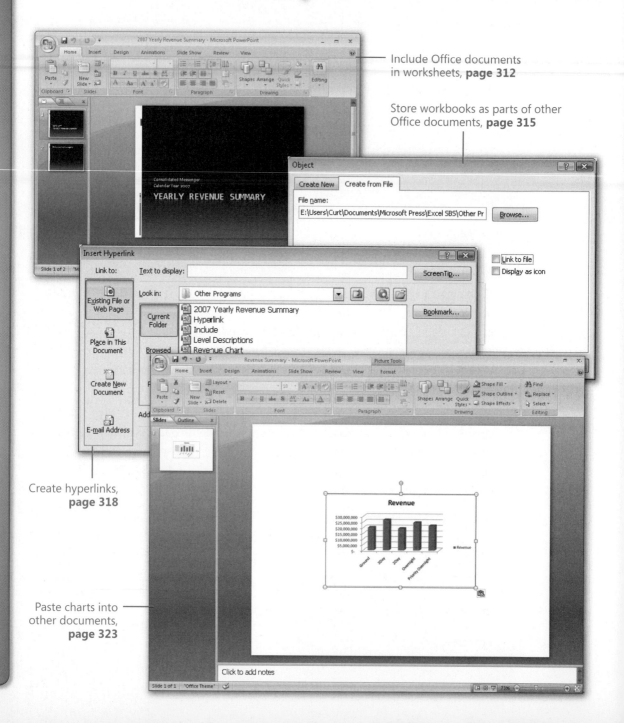

Include Office documents in worksheets, **page 312**

Store workbooks as parts of other Office documents, **page 315**

Create hyperlinks, **page 318**

Paste charts into other documents, **page 323**

14 Working with Other Microsoft Office System Programs

In this chapter you will learn to:

✔ Include Office documents in worksheets.

✔ Store workbooks as parts of other Office documents.

✔ Create hyperlinks.

✔ Paste charts into other documents.

By itself, Microsoft Office Excel 2007 provides a broad range of tools so that you can store, present, and summarize your financial data. Other 2007 Microsoft Office system programs extend your capabilities even further, enabling you to create databases, presentations, written reports, and custom Web pages through which you can organize and communicate your data in print and over networks.

All the Microsoft Office system programs interact in many useful ways. For example, you can include a file created with another Microsoft Office system program in an Excel 2007 worksheet. If you use Microsoft Office Word 2007 to write a quick note about why a customer's shipping expenditures decreased significantly in January, you can include the report in your workbook. Similarly, you can include your Excel 2007 workbooks in documents created with other Microsoft Office system programs. If you want to copy only part of a workbook, such as a chart, to another Microsoft Office system document, you can do that as well.

Excel 2007 integrates well with the Web. If you know of a Web-based resource that would be useful to someone who is viewing a document, you can create a *hyperlink*, or connection from a document to a place in the same file or to another file anywhere on a network or the Internet that the user's computer can reach.

In this chapter, you will learn how to include a Microsoft Office system document in a worksheet, store an Excel 2007 workbook as part of another Office document, create hyperlinks, and paste an Excel 2007 chart into another document.

See Also Do you need only a quick refresher on the topics in this chapter? See the Quick Reference section at the beginning of this book.

> **Important** Before you can use the practice files in this chapter, you need to install them from the book's companion CD to their default location. See "Using the Companion CD" at the beginning of this book for more information.

Including Office Documents in Worksheets

A benefit of working with Excel 2007 is that because it is part of the Microsoft Office system, it is possible to combine data from Excel 2007 and other Microsoft Office system programs to create informative documents and presentations. Just like combining data from more than one Excel 2007 document, combining information from other Microsoft Office system files with an Excel 2007 workbook entails either pasting another Microsoft Office system document into an Excel 2007 workbook or creating a link between a workbook and the other document.

There are two advantages of creating a link between your Excel 2007 workbook and another file. The first benefit is that linking to the other file, as opposed to copying the entire file into your workbook, keeps your Excel 2007 workbook small. If the workbook is copied to another drive or computer, you can maintain the link by copying the linked file along with the Excel 2007 workbook, re-creating the link if the linked file is on the same network as the Excel 2007 workbook. It is also possible to use the workbook without the linked file. The second benefit of linking to another file is that any changes in the file to which you link are reflected in your Excel 2007 workbook.

> **Tip** You usually have to close and reopen a workbook for any changes in the linked document to appear in your workbook. The exception to this rule occurs when you open the file for editing from within your Excel 2007 workbook (as discussed later in this chapter).

You create a link between an Excel 2007 workbook and another Microsoft Office system document by clicking the Insert tab and then, in the Text group, clicking Object to display the Object dialog box. In the Object dialog box, click the Create From File tab.

Clicking the Browse button on the Create From File tab opens the Browse dialog box, from which you can browse to the folder containing the file you want to link to. After you locate the file, double-clicking it closes the Browse dialog box and adds the file's name and path to the File Name box of the Object dialog box. To create a link to the file, select the Link To File check box, and click OK. When you do, the file appears in your workbook.

If you want to link a file to your workbook but don't want the file image to take up much space on the screen, you can also select the Display As Icon check box. After you select the file and click OK, the file will be represented by the same icon used to represent it in Windows.

After you have linked a file to your Excel 2007 workbook—for example, a Microsoft Office PowerPoint 2007 file—you can edit the file by right-clicking its image in your workbook and then, on the shortcut menu that appears, pointing to the appropriate Object command and clicking Edit. For an Office PowerPoint file, you point to Presentation Object. The file will open in its native application. When you finish editing the file, your changes appear in your workbook.

> **Tip** The specific menu item you point to changes to reflect the program used to create the file to which you want to link. For an Office Word 2007 document, for example, the menu item you point to is Document Object.

In this exercise, you will link a PowerPoint 2007 presentation showing a business summary to an Excel 2007 workbook and then edit the presentation from within Excel 2007.

> **Important** You must have PowerPoint 2007 installed on your computer to complete this exercise.

USE the *Summary Presentation* workbook and the *2007 Yearly Revenue Summary* presentation. These practice files are located in the *Documents\Microsoft Press\Excel2007SBS\Other Programs* folder.

BE SURE TO start Excel 2007 and PowerPoint 2007 before beginning this exercise.

OPEN the *Summary Presentation* workbook.

1. On the **Insert** tab, in the **Text** group, click **Object**.

   The Object dialog box opens.

2. Click the **Create from File** tab.

   The Create From File tab appears.

3. Click **Browse**.

   The Browse dialog box opens.

4. Browse to the *Documents\Microsoft Press\Excel2007SBS\Other Programs* folder, click *2007 Yearly Revenue Summary.pptx*, and then click **Insert**.

   The Browse dialog box closes, and the full file path of the *2007 Yearly Revenue Summary* presentation appears in the File Name box.

5. Select the **Link to file** check box, and then click **OK**.

   Excel 2007 creates a link from your workbook to the presentation.

6. Right-click the presentation, point to **Presentation Object**, and then click **Edit**.

   The presentation opens in a PowerPoint 2007 window.

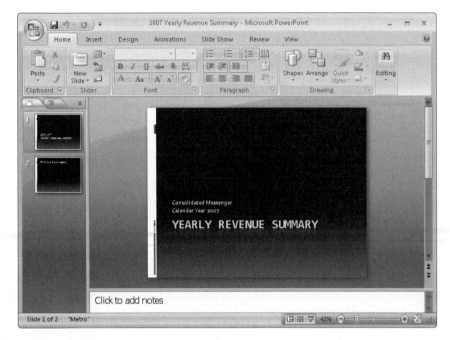

7. Click **Consolidated Messenger FY2007**.

   The text box containing Consolidated Messenger FY2007 is activated.

8. Select the *FY2007* text, and then type Calendar Year 2007.

Save

9. In PowerPoint 2007, on the **Quick Access Toolbar**, click the **Save** button.

   PowerPoint 2007 saves your changes, and Excel 2007 updates the linked object's appearance to reflect the new text.

10. Click the **Microsoft Office Button**, and then click **Save**.

Microsoft Office
Button

> **CLOSE** the *Summary Presentation* workbook and the *2007 Yearly Revenue Summary* presentation, and then exit PowerPoint 2007.

Storing Workbooks as Parts of Other Office Documents

In this chapter's preceding section, you learned how to link to another file from within your Excel 2007 workbook. The advantages of linking to a second file are that the size of your workbook is kept small and any changes in the second document will be reflected in your workbook. The disadvantage is that the second document must be copied with the workbook—or at least be on a network-accessible computer. If Excel 2007 can't find or access the second file where the link says it is located, Excel 2007 can't display it. You can still open your workbook, but you won't see the linked file's contents.

If file size isn't an issue, and you want to ensure that the second document is always available, you can *embed* the file in your workbook. Embedding another file in an Excel 2007 workbook means that the entirety of the other file is saved as part of your work-book. Wherever your workbook goes, the embedded file goes along with it. Of course, the embedded version of the file is no longer connected to the original file, so changes in one aren't reflected in the other.

> **Important** To view the embedded file, you need to have the program used to create it installed on the computer where you open the workbook.

You can embed a file in an Excel 2007 workbook by following the procedure described in the preceding section, except that the Link to file check box should not be selected.

It is also possible to embed your Excel 2007 workbooks in other Microsoft Office system documents. In PowerPoint 2007, for example, you can embed an Excel 2007 file in a pre-sentation by displaying the Insert tab in PowerPoint and then clicking Object to display the Object dialog box. Then in the Object dialog box, click Create From File.

To identify the file you want to embed, click the Browse button and then, in the Browse dialog box that opens, navigate to the folder where the file is stored and double-click the file. The Browse dialog box closes, and the file appears in the File Name box. Click OK to embed your workbook in the presentation.

If you want to embed a workbook in a file created with another program, but you don't want the worksheet to take up much space on the screen, select the Display As Icon check box. After you select the file to embed and click OK, the file is represented by the same icon used to represent it in Windows. Double-clicking the icon opens the embedded document in its original application.

To edit the embedded Excel 2007 workbook, right-click the workbook (or the icon representing it) and then, on the shortcut menu that appears, point to Worksheet Object and click Edit. The workbook opens for editing. After you finish making your changes, you can click anywhere outside the workbook to return to the presentation.

In this exercise, you will embed an Excel 2007 workbook containing sales data in a PowerPoint 2007 presentation and then change the formatting of the workbook from within PowerPoint 2007.

> **Important** You must have PowerPoint 2007 installed on your computer to complete this exercise.

USE the *2007 Yearly Revenue Summary* presentation and the *RevenueByServiceLevel* workbook. These practice files are located in the *Documents\Microsoft Press\Excel2007SBS\ Other Programs* folder.
BE SURE TO start PowerPoint 2007 before beginning this exercise.
OPEN the *2007 Yearly Revenue Summary* presentation.

1. In the **Slides** panel of the presentation window, click the second slide.

   The second slide appears.

2. On the **Insert** tab, in the **Text** group, click **Object**.

   The Insert Object dialog box opens.

3. Click **Create from file**.

   The Insert Object dialog box changes to allow you to enter a file name.

4. Click **Browse**.

   The Browse dialog box opens.

5. Browse to the *Documents\Microsoft Press\Excel2007SBS\Other Programs* folder, and then double-click the *RevenueByServiceLevel* workbook.

   The Browse dialog box closes, and the file's full path appears in the File Name box.

6. Click **OK**.

   The workbook appears in your presentation.

> **CLOSE** the *RevenueByServiceLevel* workbook and the *2007 Yearly Revenue Summary* presentation, and exit PowerPoint 2007.

Creating Hyperlinks

One of the hallmarks of the Web is that documents published on Web pages can have references, or hyperlinks, to locations in the same document or to other Web documents. A hyperlink functions much like a link between two cells or between two files, but hyperlinks can reach any computer on the Web, not just those on a corporate network. Hyperlinks that haven't been clicked usually appear as under-lined blue text, and followed hyperlinks appear as underlined purple text, but those settings can be changed.

To create a hyperlink, click the cell in which you want to insert the hyperlink and then, on the Insert tab, click Hyperlink. The Insert Hyperlink dialog box opens.

> **Tip** You can also open the Insert Hyperlink dialog box by pressing Ctrl+K.

You can choose one of four types of targets, or destinations, for your hyperlink: an existing file or Web page, a place in the current document, a new document you create on the spot, or an e-mail address. By default, the Insert Hyperlink dialog box displays the tools to connect to an existing file or Web page.

To create a hyperlink to another file or Web page, you can use the Look In box navigation tool to locate the file. If you recently opened the file or Web page to which you want to link, you can click either the Browsed Pages or the Recent Files button to display the Web pages or files in your History list.

If you want to create a hyperlink to another place in the current Excel 2007 workbook, you click the Place In This Document button to display a list of available targets in the current workbook.

To select the worksheet to which you want to refer, you click the worksheet name in the Or Select A Place In This Document box. When you do, a 3-D reference with the name of the worksheet and cell A1 on that worksheet appears in the Text To Display box.

If you want to refer to a specific cell on a worksheet, click the worksheet name in the Or Select A Place In This Document box, and then change the cell reference in the Type The Cell Reference box.

You can also create hyperlinks that generate e-mail messages to an address of your choice. To create this type of hyperlink, which is called a *mailto* hyperlink, click the E-mail Address button.

In the dialog box that appears, you can type the recipient's e-mail address in the E-mail Address box and the subject line for messages sent via this hyperlink in the Subject box.

> **Tip** If you use Windows Mail, Microsoft Office Outlook, or Microsoft Outlook Express as your e-mail program, a list of recently used addresses will appear in the Recently Used E-Mail Addresses box. You can insert any of those addresses in the E-mail Address box by clicking the address.

Clicking a mailto hyperlink causes the user's default e-mail program to open and create a new e-mail. The e-mail message is addressed to the address you entered in the E-mail Address box, and the subject is set to the text you typed in the Subject box.

Regardless of the type of hyperlink you create, you can specify the text you want to represent the hyperlink in your worksheet. You type that text in the Text To Display box. When you click OK, the text you type there appears in your worksheet, formatted as a hyperlink.

> **Tip** If you leave the Text To Display box empty, the actual link will appear in your worksheet.

To edit an existing hyperlink, click the cell containing the hyperlink and then, on the shortcut menu that appears, click Edit Hyperlink. You can also click Open Hyperlink to go to the target document or create a new e-mail message, or click Remove Hyperlink to delete the hyperlink.

> **Tip** If you delete a hyperlink from a cell, the text from the Text To Display box remains in the cell, but it no longer functions as a hyperlink.

In this exercise, you will create a hyperlink to another document and then a second hyperlink to a different location in the current workbook.

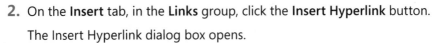

USE the *Hyperlink* and *Level Descriptions* workbooks. These practice files are located in the *Documents\Microsoft Press\Excel2007SBS\Other Programs* folder.
OPEN the *Hyperlink* workbook.

1. On the Revenue by Level worksheet, click cell B9.
2. On the **Insert** tab, in the **Links** group, click the **Insert Hyperlink** button.

   The Insert Hyperlink dialog box opens.

Hyperlink

Insert Hyperlink

3. If necessary, click the **Existing File or Web Page** button.

4. If necessary, use the controls to the right of the **Look in** box to navigate to the *Documents\Microsoft Press\Excel2007SBS\Other Programs* folder.

The files in the target folder appear in the Insert Hyperlink dialog box.

5. In the file list, click the **Level Descriptions** workbook, and then click **OK**.

The workbook's full path appears in the Text To Display box and the Address box.

6. In the **Text to display** box, edit the value so that it reads Level Descriptions.

Insert Hyperlink	? ✕

Link to: Text to display: Level Descriptions   ScreenTip...

Look in: Other Programs

Existing File or Web Page

Current Folder
- 2007 Yearly Revenue Summary
- Hyperlink
- Include
- Level Descriptions
- Revenue Chart
- Revenue Summary
- RevenueByServiceLevel
- Summary Presentation

Browsed Pages

Recent Files

Place in This Document

Create New Document

Bookmark...

Address: Level Descriptions.xlsx

E-mail Address

OK   Cancel

7. Click **OK**.

8. Click the hyperlink in cell B9.

The *Level Descriptions* workbook appears.

Microsoft Office Button

9. In the *Level Descriptions* workbook, click the **Microsoft Office Button**, and then click **Close**.

The *Level Descriptions* workbook closes.

10. Right-click cell B11, and then click **Hyperlink**.

The Insert Hyperlink dialog box opens.

11. In the **Link to** pane, click **Place in This Document**.

The document elements to which you can link appear in the dialog box.

12. In the **Or select a place in this document** pane, click **Notes**.

13. Click **OK**.

    The Insert Hyperlink dialog box closes, and Excel 2007 creates a hyperlink in cell B11.

14. Right-click cell B11, and then click **Edit Hyperlink**.

    The Edit Hyperlink dialog box opens.

15. Edit the **Text to display** box's value so it reads Revenue Notes.

16. Click **OK**.

    The Edit Hyperlink dialog box closes, and the text in cell B11 changes to *Revenue Notes*.

17. On the **Quick Access Toolbar**, click the **Save** button to save your work.

Save

> **CLOSE** the *Hyperlink* and *Level Descriptions* workbooks.

Pasting Charts into Other Documents

A final way to include objects from one workbook in another workbook is to copy the object you want to share and then paste it into its new location. Copying Excel 2007 charts to Word 2007 documents and PowerPoint 2007 presentations enables you to reuse your data without inserting a worksheet into the file and re-creating your chart in that new location.

When you want to copy the image of the chart in its current form to another document, you just right-click the chart, click Copy on the shortcut menu that appears, and then paste the image into the other document. After the other Microsoft Office system program completes the paste operation, it displays the Paste Options button. Clicking the Paste Options button enables you to choose whether to paste the chart as a chart that remains linked to the worksheet that provides its data, to paste the entire workbook, or to paste an image of the chart in its current state.

> **Tip** In previous versions of Microsoft Office, the default option was to paste an image of the chart. In the 2007 release, the programs assume that you want to paste the chart and retain its connection to the source workbook.

In this exercise, you will copy a chart containing sales information to the Clipboard and paste an image of the chart into a PowerPoint 2007 presentation.

> **Important** You must have PowerPoint 2007 installed on your computer to complete this exercise.

USE the *Revenue Chart* workbook and the *Revenue Summary* presentation. These practice files are located in the *Documents\Microsoft Press\Excel2007SBS\Other Programs* folder.
OPEN the *Revenue Chart* workbook and the *Revenue Summary* presentation.

1. In the *Revenue Chart* workbook, right-click the chart, and then click **Copy**.

   Excel 2007 copies the workbook to the Clipboard.

2. Display the *Revenue Summary* presentation.

3. Right-click a blank spot in the visible slide, and click **Paste**.

   The chart appears in the presentation, and PowerPoint 2007 displays a Paste Options button.

Paste Options

4. In the **Paste Options** list, click **Paste as Picture**.

   The chart appears as a static image.

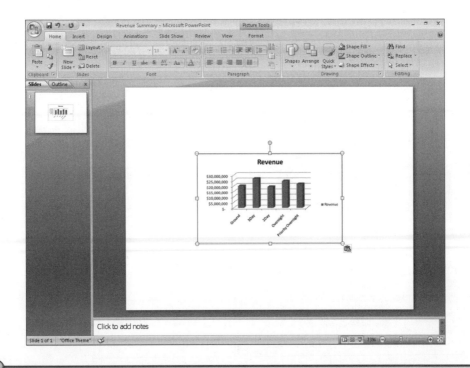

CLOSE the *Revenue Chart* workbook and the *Revenue Summary* presentation, and exit PowerPoint 2007. If you are not continuing directly to the next chapter, exit Excel.

Key Points

- Excel 2007 is a versatile program. You can exchange data between Excel 2007 and quite a few other programs in just a few steps.

- One benefit of Excel 2007 being part of the Microsoft Office system is that you can embed Excel 2007 worksheets in other Office documents and embed other Office documents (such as PowerPoint 2007 presentations) in Excel 2007 workbooks.

- Excel 2007 works smoothly with the Web; adding hyperlinks to Web pages, other documents, or specific locations in the current workbook is possible through the Insert Hyperlink dialog box.

- After you create a hyperlink, you can change any part of it.

- Excel 2007 is the easiest Microsoft Office system program in which to create charts. After you create a chart in Excel 2007, you can paste it directly into another Office document.

Chapter at a Glance

Manage comments, **page 331**

Share data lists, **page 328**

Track and manage colleagues' changes, **page 335**

Protect workbooks and worksheets, **page 339**

Authenticate workbooks, **page 344**

Save workbooks for the Web, **page 346**

15 Collaborating with Colleagues

In this chapter you will learn to:

✔ Share data lists.

✔ Manage comments.

✔ Track and manage colleagues' changes.

✔ Protect workbooks and worksheets.

✔ Authenticate workbooks.

✔ Save workbooks for the Web.

Even though a single individual might be tasked with managing a company's financial data and related information, many people have input when making future revenue projections. You and your colleagues can enhance the workbook data you share by adding comments that offer insight into the information the data represents, such as why revenue was so strong during a particular month or whether a service level might be discontinued. If the workbook in which those projections and comments will be stored is available on a network or an intranet, you can allow more than one user to access the workbook at a time by turning on workbook sharing. After a workbook has been shared with your colleagues, you can have the workbook mark and record any changes made to it. After all changes have been made, the workbook's administrator can decide which changes to keep and which to reject.

If you prefer to limit the number of colleagues who can view and edit your workbooks, you can add password protection to a workbook, worksheet, cell range, or even an individual cell. By adding password protection, you can prevent changes to critical elements of your workbooks. You can also hide formulas used to calculate values.

If you work in an environment in which you and colleagues, both inside and outside your organization, exchange files frequently, you can use a digital signature to help verify that your workbooks and any macros they contain are from a trusted source.

Finally, if you want to display information on a Web site, you can do so by saving a workbook as a Web page. Your colleagues won't be able to edit the information, but they will be able to view it, and comment by e-mail or phone.

In this chapter, you'll learn how to share a data list, manage comments in workbook cells, track and manage changes made by colleagues, protect workbooks and worksheets, and digitally sign your workbooks.

See Also Do you need only a quick refresher on the topics in this chapter? See the Quick Reference section at the beginning of this book.

> **Important** Before you can use the practice files in this chapter, you need to install them from the book's companion CD to their default location. See "Using the Companion CD" at the beginning of this book for more information.

Sharing Data Lists

To enable several users to edit a workbook simultaneously, you must turn on workbook sharing. Enabling more than one user to edit a workbook simultaneously is perfect for an enterprise such as Consolidated Messenger, whose employees need to look up customer information, shipment numbers, and details on mistaken deliveries.

To turn on workbook sharing, on the Review tab, in the Changes group, click Share Workbook. In the Share Workbook dialog box, turn on workbook sharing by selecting the Allow Changes By More Than One User At The Same Time check box. You can then set the sharing options for the active workbook by clicking the Advanced tab.

> **Important** You can't share a workbook that contains a data table. To share the workbook, convert the table to a regular cell range by clicking the table, clicking the Design tab and then, in the Tools group, clicking Convert To Range. Click Yes in the dialog box that appears to confirm the change.

On the Advanced tab of the Share Workbook dialog box, two settings are of particular interest. The first determines whether Microsoft Office Excel 2007 should maintain a history of changes made to the workbook and, if so, for how many days it should keep the changes. The default setting is to retain a record of all changes made in the past 30 days, but you can enter any number of days you like. Unless it's critical that you keep all changes made to a workbook, you should probably stay with the default setting of 30 days so the list doesn't become too large and unwieldy.

The other important setting on this tab deals with how Office Excel 2007 decides which of two conflicting changes in a cell should be applied. For example, a service level's price might change, and two of your colleagues might type in what they think the new price should be. Selecting the Ask Me Which Changes Win option enables you to decide which price to keep.

Another way to share a workbook is to send a copy of it to your colleagues via e-mail. Although the specific command to attach a file to an e-mail message is different in every program, the most common method of attaching a file is to create a new e-mail message and then click the Attach button, as in Microsoft Office Outlook 2007.

In this exercise, you will turn on workbook sharing and then attach the file to an Office Outlook 2007 e-mail message.

> **Tip** You must have Outlook 2007 installed on your computer to follow this procedure exactly.

USE the *Cost Projections* workbook. This practice file is located in the *Documents\Microsoft Press\Excel2007SBS\Sharing* folder.

BE SURE TO start Excel 2007 and Outlook 2007 before beginning this exercise.

OPEN the *Cost Projections* workbook.

1. On the **Review** tab, in the **Changes** group, click **Share Workbook**.

   The Share Workbook dialog box opens.

2. Select the **Allow changes by more than one user at the same time** check box.

3. Click **OK**.

   A message box appears, indicating that you must save the workbook for the action to take effect.

4. Click **OK**.

   Excel 2007 saves and shares the workbook.

Microsoft Office Button

5. Click the **Microsoft Office Button**, point to **Send**, and then click **E-mail**.

   A new e-mail message opens with the *Cost Projections* workbook attached.

[Screenshot of e-mail message window "Cost Projections.xlsx - Message (HTML)" with Subject: Cost Projections.xlsx and Attached: Cost Projections.xlsx (17 KB)]

6. Type an address in the **To** box.

7. Click **Send**.

   Your e-mail program sends the message. If Excel 2007 had to open your e-mail program to send the message, the program closes.

CLOSE the *Cost Projections* workbook.

Managing Comments

Excel 2007 makes it easy for you and your colleagues to insert comments in workbook cells, adding insights that go beyond the cell data. For example, if a regional processing center's package volume is exceptionally high on a particular day, the center's manager can add a comment to the cell in which shipments are recorded for that day, noting that two exceptionally large bulk shipments accounted for the disparity.

When you add a comment to a cell, a flag appears in the upper-right corner of the cell. When you point to a cell with a comment, the comment appears in a box next to the cell, along with the name of the user logged on to the computer at the time the comment was created.

> **Important** Note that the name attributed to a comment might not be the same as the person who actually created it. Enforcing access controls, such as requiring users to enter account names and passwords when they access a computer, can help track the person who made a comment or change.

You can add a comment to a cell by clicking the cell, clicking the Review tab, and then clicking New Comment. When you do, the comment flag appears in the cell, and a comment box appears next to the cell. You can type the comment in the box and, when you're done, click another cell to close the box for editing. When you point to the cell that contains the comment, the comment appears next to the cell.

If you want a comment to be shown the entire time the workbook is open, click the cell that contains the comment, click the Review tab and then, in the Comments group, click Show/Hide Comment. You can hide the comment by clicking the same button when the comment appears in the workbook, and delete the comment by clicking the Review tab and then, in the Comments group, clicking Delete. Or you can open the comment for editing by clicking Edit Comment in the Comments group.

> **Important** When someone other than the original user edits a comment, that person's input is marked with the new user's name and is added to the original comment.

If you want to select every cell that contains a comment, you can do so by using the Go To Special dialog box. To display the Go To Special dialog box, click Find & Select in the Editing group on the Home tab, and then click Go To Special. In the Go To Special dialog box, click Comments, and then click OK. Excel 2007 then selects every cell that contains a comment.

In this exercise, you will add comments to two cells. You will then highlight the cells that contain comments, review a comment, and delete that comment.

> **USE** the *Projections for Comment* workbook. This practice file is located in the *Documents\Microsoft Press\Excel2007SBS\Sharing* folder.
>
> **OPEN** the *Projections for Comment* workbook.

1. Click cell E6.

2. On the **Review** tab, in the **Comments** group, click **New Comment**.

   A red comment flag appears in cell E6, and a comment box appears next to the cell.

3. In the comment box, type Seems optimistic; move some improvement to the next year?

4. Click any cell outside the comment box.

   The comment box disappears.

5. Click cell G7.

6. On the **Review** tab, in the **Comments** group, click **New Comment**.

   A red comment flag appears in cell G7, and a comment box appears next to the cell.

7. In the comment box, type Should see more increase as we integrate new processes.

8. Click any cell outside the comment box.

   The comment box disappears.

9. On the **Home** tab, in the **Editing** group, click **Find & Select**, and then click **Go To Special**.

   The Go To Special dialog box opens.

Go To Special
Select

Select:
- ⦿ Comments
- ○ Constants
- ○ Formulas
  - ☑ Numbers
  - ☑ Text
  - ☑ Logicals
  - ☑ Errors
- ○ Blanks
- ○ Current region
- ○ Current array
- ○ Objects

- ○ Row differences
- ○ Column differences
- ○ Precedents
- ○ Dependents
  - ⦿ Direct only
  - ○ All levels
- ○ Last cell
- ○ Visible cells only
- ○ Conditional formats
- ○ Data validation
  - ⦿ All
  - ○ Same

[OK] [Cancel]

10. Click **Comments**, and then click **OK**.

   Excel 2007 selects all cells that contain comments.

11. Click any unselected cell.

   Excel 2007 removes the previous selection.

12. Click cell G7.

13. On the **Review** tab, in the **Comments** group, click **Delete**.

   Excel 2007 deletes the comment.

✕ **CLOSE** the *Projections for Comment* workbook.

Tracking and Managing Colleagues' Changes

Whenever you collaborate with a number of your colleagues to produce or edit a document, you should consider tracking the changes each user makes. When you turn on change tracking, any changes made to the workbook are highlighted in a color assigned to the user who made the changes. One benefit of tracking changes is that if you have a question about a change, you can quickly identify who made the change and verify that it is correct. In Excel 2007, you can turn on change tracking in a workbook by clicking the Review tab and then, in the Changes group, clicking Track Changes and then Highlight Changes.

In the Highlight Changes dialog box that appears, select the Track Changes While Editing check box. Selecting this check box saves your workbook, turns on change tracking, and also shares your workbook, enabling more than one user to access the workbook simultaneously.

You can use the controls in the Highlight Changes dialog box to choose which changes to track, but clearing the When, Who, and Where check boxes makes Excel 2007 track all changes. Now, whenever anyone makes a change to the workbook, the change is attributed to the user logged in to the computer from which the change was made. Each user's changes are displayed in a unique color. As with a comment, when you point to a change, the date and time when the change was made and the name of the user who made it appear as a ScreenTip.

After you and your colleagues finish modifying a workbook, you can decide which changes to accept and which changes to reject. To start the process, click the Review tab. In the Changes group, click Track Changes, and then click Accept Or Reject Changes. After you clear the message box that indicates Excel 2007 will save your workbook, the Select Changes To Accept Or Reject dialog box opens. From the When list, you can choose which changes to review. The default choice is Not Yet Reviewed, but you can also click Since Date to open a dialog box, into which you can enter the starting date of changes you want to review. To review all changes in your workbook, clear the When, Who, and Where check boxes.

When you are ready to accept or reject changes, click OK. The Accept Or Reject Changes dialog box opens, with the first change described in the body of the dialog box. Clicking the Accept button institutes the change; whereas clicking the Reject button removes the change, restores the cell to its previous value, and erases any record of the change. Clicking Accept All or Reject All implements all changes or restores all cells to their original values, but you should choose one of those options only if you are absolutely certain you are doing the right thing.

If you want an itemized record of all changes you have made since the last time you saved the workbook, you can add a History worksheet to your workbook. To add a History worksheet, click Track Changes in the Changes group, and then click Highlight Changes to open the Highlight Changes dialog box. Select the List Changes On A New Sheet check box. When you click OK, a new worksheet named History appears in your workbook. The next time you save your workbook, Excel 2007 will delete the History worksheet.

In this exercise, you will turn on change tracking in a workbook, make changes to the workbook, accept or reject changes, and create a History worksheet.

> **USE** the *Projection Change Tracking* workbook. This practice file is located in the *Documents\Microsoft Press\Excel2007SBS\Sharing* folder.
>
> **OPEN** the *Projection Change Tracking* workbook.

1. On the **Review** tab, in the **Changes** group, click **Track Changes**, and then click **Highlight Changes**.

   The Highlight Changes dialog box opens.

2. Select the **Track changes while editing. This also shares your workbook** check box.

   The Highlight Which Changes area controls become active.

3. Click **OK**.

A message box appears, indicating that Excel 2007 will save the workbook.

4. Click **OK**.

The message box closes. Excel 2007 saves the workbook and begins tracking changes.

5. In cell E6, type 15%, and then press Enter .

A blue flag appears in the upper-left corner of cell E6.

6. In cell E7, type 12%, and then press Enter .

A blue flag appears in the upper-left corner of cell E7.

7. On the **Quick Access Toolbar**, click the **Save** button to save your work.

Save

8. On the **Review** tab, in the **Changes** group, click **Track Changes**, and then click **Highlight Changes**.

The Highlight Changes dialog box opens.

9. Select the **List changes on a new sheet** check box, and then click **OK**.

Excel 2007 creates and displays a worksheet named *History*, which contains a list of all changes made since the last time a user accepted or rejected changes.

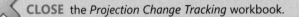

10. Click the **Sheet1** sheet tab.

    The *Sheet1* worksheet appears.

11. On the **Review** tab, in the **Changes** group, click **Track Changes**, and then click **Accept/Reject Changes**.

    The Select Changes To Accept Or Reject dialog box opens.

12. Click **OK**.

    The Select Changes To Accept Or Reject dialog box displays the first change.

13. Click **Accept**.

    Excel 2007 keeps the change and then displays the next change.

14. Click **Accept**.

    Excel 2007 keeps the change and deletes the *History* worksheet. The Accept Or Reject Changes dialog box closes.

CLOSE the *Projection Change Tracking* workbook.

Protecting Workbooks and Worksheets

Excel 2007 gives you the ability to share your workbooks over the Web, over a corporate intranet, or by copying files for other users to take on business trips. An important part of sharing files, however, is ensuring that only those users you want to have access to the files can open or modify them. For example, Consolidated Messenger might have a series of computers available in a processing center so supervisors can look up package volumes and handling efficiency information. Although those computers are vital tools for managing the business process, it doesn't help the company to have unauthorized personnel, even those with good intentions, accessing critical workbooks.

You can limit access to your workbooks or elements within workbooks by setting passwords. Setting a password for an Excel 2007 workbook means that any users who want to access the protected workbook must enter the workbook's password in a dialog box that appears when they try to open the file. If users don't know the password, they cannot open the workbook.

To set a password for a workbook, open the workbook to be protected, click the Microsoft Office Button, and then click Save As. The Save As dialog box opens, with the name of the open workbook in the File Name box. In the lower-left corner of the dialog box, click the Tools button and then click General Options to open the Save Options dialog box. In the Save Options dialog box, you can require users to enter one password to open the workbook and another to modify it. After you click OK, the Confirm Password dialog box opens, in which you can verify the passwords required to access and modify the workbook. After you have confirmed the passwords, click Save in the Save As dialog box to finish adding password protection to the workbook. To later remove the passwords from a workbook, repeat these steps, but delete the passwords from the Save Options dialog box and save the file.

> **Tip** The best passwords are random strings of characters, but random characters are hard to remember. One good method of creating hard-to-guess passwords is to combine elements of two words with a number in between. For example, you might have a password wbk15pro, which could be read as "workbook, Chapter 15, protection." In any event, avoid dictionary words in English or any other language, as they can be found easily by password-guessing programs available on the Internet.

If you want to allow anyone to open a workbook but want to prevent unauthorized users from editing a worksheet, you can protect a worksheet by displaying that worksheet, clicking the Review tab and then, in the Changes group, clicking Protect Sheet to open the Protect Sheet dialog box.

In the Protect Sheet dialog box, you select the Protect Worksheet And Contents Of Locked Cells check box to protect the sheet. You can also set a password that a user must type in before protection can be turned off again and choose which elements of the worksheet a user can change while protection is turned on. To enable a user to change a worksheet element without entering the password, select the check box next to that element's name.

The check box at the top of the worksheet mentions locked cells. A locked cell is a cell that can't be changed when worksheet protection is turned on. You can lock or unlock a cell by right-clicking the cell and clicking Format Cells on the shortcut menu that appears. In the Format Cells dialog box, you click the Protection tab and select the Locked check box.

When worksheet protection is turned on, selecting the Locked check box prevents unauthorized users from changing the contents or formatting of the locked cell, whereas selecting the Hidden check box hides the formulas in the cell. You might want to hide the formula in a cell if you draw sensitive data, such as customer contact information, from another workbook and don't want casual users to see the name of the workbook in a formula.

Finally, you can password-protect a cell range. For example, you might want to let users enter values in most worksheet cells but also want to protect the cells with formulas that perform calculations based on those values. To password-protect a range of cells, select the cells to protect, click the Review tab and then, in the Changes group, click Allow Users To Edit Ranges. The Allow Users To Edit Ranges dialog box opens.

To create a protected range, click the New button to display the New Range dialog box. Type a name for the range in the Title box, and then type a password in the Range Password box. When you click OK, Excel 2007 asks you to confirm the password; after you do, click OK in the Confirm Password dialog box and again in the Allow Users To Edit Ranges dialog box to protect the range. Now, whenever users try to edit a cell in the protected range, they are prompted for a password.

> **Tip** Remember that a range of cells can mean just one cell!

In this exercise, you will password-protect a workbook, a worksheet, and a range of cells. You will then hide the formula in a cell.

> **USE** the *SecureInfo* workbook. This practice file is located in the *Documents\Microsoft Press\Excel2007SBS\Sharing* folder.
> **OPEN** the *SecureInfo* workbook.

Microsoft Office
Button

1. Click the **Microsoft Office Button**, and then click **Save As**.

   The Save As dialog box opens.

2. Click the **Tools** button, and then click **General Options**.

   The General Options dialog box opens.

3. Type work15pro in the **Password to open** box.

4. Type pro15work in the **Password to modify** box.

5. Click **OK**.

   The Confirm Password dialog box opens.

6. In the **Reenter password to proceed** box, type work15pro.

7. Click **OK**.

   The Confirm Password dialog box changes to ask you to reenter the password to modify the workbook.

8. In the **Reenter password to modify** box, type pro15work.

9. Click **OK**.

   The Confirm Password dialog box closes.

10. Click **Save**.

    Excel 2007 saves the workbook.

11. If necessary, click the **Performance** sheet tab.

    The Performance worksheet appears.

12. Right-click cell B8, and then click **Format Cells**.

    The Format Cells dialog box opens.

13. Click the **Protection** tab.

    The Protection tab appears.

14. Select the **Hidden** check box, and then click **OK**.

Excel 2007 formats cell B8 so that it won't display its formula after you protect the worksheet.

15. On the **Review** tab, in the **Changes** group, click **Protect Sheet**.

The Protect Sheet dialog box opens.

16. In the **Password to unprotect sheet** box, type prot300pswd.

17. Clear the **Select locked cells** and **Select unlocked cells** check boxes, and then click **OK**.

The Confirm Password dialog box opens.

18. In the **Reenter password to proceed** box, type prot300pswd, and then click **OK**.

19. Click the **Weights** sheet tab.

The Weights worksheet appears.

20. Select the cell range B2:C7.

21. On the **Review** tab, in the **Changes** group, click **Allow Users to Edit Ranges**.

The Allow Users To Edit Ranges dialog box opens.

22. Click **New**.

The New Range dialog box opens, with the range B2:C7 called out in the Refers To Cells box.

23. In the **Title** box, type AllWeights.

24. In the **Range password** box, type work15pro, and then click **OK**.

25. In the **Confirm Password** dialog box, reenter the password work15pro.

The range appears in the Allow Users To Edit Ranges box.

26. Click **Protect Sheet**.

The Protect Sheet dialog box opens.

27. In the **Password to unprotect sheet** box, type work15pro, and then click **OK**.

28. In the **Confirm Password** dialog box, reenter the password work15pro, and then click **OK**.

> **CLOSE** the *SecureInfo* workbook, saving your changes.

Authenticating Workbooks

The unfortunate reality of exchanging files over networks, especially over the Internet, is that you need to be sure you know the origin of the files you're working with. One way an organization can guard against files with viruses or substitute data is to authenticate every workbook using a digital signature. A *digital signature* is a value created by combining a user's unique secret digital signature file mathematically with the contents of the workbook, which programs such as Excel 2007 can recognize and use to verify the identity of the user who signed the file. A good analog for a digital signature is a wax seal, which was used for thousands of years to verify the integrity and origin of a document.

> **Tip** The technical details of and procedure for managing digital certificates are beyond the scope of this book, but your network administrator should be able to create a digital certificate for you. You can also directly purchase a digital signature from a third party, which can usually be renewed annually for a small fee. For the purposes of this book, you'll use the selfcert.exe Microsoft Office system accessory program to generate a certificate with which to perform the exercise at the end of the chapter. This type of certificate is useful for certifying a document on your own computer, but it is not a valid certificate to verify yourself to others across your network or on the Internet.

To create a digital certificate you can use as a demonstration, open the Start menu, click All Programs, click Microsoft Office, click Microsoft Office Tools, and then click Digital Certificate For VBA Projects. In the Create Digital Certificate dialog box, type a name for your certificate and click OK to have the program create your trial certificate. Then, in Excel 2007, click the Microsoft Office Button, click Prepare, and click Add A Digital Signature. In the Sign dialog box, type your purpose for signing the document, and then click Sign to sign your workbook.

> **Tip** After you click Add A Digital Signature, Excel 2007 displays a dialog box, indicating that you can buy digital signatures from third-party providers. To get information about those services, click the Signature Services From The Office Marketplace button. To bypass the message, click OK; to prevent the dialog box from appearing again, select the Don't Show This Message Again check box, and then click OK.

If you have several certificates from which to choose, and the desired certificate doesn't appear in the Sign dialog box, you can click Change to display the Select Certificate dialog box. In the Select Certificate dialog box, click the certificate with which you want to sign the workbook, and then click OK. The Select Certificate dialog box closes, and the certificate with which you signed the workbook appears in the Sign dialog box. As before, click Sign to sign your document using the digital certificate.

In this exercise, you will create a digital certificate and digitally sign a workbook using the certificate.

USE the *Projections Signed* workbook. This practice file is located in the *Documents\ Microsoft Press\Excel2007SBS\Sharing* folder.

OPEN the *Projections Signed* workbook.

1. On the **Start** menu, click **All Programs**, click **Microsoft Office**, click **Microsoft Office Tools**, and then click **Digital Certificate for VBA Projects**.

   The Create Digital Certificate dialog box opens.

2. In the **Your certificate's name** box, type Excel2007SBS, and then click **OK**.

   A message box indicates that the program created your certificate successfully.

3. Click **OK**.

   The message box closes.

Microsoft Office
Button

4. Click the **Microsoft Office Button**, click **Prepare**, and then click **Add a Digital Signature**.

   A message box appears, offering the opportunity to view signature services on Office Marketplace.

5. Click **OK**.

   The message box closes, and the Sign dialog box opens.

6. In the **Purpose for signing this document** box, type Testing.

7. Verify that the *Excel2007SBS* certificate appears in the **Signing as** area of the dialog box, and then click **Sign**.

   The Signature Confirmation dialog box opens.

8. Click **OK**.

   The Signatures task pane appears.

CLOSE the *Projections Signed* workbook.

Saving Workbooks for the Web

Excel 2007 enables you to save Excel 2007 workbooks as Web documents, so you and your colleagues can view workbooks over the Internet or a corporate intranet. For a document to be viewed on the Web, the document must be saved as a Hypertext Markup Language (HTML) file. HTML files, which end with either the *.htm* or the *.html* extension, include tags that tell a Web browser such as Microsoft Internet Explorer how to display the contents of the file.

For example, you might want to set the data labels in a workbook apart from the rest of the data by having the labels displayed with bold text. The coding in an HTML file that indicates text to be displayed as bold text is *...*, where the ellipsis points between the tags are replaced by the text to be displayed. So the following HTML fragment would be displayed as **Excel**:

```
<b>Excel</b>
```

You can create HTML files in Excel 2007 by clicking the Microsoft Office Button and clicking Save As to display the Save As dialog box. To save a workbook as an HTML file, select the Entire Workbook option, type a name for the file in the File Name box and then, in the Save As Type list, click Web Page (*.htm; *.html). With the file type set to Web Page, you can then click Save to have Excel 2007 create an HTML document for each sheet in the workbook.

> **Tip** If your workbook contains data only on the sheet displayed when you save the workbook as a Web page, only that worksheet is saved as a Web page.

After you save an Excel 2007 workbook as a series of HTML documents, you can open it in your Web browser. To open the Excel 2007 file, start Internet Explorer, and then click Open on the File menu to display the Open dialog box. In the Open dialog box, click the Browse button to open the Microsoft Internet Explorer dialog box. You can use the controls in that dialog box to identify the file you want to open.

When you double-click the file you want to open, the Microsoft Internet Explorer dialog box closes and the file's name and path appear in the Open box. To display the Excel 2007 workbook, click OK, and the workbook appears in Internet Explorer. You can move among the workbook's worksheets by clicking the sheet tabs in the lower-left corner of the page.

Saving a workbook to an organization's intranet site enables you to share data with your colleagues. For example, Consolidated Messenger's chief operating officer, Jenny Lysaker, could save a daily report on package misdeliveries to her team's intranet so that everyone could examine what happened, where the problem occurred, and how to fix the problem. It's also possible to save a workbook as a Web file that retains a link to the original workbook. Whenever someone updates the workbook, Excel 2007 updates the Web files to reflect the new content.

To publish a workbook to the Web, click the Microsoft Office Button, click Save As and then, in the Save As Type list, click Web Page. When you do, Excel 2007 displays the Publish button; clicking the Publish button displays the Publish As Web Page dialog box.

The controls in the Publish As Web Page dialog box enable you to select which elements of your workbook you want to publish to the Web. Clicking the Choose arrow displays a list of publishable items, including the option to publish the entire workbook, items on specific sheets, a PivotTable dynamic view, or a range of cells. To have Excel 2007 update the Web page whenever someone updates the source workbook, select the AutoRepublish Every Time This Workbook Is Saved check box. You can also specify which text appears on the Web page's title bar. To do so, click the Change button, type the page title in the Set Title dialog box, and click OK. When you save a workbook that has AutoRepublish turned on, Excel 2007 displays a dialog box indicating that the changes will update the associated Web file.

> **Important** When you save a PivotTable to the Web, the PivotTable doesn't retain its interactivity. Instead, Excel 2007 publishes a static image of the PivotTable's current configuration.

In this exercise, you will save a workbook as a Web page and then publish a worksheet's PivotTable to the Web.

> **USE** the *Shipment Summary* workbook. This practice file is located in the *Documents\ Microsoft Press\Excel2007SBS\Sharing* folder.
> **OPEN** the *Shipment Summary* workbook.

Microsoft Office
Button

1. Click the **Microsoft Office Button**, and then click **Save As**.

   The Save As dialog box opens.

2. In the **File name** box, type Shipment Summary Web.

3. In the **Save as type** list, click **Web Page**.

   The Save As dialog box changes to reflect the Web Page file type.

Save As
« Excel SBS ▶ Web ▶   ▾ ✦₊ Search   🔎
File name: Shipment Summary Web   ▾
Save as type: Web Page   ▾
Authors: Curt   Tags: Add a tag
Save: ⦿ Entire Workbook   Page title: [   ]
◯ Selection: Sheet   [Change Title...]
[Publish...]   ☐ Save Thumbnail
▾ Browse Folders   Tools ▾ [Save] [Cancel]

4. Click **Save**.

   A warning message box appears, indicating that the workbook might contain elements that can't be saved in a Web page.

5. Click **Yes** to save the workbook as a Web file.

   The message box closes, and Excel 2007 saves the workbook as a Web page.

6. Click the **Microsoft Office Button**, and then click **Close**.

7. Click the **Microsoft Office Button** and then, in the list of recently viewed files, click **Shipment Summary**.

   The *Shipment Summary* workbook opens.

8. Click the **Microsoft Office Button**, and then click **Save As**.

   The Save As dialog box opens.

9. In the **File name** box, type Shipment Summary Publish.

10. In the **Save as type** list, click **Web Page**.

    The Save As dialog box changes to reflect the Web Page file type.

11. Click **Publish**.

    The Publish As Web Page dialog box opens.

12. In the **Choose** list, click **Items on Sheet 2**.

    The available items on Sheet2 appear.

Publish as Web Page		? ✕
Item to publish		
Choose:	Items on Sheet2 ▾	
	Sheet	All contents of Sheet2
	PivotTable	PivotTable1 ($A$1:$E$15)
Publish as		
Title:		Change...
File name:	E:\Users\Curt\Documents\Microsoft Press\Excel SBS\Web\Shipn	Browse...
☐ AutoRepublish every time this workbook is saved		
☐ Open published web page in browser	Publish	Cancel

13. In the **Item to Publish** list, click **PivotTable**.

14. Select the **AutoRepublish every time this workbook is saved** check box.

15. Click **Publish**.

Excel 2007 publishes the PivotTable to a Web page. Excel 2007 will update the contents of the Web page whenever a user saves the *Shipment Summary* workbook.

CLOSE the *Shipment Summary* workbook, and exit Excel.

Saving a Workbook for Secure Electronic Distribution

You can create a secure, read-only copy of a workbook for electronic distribution by saving it as a Portable Document Format (PDF) or XML Print Specification (XPS) file. To do so, you must first install the Save As PDF Or XPS add-in from the Microsoft Download Center. To install the add-in, click the Microsoft Office Button, point to Save As, and click Find Add-Ins For Other File Formats. Then follow the instructions on the Web site to install the add-in.

Tip If PDF Or XPS appears on the Save As menu, the add-in is already installed.

To save a workbook as a PDF or XPS file:

1. Install the **Save As PDF or XPS** add-in.
2. Click the **Microsoft Office Button**, point to **Save As**, and then click **PDF or XPS**.
3. In the **Publish as PDF or XPS** dialog box, select the file format you want.
4. If you plan to distribute the file online but not print it, click **Minimum size**.
5. If you want to specify what portion of the workbook or types of content to publish, click the **Options** button, make your selections, and then click **OK**.
6. Click **Publish**.

Finalizing a Workbook

With the new features in Excel 2007, you can inspect a workbook for information you might not want to distribute to other people, and create a read-only final version that prevents other people from making changes to the workbook content.

Using the Document Inspector, you can quickly locate comments and annotations, document properties and personal information, custom XML data, headers and footers, hidden rows and columns, hidden worksheets, and invisible content. You can then easily remove any hidden or personal information that the Document Inspector finds.

To inspect and remove hidden or personal information, follow these steps:

1. Save the file.

2. Click the **Microsoft Office Button**, point to **Prepare**, and then click **Inspect Document**.

3. In the **Document Inspector** window, clear the check box of any content type you don't want to locate. Then click **Inspect**.

4. In the inspection results list, click the **Remove All** button to the right of any category of data you want to remove.

Marking a workbook as final sets the status property to Final and turns off data entry, editing commands, and proofreading marks.

To mark a workbook as final, follow these steps:

1. Click the **Microsoft Office Button**, point to **Prepare**, and then click **Mark as Final**.

2. In the message box indicating that the file will be marked as final and then saved, click **OK**.

3. In the message box indicating that the file has been marked as final, click **OK**.

   To restore functionality to a workbook that has been marked as final, click the Microsoft Office Button, point to Prepare, and then click Mark As Final.

Key Points

- Sharing a workbook enables more than one user to view and edit the data at one time, which is useful in group projects in which each member has a distinct area of responsibility.

- Sending files by e-mail is a very efficient means of collaborating with colleagues.

- Adding comments to cells is a quick way to let your colleagues know what you're thinking without taking up valuable space in a cell.

- Use the Go To Special dialog box to find cells with special contents, such as comments, constants, or formulas.

- Tracking changes is vital when you share responsibility for a workbook with several other people.

- When your workbook's data is too important to leave lying around in the open, use passwords to protect all or part of the file!

- Authenticating workbooks with digital signatures helps to identify the source of your files, so you won't have to guess about the origins of that next attachment in your e-mail inbox.

- Saving a workbook as a Web-accessible HTML document is as easy as saving it as a regular Excel 2007 file, and opening a workbook saved for the Web is just as easy as opening any other Web page.

- Use the AutoRepublish facility to update Excel 2007 files on the Web. Whenever anyone changes the original workbook, Excel 2007 writes the edits to the HTML version of the file.

Glossary

3-D reference A pattern for referring to the workbook, worksheet, and cell from which a value should be read.

active cell The cell that is currently selected and open for editing.

add-in A supplemental program that can be used to extend Excel's functions.

alignment The manner in which a cell's contents are arranged within that cell (for example, centered).

arguments The specific data a function requires to calculate a value .

aspect ratio The relationship between a graphic's height and width.

auditing The process of examining a worksheet for errors.

AutoComplete The ability to complete data entry for a cell based on similar values in other cells in the same column.

AutoFill The ability to extend a series of values based on the contents of a single cell.

AutoFilter A Microsoft Excel tool you can use to create filters.

AutoRepublish An Excel technology that maintains a link between a Web document and the worksheet on which the Web document is based and updates the Web document whenever the original worksheet is saved.

browser A program that lets users view Web documents.

cell The box at the intersection of a row and a column.

cell range A group of cells.

cell reference The letter and number combination, such as C16, that identifies the row and column intersection of a cell.

charts Visual summaries of worksheet data, also called graphs.

columns Cells that are on the same vertical line in a worksheet.

conditional formats Formats that are applied only when cell contents meet certain criteria.

conditional formula A formula that calculates a value using one of two different expressions, depending on whether a third expression is true or false.

data consolidation Summarizing data from a set of similar cell ranges.

data list One or more columns of data depicting multiple instances of a single thing (such as an order).

data table A new Microsoft Office Excel 2007 object that enables you to store and refer to data based on the name of the table and the names of its columns and rows.

dependents The cells with formulas that use the value from a particular cell.

driver A program that controls access to a file or device.

dynamic-link library A file with programming code that can be called by a worksheet function.

embed To save a file as part of another file, as opposed to linking one file to another.

error code A brief message that appears in a worksheet cell, describing a problem with a formula or a function.

Extensible Markup Language (XML) A content-marking system that lets you store data about the contents of a document in that document.

field A column in a data list.

fill handle The square at the lower right corner of a cell you drag to indicate other cells that should hold values in the series defined by the active cell.

Fill Series The ability to extend a series of values based on the contents of two cells, where the first cell has the starting value for the series and the second cell shows the increment.

filter A rule that Excel uses to determine which worksheet rows to display.

formats Predefined sets of characteristics that can be applied to cell contents.

formula An expression used to calculate a value.

Formula AutoComplete The ability to enter a formula quickly by selecting functions, named ranges, and table references that appear when you begin to type the formula into a cell.

freeze To assign cells that will remain at the top of a worksheet regardless of how far down the worksheet a user scrolls.

function A predefined formula.

Goal Seek An analysis tool that finds the value for a selected cell that would produce a given result from a calculation.

graphs Visual summaries of worksheet data, also called charts.

HTML See *Hypertext Markup Language*.

hyperlink A reference to a file on the Web.

Hypertext Markup Language (HTML) A document-formatting system that tells a Web browser such as Internet Explorer how to display the contents of a file.

landscape mode A display and printing mode whereby columns run parallel to the short edge of a sheet of paper.

link A formula that has a cell show the value from another cell.

locked cells Cells that cannot be modified if their worksheet is protected.

macro A series of recorded automated actions that can be replayed.

mailto A special type of hyperlink that lets a user create an e-mail message to a particular e-mail address.

Merge and Center An operation that combines a contiguous group of cells into a single cell. Selecting a merged cell and clicking the Merge And Center button splits the merged cells into the original group of separate cells.

metadata Data that describes the contents of a file.

named range A group of related cells defined by a single name.

Open Database Connectivity (ODBC) A protocol that facilitates data transfer between databases and related programs.

Paste Options A button that appears after you paste an item from the Clipboard into your workbook and provides options for how the item appears in the workbook.

Pick from List The ability to enter a value into a cell by choosing the value from the set of values already entered into cells in the same column.

pivot To reorganize the contents of a PivotTable.

PivotChart A chart that is linked to a PivotTable and that can be reorganized dynamically to emphasize different aspects of the underlying data.

PivotTable A dynamic worksheet that can be reorganized by a user.

portrait mode A display and printing mode whereby columns run parallel to the long edge of a sheet of paper.

precedents The cells that are used in a formula.

primary key A field or group of fields with values that distinguish a row in a data list from all other rows in the list.

property A file detail, such as an author name or project code, that helps identify the file.

query A statement that locates records in a database.

range A group of related cells.

refresh To update the contents of one document when the contents of another document are changed.

relative reference A cell reference in a formula, such as =B3, that refers to a cell that is a specific distance away from the cell that contains the formula. For example, if the formula =B3 were in cell C3, copying the formula to cell C4 would cause the formula to change to =B4.

report A special document with links to one or more worksheets from the same workbook.

rows Cells that are on the same horizontal line in a worksheet.

scenarios Alternative data sets that let you view the impact of specific changes on your worksheet.

schema A document that defines the structure of a set of XML files.

sharing Making a workbook available for more than one user to open and modify simultaneously.

sheet tab The indicator for selecting a worksheet, located at the bottom of the workbook window.

smart tags A Microsoft Office technology that recognizes values in a spreadsheet and finds related information on the Web.

sort To reorder the contents of a worksheet based on a criterion.

split bar A line that defines which cells have been frozen at the top of a worksheet.

subtotals Partial totals for related data in a worksheet.

tables Data lists in a database.

tags Marks used to indicate display properties or to communicate data about the contents of a document.

template A workbook used as a pattern for creating other workbooks.

theme A predefined format that can be applied to a worksheet.

trendline A projection of future data (such as sales) based on past performance.

validation rule A test that data must pass to be entered into a cell without generating a warning message.

what-if analysis Analysis of the contents of a worksheet to determine the impact that specific changes have on your calculations.

workbook The basic Excel document, consisting of one or more worksheets.

worksheet A page in an Excel workbook.

workspace An Excel file type (.xlw) that allows you to open several files at once.

XML See *Extensible Markup Language*.

Index

A

absolute references, 68–69
Accept Or Reject Changes dialog box, 336
access controls, 332, 339. *See also* security
accuracy, 237. *See also* validation rules
active cells, 41, 75, 120
Add Scenario dialog box, 179
add-ins, 2, 190, 195, 350
Advanced Filter dialog box, 128
advertising, 113
Allow Users To Edit Ranges dialog box, 340–341
alternative data sets, 178–185
Analysis ToolPak, 195
appearance, workbook. *See also* formatting; layout
  about, 84–86
  cell formatting, 86–91
  of charts, 10, 235, 242–247
  color coding, 106–113
  corporate images, 113–116
  quick reference, xxxviii–xlii
  readability, 102–106, 221
  spacing, 21
  styles, 92–96
  table styles, 98–101
  themes, 96–98
arguments, 65, 152
arrangement, multiple windows, 27
Assign Macro dialog box, 303
assistance with Excel, xix
attribution of changes, 335
audits, worksheet, 76
Auto Header & Footer, 267
Auto_Open, 306
AutoCalculate, xliii, 126
AutoComplete, xxxii, xxxvi, 37–38, 66
AutoCorrect Options, 54
AutoFill, xxxii, 36–37, 38–39
AutoFilter, 120
autoformats, 223
AutoHeader, lvi
automation, 3. *See also* macros
AutoRepublish, 348
AVERAGE (function), 65, 126, 127

AVERAGEIF/AVERAGEIFS (function), 8, 71–73
averages, 54–55
axis changes, 237
Axis Labels dialog box, 238

B

background color, xxxviii
background images, 114
backups, 182
banding (formatting), 223
blank pages, 283
borders, cell, xxxviii, 87–88
boundaries between sections, 271
Browse dialog box, 313
browsers, 347
business certification program (Microsoft), xxi–xxv
buttons, adding, 28

C

calculations on data
  about, 58–60
  corrections, 75–82
  data group names, 60–63
  formulas, 64–70
  quick reference, xxxv–xxxviii
  for specific conditions, 71–74
Calibri (font), 88
case matching (in searches), 45
case sensitive sorting, 140
caveats. *See* quirks
Cell Styles gallery, 92–93
cells
  active, 41, 75, 120
  appearance of, xxxviii–xxxix
  with comments, lxi, 333
  copying and pasting, xxxii
  delimiters, 228
  editing, xxxiii
  formatting, 5–6, 86–91
  inserting/deleting, 22
  linking, xlviii, 320

cells *(continued)*
  location changes, 23
  locked, 340
  precedents, 76
  quick reference, xxix–xxx, xl–xlii
  ranges, 41, 60–63, 66
  security, lxiii
  value monitoring, 78
centering print areas, lvii, 282
certificates, digital, 344–345
certification, professional, xxi–xxv
Change Chart Type dialog box, 252
change history, lxii, 329, 336
change tracking, lxii, 335–338
charts
  about, 234–236
  appearance of, 10, 242–247
  creating, 236–241
  in Office documents, lx–lxi, 323–325
  PivotCharts, 251–256
  printing, lviii, 286–287
  quick reference, lii–lv
  SmartArt diagrams, 256–263
  trends in, 248–250
Choose A SmartArt Graphic dialog box, 256–258
coding sample, 293
col_index_num, 152
collaboration
  about, 326–328
  change tracking, 335–338
  comments, managing, 331–334
  data list sharing, 328–331
  quick reference, lxi–lxiii
  security, 339–344
  workbook authentication, 344–346
  workbooks as Web documents, 346–350
color
  about, 5
  background, xxxviii
  palettes, 97
  scales, xlii, 109
  themes, xxxix
color coding, 9, 19, 88, 106–113
columns
  alignment, 272
  copying and pasting, xxxii
  headings, repeated, 283
  labeling, 29, 120
  limitations on, 3
  modifying, 19
  quick reference, xxix, xxxi
  referencing, xxxvi
  rows, transposing to, 43
  searching by, 45
  selecting, 41
  sorting, 140

  in table manipulations, 54
  top/bottom values, xliii
  Total, xxxiv–xxxv
commands, organization of, 2
commas (as delimiters), 228
comments, managing, lxi, 331–334
compatibility packs, 4
conditional formats
  color coding, 9, 106–107
  limitations on, 3, 107
  PivotTables, li, 222
  quick reference, xli
  rules, xli
Conditional Formatting Rules Manager,
    107–108, 109
conditional formulas, xxxvii, 71–74
Confirm Password dialog box, 339, 341
conflicting changes, 329
Consolidate dialog box, 170–171
consolidation, data, 170–173
convenience, 27, 28. *See also* Quick Access Toolbar
conventions, xi–xii
copying and pasting
  Auto Fill Options, 39
  charts, 323–324
  columns, 41
  eliminating, 36
  with formatting, xxxix, 93
  formulas, 68, 73
  options, 42
  quick reference, xxxii
  sorting levels, 140
  within workbooks, 41–43
  worksheets, xxviii, 18
corporate identity, 113
corrections, 48–53, 75–82
COUNT (function), 65, 127
COUNTA (function), 127
COUNTIFS (function), 8, 71–73
Create Charts dialog box, 244
Create Digital Certificate dialog box, 344
Create Names From Selection dialog box, 61
Create PivotTable dialog box, 202–203
currency, xl
customization
  charts, 242–247
  conditional formats, 106–107
  data lists, xlvi
  enhancements, 4
  filters, xliii, 122
  headers, 268
  macro access, lix, 301, 302, 303
  margins, 271
  numeric formats, 103–104
  PivotTables, 223
  program windows, 26–32

properties, xxvii, 15–16
Quick Access Toolbar, 28–29
sorting, 140, 141
spelling checker, 48–49
user-defined functions, 7
workbooks, 26–32
cutting and pasting
columns, 41–43
eliminating, 33, 36
shapes, 259
cycle diagrams, 257

D

data
about, 34–36
chart options, 252
collections, 3
color coding, 106–113
correcting/expanding, 48–53
destruction potential, 178, 179
entering/revising, 36–41, 54, 119
from external sources, lii
finding and replacing, 44–48
group names, 60–63
moving, 41–44
from multiple Office applications, 312
quick reference, xxxii–xxxv
series, lii–liii
substitutions, 344
summaries, 8
transposition of, xxxii
trends, 248–250
Data Analysis item, 195
data bars, xli, 109
data combining
about, 156–158
consolidation, 170–173
list templates, 158–164
quick reference, xlvii–xlviii
set groupings, 173–175
sources, linking, 164–169
data filters
about, 118–120
creating, 120–125
list manipulation, 125–130
multiple values, 212
of named ranges, 62
PivotCharts, 251–252
PivotTables, l, 209–215, 251–252
quick reference, xlii–xliv
validation rules, 130–135
data lists. *See also* PivotTables
evolution of, 53
manipulation, 125–130

organization of, 151–155
PivotTables from, l
printing, 279–286
quick reference, xlv–xlvii, xlvi
sharing, 328–331
templates, 158–164
data organization
about, 136–138
levels, 145–150
limitations, 199, 201
lists, 151–155
in PivotTables, 204–206, 211–212
quick reference, xlv–xlvii
sorting, 138–145
data set analysis
about, 176–178
alternative sets, 178–181
descriptive statistics, 194–196
Goal Seek, 185–188
multiple alternatives, 181–185
quick reference, xlviii–xlix
Solver, 189–194
data tables
linking to, 166
managing, 6–7
names of, 54–55
PivotTable interface, 201–202
quick reference, xxxiv
renaming, xxxv
setting up, 53–56
sharing limitations, 328
styles, xl, 98–99
Data Validation dialog box, 131
defaults
change history, 329
change tracking, 335
charts, 324
margins, 271
page printing order, 275
security, 292
sorting, 139, 140
styles, 98, 223
templates, 159
themes, 97
values, 179
workbooks, 14
worksheet names, 18
Delete dialog box, 23
deletion
cell formatting, 87
comments, lxi
formatting rules, xli
links, lxi
named ranges, xxxvi
rows/columns/cells, xxix, xxx, 22
sorting levels, vl

deletion *(continued)*
  styles, xxxix
  window watches, xxxviii
  worksheets, xxix
delimiters, 228, 229, 230
descriptive statistics, xlix, 194–196
design themes. *See* themes
destinations, hyperlink, 319
Developer tab, 2
diagrams, lv, 257. *See also* charts
dialog boxes
  Assign Macro, 303
  Browse, 313
  Confirm Password, 339, 341
  Create Digital Certificate, 344
  Create Names From Selection, 61
  Excel Options, 2, 37, 43, 88, 190, 195, 292, 301–302
  Go To Special, 333
  Goal Seek Status, 186
  Macro, 293, 294, 301, 302
  Name Manager, 61, 62
  New Name, 61, 62
  New Range, 341
  New Workbook, 159
  Object, 312–313, 316
  Open, 347
  Print, 281, 286
  Protect Sheet, 340
  Publish As Web Page, 347
  Record Macro, 297
  Scenario Summary, 182
  Security Options, 291
  Select Certificate, 345
  Set Title, 348
  Share Workbook, 328–329
  Sign, 344–345
  Solver Parameters, 190
dialog boxes, charts
  Axis Labels, 238
  Change Chart Type, 252
  Create Charts, 244
  Create PivotTable, 202–203
  Move Chart, 239
  New PivotTable QuickStyle, 223
  New Table Quick Style, 98
dialog boxes, data functions
  Advanced Filter, 128
  Consolidate, 170–171
  Data Validation, 131
  Error Checking, 77
  Evaluate Formula, 78
  Select Data Source, 237, 238
  Sort, 139, 140
  Sort Options, 140
  Subtotal, 145
  Top 10 AutoFilter, 122
  Value Field Settings, 217

dialog boxes, editing
  Accept Or Reject Changes, 336
  Allow Users To Edit Ranges, 340, 341
  Delete, 23
  Edit Name, 62
  Find And Replace, 44–45
  Highlight Changes, 335
  Move Or Copy, 18
  Paste Special, 43
  Save As, 15, 339, 346
  Save Options, 339
  Save Workspace, 173
  Select Changes To Accept Or Reject, 335
dialog boxes, formatting
  Find Format, 45
  Format, 243
  Format Cells, 92, 98, 102, 103, 221, 223, 340
  Format Shape, 260
  Page Setup, 267, 271, 273, 275, 279, 281, 282, 283
  Style, 92
  Templates, 159
dialog boxes, insertion functions
  Add Scenario, 179
  Choose A SmartArt Graphic, 256–258
  Import Text File, 228–229
  Insert, 23, 160
  Insert Function, 7
  Insert Hyperlink, 318–319, 320
dictionary (spelling checker), 48–49
digital certificates, 344–345
digital signatures, lxiii, 328, 344
displays, worksheet, 19
distribution, electronic, 350
#DIV/0!, 76
Document Inspector, 351
dynamic analysis, 200–208, 235, 251–256
dynamic lists. *See* PivotTables

E

Edit Name dialog box, 62
electronic distribution, 350
elements, chart, 243
e-mail, 320–321, 329
embedding, lx, 286, 316–317
Encarta encyclopedia, 49
entering data, 36–41
Error Checking dialog box, 77
error messages, 132, 152, 166, 252
errors
  in data entry, 119
  error codes table, 76
  finding, xxxvii–xxxviii
  identifying, 75–78
  printing options, 279

Evaluate Formula dialog box, 78
Excel 2007 changes, lxiv, 1–11, 266–267. *See also* specific features
Excel 2007 workbook template (.xltm), 159. *See also* templates; workbooks; worksheets
Excel 2007 workbook (.xlsx), 5, 158–159, 165, 291. *See also* workbooks; worksheets
Excel 97–2003 (.xlt), 159
Excel binary workbook (.xlsb), 5
Excel macro-enabled template (.xltxm), 5, 291. *See also* templates
Excel macro-enabled workbook (.xlsm), 5, 291. *See also* workbooks; worksheets
Excel Options dialog box, 2, 37, 43, 88, 190, 195, 292, 301–302
Excel tables. *See* data tables
Excel template (.xltx), 5, 158–159, 291. *See also* templates
exercises
    charts, 239–241, 245–247, 250, 253–256, 260–263
    collaboration, 330–331, 333–334, 336–338, 341–344, 345–346, 348–350
    data calculations, 62–63, 69–70, 73–74, 79–82
    data combining, 161–164, 166–169, 174–175
    data entry/manipulation, 39–41, 43–44, 46–48, 51–53, 55–56
    data filters, 122–125, 128–130, 132–135
    data organization, 141–145, 148–150, 154–155
    data set analysis, 180–181, 183–185, 187–188, 191–194, 195–196
    macros, 294–297, 298–301, 304–306, 307–309
    Office applications, 314–315, 317–318, 321–323, 324–325
    PivotTables, 207–208, 213–215, 218–221, 224–228, 231–232
    printing, 268–270, 277–278, 280–281, 283–286, 286–287
    workbook appearance, 89–91, 93–96, 99–101, 104–106, 110–113, 115–116
    workbook setup, 16–17, 19–21, 23–25, 29–32
expansion, data/worksheets, 48–53
exponential distribution, 248
Extensible Markup Language (XML), 4–5
extrapolation, 235

F

features, xi–xii
fields (in PivotTables), 204
file properties, xxvii, 4, 15–16
fill handles, xxxii, 36–37
Fill with/without formatting, 39
FillSeries, 37, 38, 39
filtering data. *See* data filters
financial data delimiters, 228
Find And Replace dialog box, 44–45

Find Format dialog box, 45
finding and replacing options, 44–48
fixed width files, 229
flexibility. *See* PivotTables
Font Color control, 87
fonts
    appearance of, xxxviii, xxxix
    applying changes, 89
    choices, 88
footers, 266–268
Format Cells dialog box, 92, 98, 102, 103, 221, 223, 340
Format dialog box, 243
Format Painter, 93
Format Shape dialog box, 260
formatting. *See also* appearance, workbook; conditional formats; layout
    cells, 86–91
    charts, liii, liv, 242–247
    in copying/cutting, 42–43
    data tables, 54
    diagrams, 258, 260
    with fill operations, 39
    finding, 45
    of inserted rows/columns, 22
    options, 5
    pitfalls, 306
    PivotTables, li, 221–228
    predefined, 92
    tool display, 88
Formatting Options smart tag, 222
Formula Auditing, 77, 78
Formula AutoComplete, xxxvi, 7–8, 66
formula bars, xxxi, 29
formulas
    arguments, 8
    calculations, 64–74
    conditional, xxxvii, 71–74
    creating, xxxvi–xxxvii, 7–8
    GETPIVOTDATA, 217
    hiding, 327
    quirks, 110
    RAND function, 125
    results, changes, 179
    searching by, 45
    for specific results, xlix
    SUBTOTAL (function), 126
    updating multiple locations, 27
functions (data calculations), 65

G

galleries, 1
GETPIVOTDATA formula, 217
Go To Special dialog box, 333
Goal Seek, 185–188

Goal Seek Status dialog box, 186
graphics
    effects, xxxix
    in headers and footers, 268
    icons, xlii, 109, 122
    images, lvi
    inserting/modifying, xlii, 113–114
    macro custom shapes, 303
gridlines, liii, 243
groupings, data, xlvi–xlvii, 173–175

H

hardware requirements, xv
headers, lv–lvi, 266–268
help with Excel, xix
Hide Detail buttons, 146–147
hiding
    detail levels, vlii, 146–147
    formula bars, xxxi, 29
    headings, xxxi
    PivotTable data, vlii, 209–215
    Ribbon, xxxi, 29
    rows/columns, xxix, 22
    totals, 166
    worksheets, xxviii
hierarchy diagrams, 257
Highlight Changes dialog box, 335
History worksheet, lxii, 336
HLOOKUP function, 153
Home tab, 2
horizontal axis, 237
horizontal gridlines, 243
horizontal page breaks, 274
.htm (Hypertext Markup Language), 346
.html (Hypertext Markup Language), 346
hyperlinks, lx–lxi, 311, 312–313, 318–323. *See also*
    linking
Hypertext Markup Language (.htm/.html), 346

I

icons, xlii, 109, 122
IF (function), 71
IFERROR (function), 8, 71, 72
illustrations. *See* graphics
images, corporate, 113–116
Import Text File dialog box, 228–229
importing data, li–lii
information compartmentalizing, 3
Insert dialog box, 23, 160
Insert Function dialog box, 7
Insert Hyperlink dialog box, 318–319, 320
insertion
    of graphics, xlii, 113–114

    of links, lx
    of page breaks, lvii
    of rows/columns/cells, xxix, 19–20
inspection, document, 351
Intelliprint, 283
Internet Explorer, 347
interoperability, 3
intranets, 327, 347
invalid data, finding, 131

K

knowledge base, Microsoft, xix

L

landscape mode, lvi, 272
language translation, xxxiv, 50
layout. *See also* appearance, workbook; formatting
    charts, liii, 242
    deferment, 206
    worksheets, 271
levels, data organization, xlv, 145–150
limitations
    conditional formats, 107
    data filters, 126
    data organization, 199, 201
    Excel 2007, 3
    rows, 44
    scenarios, 182
    summaries, 171
linear distribution, 248
linking
    advantages/disadvantages, 315–316
    breaks in, 303
    cells, xlviii
    data sources, 164–169
    Excel with Web sites, 311
    Office documents, lx–lxi, 312–313, 318–323
    PivotCharts, 251
    PivotTables, 206, 217
    worksheets, 157–158
lists. *See* data lists
location changes
    cells, 23
    charts, 239, 243
    shapes, 258
    worksheets, 19
locked cells, 340
logarithmic distribution, 248
logical consistency, 109
Logo Builder, xxv
logos, 113
lookup_value, 152

M

Macro dialog box, 293, 294, 301, 302
macro-enabled template (.xltxm), 5, 291
macro-enabled workbook (.xlsm), 5, 291
macros
  about, 288–297
  with button access, 301–306
  creating/modifying, 297–301
  quick reference, lviii–lx
  tips, 2
  with workbooks, 306–309
magnification levels, 26
mailto hyperlinks, 320, 321
malware, 290, 292, 344
margins, lvi, 271
matches, exact, 45
mathematical computations, 248
mathematical operations, 43
matrix diagrams, 257
MAX (function), 65, 127
maximums, 54–55
Microsoft Business Certification program, xxi–xxv
Microsoft Certified Application Professional
    (MCAP), xxi–xxii
Microsoft Certified Application Specialist (MCAS),
    xxi–xxiii
Microsoft Office Online Web site, 159
Microsoft Press Knowledge Base, xix
Microsoft Press Technical Support, xix
Microsoft Product Support Services, xix
MIN (function), 65, 127
minimums, 54–55
Move Chart dialog box, 239
Move Or Copy dialog box, 18
multiple data sources. *See* data combining
multiple windows, arranging, 27

N

#N/A error, 152
#NAME?, 76
name attribution, 332
Name Manager, xxxv
Name Manager dialog box, 61, 62
named ranges, xxxv–xxxvi, 8, 60–63, 66, 138
names
  data groups, 60–63
  link breaking changes, 303
network sharing, 327
New Name dialog box, 61, 62
New PivotTable QuickStyle dialog box, 223
New Range dialog box, 341
New Table Quick Style dialog box, 98
New Workbook dialog box, 159

noncontiguous groupings, 282
NOW() (function), 65
numbers, readability of, 102–106, 221

O

Object dialog box, 312–313, 316
Office 2007 Solution Center, xix
Office documents (other than Excel)
  about, 310–312
  charts in, 323–325
  hyperlinking, 318–323
  quick reference, lx–lxi
  workbooks in, 315–318
  in worksheets, 312–315
Office file formats, 4–5
Office Fluent user interface, 1, 301
off-the-cuff assessments, 194–195
on-the-fly changes, 201, 251
Open dialog box, 347
operations research, 248
optimization, 189–194
orientation, page, lvi
outline, worksheet, 146, 147–148
overwriting files, 14–15

P

Page Break Preview, 10
Page Layout, 10, 97, 98
Page Setup dialog box, 267, 271, 273, 275, 279,
    281, 282, 283
pages
  blanks, 283
  breaks, lvii, 10, 273–275
  orientation, lvi
  printing order, 275–277
  size of, 272
password protection, lxii–lxiii, 327, 339
Paste Options, 42–43
Paste Special dialog box, 43
Paste Values, 125
pasting
  charts, 323–324
  columns, 41
  into graphics, 259
  options, 42
  quick reference, xxxii, lxi
PDF (Portable Document Format), 350
phone numbers, xl, 102–103
Pick From Drop-down List, 37–38
pictures. *See* graphics
pitfalls. *See* quirks
PivotCharts, liv, 235, 251–256

PivotTables
    about, 198–200
    dynamic analysis with, 200–208
    editing, 216–221
    from external data, 228–232
    filtering/showing/hiding, 209–215
    formatting, 221–228
    quick reference, l–lii
    on the Web, 348
PMT() (function), 65
polynomial distribution, 248
Popular Commands, 302
Portable Document Format (PDF), 350
portrait mode, lvi, 272
PowerPoint, 313, 316
precedents, 76
presentation efficiency, 301, 306
previews, lvii, 92, 273
Print dialog box, 281, 286
printing
    about, 264–265
    charts, 286–287
    controlling, 10–11
    data lists, 279–286
    headers and footers, 266–270
    quick reference, lv–lviii
    worksheets, 271–278
process diagrams, 257
process planning, 297
PRODUCT (function), 127
product support, xix
program window customization, 26–32
properties, xxvii, 4, 15–16
Protect Sheet dialog box, 340
protection (security), lxii–lxiii, 290–292, 327,
    339–344
Publish As Web Page dialog box, 347
pyramid diagrams, 257

Q

Quick Access Toolbar
    additions to, 13
    button options, 28–29
    macro access from, lix, 289, 301–303
    quick reference, xxxi
    scenario removal, 179
    spelling checker changes, 49
quick reference
    appearance, workbook, xxxviii–xlii
    calculations on data, xxxv–xxxviii
    charts/graphics, lii–lv
    collaboration, lxi–lxiii
    data combining, xlvii–xlviii
    data filters, xlii–xliv

data organization, xlv–xlvii
data set analysis, xlviii–xlix
data/data tables, xxxii–xxxv
macros, lviii–lx
Office documents (other than Excel), lx–lxi
PivotTables, l–lii
printing, lv–lviii
workbooks, setup, xxvii–xxxi
quirks
    chart axes, 237
    conditional formats, 110
    data destruction potential, 178, 179
    language translation, 50
    link breaking changes, 303
    logical consistency, 109
quote marks (around text), 104

R

RAND function, 125
RANDBETWEEN function, 126
random values, xliii, 125–126
range_lookup, 152
ranges
    header cells, 128
    named, xxxv–xxxvi, 60–63, 66, 138
    password protection, lxiii, 340
    random values within, 126
    in subtotals, 137
    user-named, 8
readability, data, 102–106, 221
Record Macro dialog box, 297
#REF! error, 166
references, xxvii–lxiii, 68–69, 166, 173. *See also*
        hyperlinks; linking
relationship diagrams, 257
relative references, 68–69
reordering, lvii
repetition (column/row headings), 283
repetitive tasks. *See* macros
research tools, 49
resizing. *See* sizing
review comments, managing, 331–334
revision, data, 36–41
Ribbon, xxxi, 1, 29
rows
    alignment, 272
    columns, transposing to, 43
    copying and pasting, xxxii
    labels, 29, 283
    limitations on, 3, 44
    modifying, 19
    quick reference, xxix, xxxi
    referencing, xxxvi
    reordering, 138–139

searching by, 45
selecting, 125
in table manipulations, 54
Total, xxxiv–xxxv
rules
    copying, 140
    formatting, xli, 107–108, 109
    management, 107–108
    validation, xliv, 119, 130–135

S

Save As dialog box, 15, 339, 346
Save Options dialog box, 339
Save Workspace dialog box, 173
saving files
    chart templates, liv
    overwriting files, 14–15
    themes, xxix–xl, 98
    workbooks, xxvii, lviii
scaling to fit, lvi, 273, 281–282
Scenario Manager, 178–179, 181–182
Scenario Summary dialog box, 182
scenarios, xlviii–xlix
scientific applications, 248
search convenience, 15
security, lxii–lxiii, 290–292, 327, 339–344, 350
Security Options dialog box, 291
Select Certificate dialog box, 345
Select Changes To Accept Or Reject dialog box, 335
Select Data Source dialog box, 237, 238
sensitive information, 340
series
    adding, liii, 54
    extending, xxxii, 36–37, 39
    plotting, lii
    removing, lii
set groupings, 173–175
Set Title dialog box, 348
shading (color), 88
shapes
    diagrams, 259–260
    macros, lx, 303
Share Workbook dialog box, 328–329
Show Detail buttons, 146–147
Sign dialog box, 344–345
signature, digital, lxiii, 328, 344
simultaneous data entry/editing, 37–38, 328
simultaneous file access, xlviii, 173
sizing
    charts, 238–239, 243
    files, 4, 312, 315–316
    images, 313, 316
    paper, 272
    tables, xxxiv
    workbooks, 13

SmartArt diagrams, lv, 256–263
solution optimization, 189–194
Solver, 189–194
Solver Parameters dialog box, 190
Sort dialog box, 139, 140
Sort Options dialog box, 140
sorting (data lists), xlv–xlvi, 138–145
space optimization, windows, 29
spell checking, xxxiii, 48–49
spreadsheets, 161, 228
statistics, xlix, 194–196
STDEV/STDEVP (function), 127
Style dialog box, 92
styles. *See also* appearance, workbook; formatting;
        layout
    cells, xxxviii–xxxix
    charts, liii
    creating, 92–96
    PivotTables, li–lii, 223, 230
    tables, xl
substitute data, 344
SUBTOTAL, xliii, 126
Subtotal dialog box, 145
subtotals
    calculating, 145–146
    cell ranges in, 137
    PivotTables, li
SUM (function)
    about, 65
    filtering limitations, 126
    in SUBTOTAL (function), 127
    using, 66–67, 68
SUMIFS (function), 8, 71–73
summaries. *See also* data organization
    AutoCalculate, xliii
    charts as, 235, 236
    of conditional formulas, 71–74
    data, 54–55
    limitations, 171
    of multiple worksheets, 158
    PivotTables, li, 206, 216–217, 221
    quirks, 110
    scenarios, 179, 182
    SUBTOTAL, xliii, 126–127
sums, 54–55
switching documents, 27
system requirements, xi–xii

T

Tab character (as delimiter), 228
Table AutoExpansion, 54
table structure references, 8
table_array, 152
tables. *See* data tables
targets, hyperlink, 319

task automation. *See* macros
technical support, xix
technology certification, xxi–xxv
telephone numbers, xl, 102–103
templates
   charts, liv, 243
   defaults, 159
   lists, 158–164
   quick reference, xlvii–xlviii
   workbooks, 158–159
   worksheets, 160
Templates dialog box, 159
test taking tips, xxiv
text
   adding to shapes, 258
   errors presented as, 77
   in quote marks, 104
text (.txt) files, 228–231
Text To Display box, 321
themes
   about, xxxix–xl, 5–6
   of imported worksheets, 19
   style interface with, 242
   of workbooks, 96–98
thesaurus use, xxxiv, 49
3-D references, 165, 171, 320
tiled patterns, 114
tips
   Analysis ToolPak installation, 195
   background images, 114
   backups, 182
   change tracking, 166
   data distribution, 249
   diagrams, 258, 260
   digital certificates/signatures, 344
   e-mail, 321
   error checking, 78
   fill handles, 37
   filters, 121
   formatting, 21, 87, 88, 103, 108
   formulas, 68
   HLOOKUP function, 153
   linking, 165, 312, 313
   macros/add-ins, 2
   multiple scenarios, 182
   named ranges, 61
   optimization, 189
   page breaks, 273
   password choices, 339
   PivotTable, 203
   printing, 279, 281, 282
   RAND function, 125
   row/column inserts, 23
   saving files, 15
   SmartArt diagrams, 259
   Solver installation/options, 190, 191

sorting levels, 140
summaries, 127
Table AutoExpansion, 54
templates, 159, 244
Text To Display box, 321
themes, 98
trends, 249
Web pages, 346
worksheet copies, 19
zoom levels, 26
Top 10 AutoFilter dialog box, 122
totals
   calculating, 145
   finding, 126
   hiding, 166
   PivotTables, li
   quick reference, xxxiv–xxxv
tracer arrows, xxxvii, 76–77
translation, language, xxxiv, 50
transposition (columns/rows/data), xxxii, 43
trends/trendlines, liv, 235, 249
troubleshooting. *See also* quirks
   AutoComplete, 37
   formulas, 64
   language translation, 50
   number fields, 103
   Paste Options button, 43
Trust Center Settings, 292
trusted sources, 328
.txt (text) files, 228–231

U

undo
   changes, 49
   resizing, 114
   scenarios, 179, 182
   Table AutoExpansion, 54
updating, 27, 312, 315–316, 347, 348. *See also*
   linking
usability, 10
user interface, 1, 2
user-defined functions, 7

V

validation rules, xliv, 119, 130–135
#VALUE!, 76
Value Field Settings dialog box, 217
values. *See also* linking
   conditional formats, 106–113
   as decimals, 186
   for formulas, xxxvii
   monitoring, 78
   projections, 248

quick reference, xliii
reformatting, xl
replacing, xxxiii
searching by, 45
sorting, xlv–xlvii, xlvi, 140
in specific scenarios, xlix
unique, xliv, 128, 151
watching, xxxviii
VAR/VARP (function), 127
VBA (Visual Basic for Applications), 290, 293, 306
versatility. *See* PivotTables
versions, save options, 4
vertical axis, 237
vertical gridlines, 243
vertical page breaks, 274
viruses, 290, 292, 344
Visual Basic Editor, 294, 298
Visual Basic for Applications (VBA), 290, 293, 306
VLOOKUP function, 151–153

W

Watch Window, 78–79
watermarks, 114
Web-Excel integration, 311
Websites, lxiii, 318–319, 328
what-if analysis, 178, 186
windows, 27. *See also* program window
    customization
Windows, searching in, 15
wizards, 229
workbooks. *See also* appearance, workbook
  authenticating, 344–346
  data moves within, 41–44
  finalizing, 351
  on intranets, 347
  macros, lviii, lx, 289–290, 306
  Office documents in, 315–318
  security, lxii–lxiii, 339–344
  sharing, lxi, 328–329
  templates, xlvii–xlviii, 158–159
  as Web documents, 346–350
workbooks, setup
  about, 12–14
  creating, 14–18
  customization, 26–32
  modifying, 18–21
  quick reference, xxvii–xxxi

worksheets
  charts, importing, liii
  correcting/expanding, 48–53
  embedding in, 286
  formatting, 5–6
  graphics, xlii
  linking/hyperlinking, 157–158, 320
  location changes, 19
  modifying, 21–26
  names of, 18
  Office documents in, 312–315
  printing, lv–lviii, 271–278, 279–280
  quick reference, xxviii–xxxi
  removing, 158
  security, lxii–lxiii, 339–344
  templates, 160
workspace, 157, 173

X

x-axis, 237
.xlsb (Excel binary workbook), 5
.xlsm (Excel macro-enabled workbook), 5, 291
.xlsx (Excel 2007 workbook), 5, 158–159, 165, 291.
    See also workbooks; worksheets
.xlt (Excel 97–2003), 159
.xltm (Excel 2007 workbook template), 159
.xltx (Excel template), 5, 158–159, 291
.xltxm (Excel macro-enabled template), 5, 291
XML (Extensible Markup Language), 4–5
XML Print Specification (XPS), 350

Y

y-axis, 237

Z

zooming in/out, xxx, 26

What do you think of this book?

We want to hear from you!

Do you have a few minutes to participate in a brief online survey?

Microsoft is interested in hearing your feedback so we can continually improve our books and learning resources for you.

To participate in our survey, please visit:

www.microsoft.com/learning/booksurvey/

...and enter this book's ISBN-10 or ISBN-13 number (located above barcode on back cover*). As a thank-you to survey participants in the United States and Canada, each month we'll randomly select five respondents to win one of five $100 gift certificates from a leading online merchant. At the conclusion of the survey, you can enter the drawing by providing your e-mail address, which will be used for prize notification only.

Thanks in advance for your input. Your opinion counts!

*Where to find the ISBN on back cover

ISBN-13: 000-0-0000-0000-0
ISBN-10: 0-0000-0000-0

0 0 0 0 0

0

Example only. Each book has unique ISBN.